Tell Me Bad News

Collected Essays

I0565341

K. M. Patten

Tell Me Bad News

Other books by K. M. Patten

Indictments from the Convicted: Rants, Articles, Interviews and Essays
In Favor of Hatred
Staying ON During the Great Reset

Print ISBN 978-1-960405-33-3
ebook ISBN 978-1-960405-34-0

Cover Design by Guy D. Corp
www.GrafixCorp.com

STAIRWAY PRESS—APACHE JUNCTION

STAIRWAY≡PRESS

www.StairwayPress.com
1000 West Apache Trail
Suite 126
Apache Junction, AZ 85120 USA

Tell Me Bad News Introduction

WITH THE TITLE of this book, my second collection of journalism, I attempt to strike two chords at once. "Me." Contrary to what the late John Cage would have you believe, all works of art should be attached to the artist who made them.

Yes, I would like to evoke a reaction within you, but I also write so that I might figure out my own thoughts and feelings on a subject. You'll be forgiven if you deem that "therapy."

I wrote my first piece when I was five years old, a picture book. The story was not imaginary or fantastical; it was about the recent death of a family member, my grandfather. I started writing again in my late teens. These were diary entries. Some time ago, I realized that much of what I still write is like a diary, which hopefully means more than just giving opinions and scribbling down trivialities. All journalists should like to be there, to see things for themselves. Here I think of Josep Pla, who traveled around Europe and the Soviet Union, recording what he saw. Sometimes said to be Catalonia's best journalist, Pla once described his 40-some volume canon as an "enormous, personal diary."

If only we could all view our work so simply and honestly. Alas, on-the-ground reportage might soon become a lost artform. Immersive reporters are being shoved aside by all those sitting behind a computer, tapping into the Data Stream and shouting their "hot takes."

Hey, I too do online journalism.

The second chord would not shock anyone: "Bad." I'm sometimes called a cynic. No, I say, cynicism is for the warm-blooded. Relishing in the negativity, and taking it a step further, I admit to being a *misanthrope,* which is something I state plainly several times in these pages. It's the view of the misanthrope that humankind has rarely acted decently or morally.

As Voltaire said, "History is only the register of crimes and misfortunes." I assume the worst of people, and don't often find myself disappointed. One should never be surprised upon discovering that their polite neighbor has done something wicked and horrible. None are excluded from this assessment—especially not me.

But my misanthropy comes with a hopeful qualifier. I only hate humanity as it is, or was—not as it could be. In the intro to my first collection of essays, *Indictments from the Convicted*, I wrote that I take a "Nietzschen or Godwinian approach to the matter," believing "that it is the responsibility of every thinking person to push evolution along."

The perfection project is more urgent than ever. Since the publication of that book, things have only gotten worse. We're now in the Post-Covid Age. The Great Reset is upon us. We've witnessed the emergence of AI, as well as the outbreak of two new wars (Russia/Ukraine, and Israel/Palestine), all of which threaten our survival.

I've come to believe that if our species stands any chance in a future world ruled by these warmongers, technocrats, and upgraded humans, we must not only continue evolving, we must also pick up the pace. I insist that humanity at last become rational and peaceful creatures.

For that endeavor, rather than offering proposals, I try to give descriptions. If something isn't working right, it must be examined before one can begin the repairs. Although I'm very proud of my analytical pieces (my essays on Alcoholics Anonymous and the BLM riots are especially thorough), I have made my share of mistakes and errors, both in journalism and in life.

For instance, included in this collection are two microscopic pieces discussing healthcare and immigration. In the more than ten years since I wrote them, my thinking on both issues changed dramatically. The goal shouldn't be state-run healthcare. Instead, it should be for people to simply *be healthier*. This is like the mountains in the far distance: easy to see but difficult to climb. In years past, it was less obvious that we about our lives all while being bombarded with radiation and chemicals. It should be easier today to acknowledge that our endocrine systems have suffered a serious wallop, and so perhaps chronic illnesses can be prevented, if only we could separate ourselves from them. And no, I wouldn't trust even local governments to give us good healthcare, no more than I would trust them to remove those toxins.

As for immigration, I often wonder whether there will ever be a true Tower of Babel here on Earth.

Will all the peoples of the world one day live in harmony, with nonviolence and rationality as values taught and practiced universally?

Likely not.

But it seems obvious that I have a better chance of propagating these ideals to those most proximate to me, who I already share a language with. And while a case could be made for both sides of the argument, I think it's probably best to secure the southern border until we have a better respect for communal sovereignty and less welfare. You can't have a blending of cultures when one culture is poured all at once onto another culture.

Then there's the COVID pandemic, which was intended by some to be a catalyst for a techno-dystopic world, one with mass surveillance, forced vaccination, and, ultimately, a world state. Transhumanism is likely the final piece of the agenda.

My first piece on the pandemic, published in April of 2020, is a longish essay of more than 5,000 words. I no longer stand by everything I had originally written or said about that critical period. Although I criticize lockdowns and government overreach, I'm not sure I would endorse universal mask-wearing or social distancing.

Some can take solace in knowing that there's not a single person who's ever lived who got everything right the first time. Then again, I also have a "think-piece" about how tragic it is that we can't go back in time and fix the mistakes of the past; and, worse, thanks to interstellar travel and digital communications, that we might one day be assessed by an alien race.

There's been other, more profound developments.

Interestingly, my last book was published right around the time I gained full custody of my son. Since he is the centerpiece of my life, I try not to make him the cynosure of my journalism.

Nevertheless, there are a couple pieces that discuss certain aspects of his life. Specifically, his circumcision.

Come again?

How could I write about such personal matters? Imagine his embarrassment! Of course, I wish I never had to write about this event.

But the subject is unavoidable.

All diarists must acknowledge that, in the era of social media and mass surveillance, personal diaries are almost redundant. Very little remains unknown. My son's story is part of my story, and sad facts cannot long be hidden. If I had tried to hide them, I would likely one day be called a hypocrite—either by others who know, or by a Big Brother who reveals our secrets. That truth would find a way out regardless: I failed to keep my own son safe from that procedure I've been raging against for all these years.

There's nothing more to do but to bang my head against the wall a few more times, hoping for enlightenment, forgiveness, and redemption.

Still, I like to think I got a few things right, for intactivism is ancillary to my belief in peaceful parenting, which has gained traction only in the last few years.

I don't see how we can improve our condition without treating our children like rational, respectable human beings. It's my ultimate conviction that every generation that's slightly better than the one before it can be seen as a small step towards "perfection" and "utopia."

As long as we teach violence and superstition to our children, history can expect a continuous flow of conflict and turmoil. I know that if there is a perfected human ideal, my son will come close to reaching it.

If isn't obvious by now, this edition, like the last one, is eclectic. My mind wonders in many directions, and I follow it, sometimes to my peril. There's enough online activism—or should I say, article aggregation—but there's also a few firsthand accounts.

Most of these essays were edited—sometimes heavily—since they first appeared on those small blogs. As they say, "all writing is rewriting." While that old proverb is correct, it makes me wonder if they were ever truly my words.

Unlike the last collection, I include dates to the pieces, month and year. There's only two pieces for which I could not pinpoint. For those, I had to make honest guesses as to where they might fall on the chronology.

The first hundred pages are comprised of essays written during the same years as my earliest pieces from the last collection.

With the exception of 2013, there's something written for every year until 2022. That's about 13 years of writing. The last essay from the previous book was written in 2014, and it's there the pace picks up a little over a hundred pages in.

Common themes resurface, like my opposition to religion and war, and new themes are presented, like my growing skepticism towards technology, or my advocacy for separation.

A reader can read any way they like: start to finish, or picking pieces at random. If the reader gains understanding or amusement, no matter how small, then I have succeeded.

If nothing else, it's another high mark on my growing resume, to which I pray I will add more.

—K. M. Patten

Table of Contents

Join Arnold's Cannabis Crusade

THAT MIGHT BE a bit unfair. Our governor hasn't actually *endorsed* marijuana. But all you have to do is take a quick gander on YouTube and see that Arnold isn't all that unfamiliar with the stuff.

He even admits to inhaling!

This is interesting, and as we all know—the debate is lighting up! It is far past time that we declare this War on Drugs as the failure it is. We need to concede that not only would the legalization of marijuana align ourselves more closely with the American mantra of individual freedom, but it would also destroy a good portion of the underground (cartel-controlled) economy. We could curtail some of the black revenue and redirect it to a people's government, helping us out of our not-small debt.

At least one person is adamant about putting the issue on the table. Democratic assemblyman Tom Ammiano from San Francisco has proposed Bill 390—a bill that would legalization regulate, and tax marijuana in the state of California. In the same fashion as other illicit substances—namely, alcohol and tobacco—this bill would require that no one under the age of 21 would be able to buy the stuff and that there would be a hefty tax with the intention of helping to pull us out of our spiraling debt.

This is great news for pot smokers all over the Golden State (at least for those over the age of 21). Unfortunately for someone, most of the teenagers left out of the law likely already know tokers that are that age. And even though I strongly believe the age requirement should be dropped to 18 (due to that whole thing about 18 being the age of adulthood), this bill is still the best thing to be proposed in a long, long time. Many problems, I think, will vanish should it become law.

And for all those conservatives who declare a War on Drugs and at the same time enjoy their freedom, they can take solace in knowing that their hypocrisy is finally being exposed. We, as freedom-loving Americans, should be allowed to do what the hell we damn will please with our own bodies.

Toxins, you say? But how can someone argue that marijuana is worse for your health than alcohol or tobacco, considering that those two together kill more than 300,000 people a year, while some even claim that nobody has ever died from smoking cannabis?

So, let's assume for right now that cannabis is bad for you. If we're going to start outlawing products that are harmful to us, shouldn't we also do the same for McDonald's, and any other fast-food chain cooking its food in oils so dangerous that our risk of stomach cancer is greatly increased? Never mind bigger warning labels: should we decriminalize consumption altogether?

It's absurd and should not happen. Besides, how many doctors have come out now and said that marijuana not only helps ward off Alzheimer's and various cancers, but also has a positive effect on depression? Why should these parents only receive the benefits? Shouldn't those who also have to endure general hardship have the right to smoke away the intolerable tyrannies of everyday life? Like me, for example: For a long time, I couldn't even wake up in the morning without drinking a cold beer.

Now, I pack a fat bowl of high-end Kronic. This gets me through the day and saves me from liver disease. It makes me cheerful and helps me cope, which, cynically as it is to say, was just too difficult to deal with. Buds calm me down, allowing me to enjoy the little things. When the effects wear off and people once again turn into blood-thirsty brutes that they are, I just pack myself another bowl...and life is good once again.

What I'm trying to say is that if our government would stop being such incompetent fucks, and did away with all laws, violations, and punishments, then perhaps the people wouldn't be so angry or cold—and maybe they wouldn't even have the need to smoke a big 'ole fatty to enjoy life.

Anyway, please watch our governor's 1977 classic movie *Pumping Iron*. After a hard workout, Arnold lights up a fatty. I wonder what would happen if we asked Arnold back then about his thoughts on legalization. Today, as the Governator, he's calling for a debate on the matter and to see what other countries are doing as far as decriminalization and legalization. That's a start. Yet he seems hellbent on not releasing any inmates from our prison system, no matter how corrupt and how backwards the Torture Network has become.

Legalization of marijuana would also do something that is desperately needed in this state (along with all other states); that is, the elimination of part of the Underground Economy. Every year, the Mexican cartels bring in billions of dollars in cannabis revenue. Tom Ammiano's bill would tax the sale of marijuana and is estimated to redirect that billion into the state coffers. That's quite a bit, and it might help us out.

There are some who argue that street venders will start selling cannabis at a cheaper price. This argument is about as valuable as the one stating that people would soon be growing it themselves.

If it were so easy, so readily done, then the Cartels would already be out of business, because so many independent dealers would be harvesting right from their own gardens. No: people would much rather do it legally and easily, instead of resorting to gangbangers who thrive on the profit.

So please, tell your senators and representatives to support the passing of Assembly Bill 390. Then we can all go out and smoke some of Mother Nature's finest herb. Just say NO…to drug prohibition.

(May 2009)

Interview with Shadow Hare

K.M. Patten: Many people are compelled to do different things in life: writers, activists, protesters…things they feel they could help make a difference in the world. What compelled you personally to do what you do in the Streets of Cincinnati? You've said before that you were abused as a young child? Was that the only thing or is there something more?

Shadow Hare: Yes, I was abused as a child, but there is so much more than that as well. I look around the streets of Cincinnati, and across the country and I have seen that apathy has taken over as well. I believe if more people take action to do things to help someone else rather than just being a witness then this world will be a better place.

KMP: On your Blog on Myspace, you mentioned that you were going to school. What classes are you taking, or which ones do you plan on taking in the future? Why did you decide to take these classes?

SH: I wish not to reveal this because it will reveal a future career that I wish to pursue on the sidelines of doing what I do which would make it easier to trace me in the near future.

KMP: How much time out of the day do you devote to this endeavor? Is it only during the day, or do you spend more time out at night? Tell me what an average day consists of.

SH: I do both day and night patrols. Day patrols are more out in the open sort of thing so that I can show the people that I am there. During the night I wish not to be seen so I remain stealthy. Nighttime is where more violence occurs most of the time.

KMP: Aside from being Shadow Hare, is there a personal life outside of this ambition that you enjoy? How do you manage two lives? Does the man behind the mask still have time for pizza and movies?

SH: The man behind the mask works a full-time job and still enjoys the occasional quality time with friends. I also take time to study criminal statistics on the computer while not in uniform."

KMP: Anyone who spends that much time dedicated to a cause must have strong feelings on morals and justice. Can you name 5 specific things that you feel are the most detrimental elements to either society and/or our World? And what do you think that either you, or all of us, can do to help?

SH: Vigilance: Always be on watch anything can happen anytime or anywhere. Compassion: Be willing to help out anyone no matter who they are. Truth: Be honest to not only others but also to yourself. Bravery: The world is a dark place but that doesn't mean that you still can't stand strong. Sacrifice: Be willing to do this for what you truly believe in. Everyone can do their part by just being there for others who are in need even if it is just something small. But that small thing can be a big deal for someone else."

KMP: Give me a brief overview of your political beliefs. How do you feel about gun rights and citizens being able to defend themselves? Do you believe in a bigger Welfare program to feed the poor and impoverished?

SH: Gun laws do not matter in my opinion because if a criminal really wants a gun then that person will get one. We don't need a bigger welfare program. What we need is more jobs out there.

KMP: Are you a religious person? Do you feel there is a Supreme Being that is watching over the actions of us all? Do you feel that it can help us come to a better World?

SH: I do believe in a higher power, but I believe that power doesn't want us to just kneel and pray while people are suffering, I believe that power would like us to take actions ourselves. That power can give us power to do what we need to do to get through life though.

KMP: What do you see yourself doing in 10-15 years? Will you continue to fight injustice and for your cause, or will you move on? Perhaps it will evolve?

SH: I will do this for the rest of my life. I have a feeling that it will become more evolved. I believe the people will have more power than they do now.

KMP: A lot of people might feel that the mask is a prop, sort of like a starvation for attention. Of course, a lot of the time there is a necessity for privacy. Why do you wear the mask?

SH: I wear a mask to show that I am not just a man but I do this as an idea, a symbol. Man can be corrupted but an idea cannot. I wear it to show no emotion as I go through the streets."

(May 2009)

Standing Side-by-Side with California's Nazi: A Letter to the Governator

STAND WITH YOU? Stand with you!? That proposition doesn't sound very enticing to me, Mr. Schwarzenegger. And I have some very good reasons for me feeling that way. But before I get into all that, I want you to know that the only reason I'm writing this letter is because you are the one who has endorsed involvement of the California citizenry. You constantly tell us to "contact our senators, our representatives; to call them, write letters"—and so on. So I, as a First Amendment sort of guy, have decided to do just that: exercise my right to participate in our democracy. And so here I go....

For starters: I don't believe that any state budget is going to rectify our problems here in the Golden State. The Elites can sit in their offices and do all these things with the budget, and no matter what they come up with I will not be satisfied. And for good reason: there is no justification to be given, as to why the Guard's Union—the C.C.P.O.A.—should be paid anywhere close to $100,000 a year. The number is astronomical and serves as an insult to the millions of other people who work hard in this state. On top of that salary, they get health benefits, vacation, etc. They sit at their tables, kick their feet up, and occasionally they have to get up and blast with mace *en masse*. That assessment has made by a true, first-hand observer: *me*. The situation is made worse by the failure to make the necessary adjustments.

"Criminals produce more criminals." So easy to understand, even you should be able to get it. Being a Republican, I would certainly expect you to fall right in line when the other Neo-Cons and sanction Nazi-related crimes— like the crime of producing more criminals. It's more subtle over here in America…we criminalize drugs then lock them up with harder criminals where they become…gasp…better criminals! What a shocker. Hitler had his Nuremburg rallies, where he induced the masses into believing all his bullshit, creating monsters, and now you are doing the same thing when you pay the Union to assemble their monsters. All under a different banner. This one being "rehabilitation."

But you know all about Hitler, don't you? You were friends with one of his comrades: Mr. Kurt Waldeim, I believe. He could lie about it all he wants, but the medals, the signatures attached to all those deportation slips, witness accounts, his initiation to the National Socialist German Student League, not to mention that the U.N. said he was a war criminal: these facts say otherwise. And it's unfortunate that the (numerous) articles written about your connection with him have gone mostly unnoticed. But that's no surprise, seeing as our media is a well-oiled propaganda machine. The people, subsequently, fall into a circle of ignorance and apathy. The only thing they do pay attention to is the stuff that affects their immediate life…like health care, or the economy, or the crime statistics, etc.

Fortunately, you have managed to screw up a great number of these things. You have just recently exercised your state privilege to veto some of the budget measures—including funds for MEDI-CAL and state parks—while allowing for the construction of a new wing on death row. On top of that, the tentative release of 58,000 inmates will also soon face your veto power. So instead of my first suggestion of cutting the salaries of the guards Union and implementing more rehabilitative programs inside the prisons, you'd rather just "cut, cut, cut," but always making sure to have enough money to lock up more inmates and fill the pockets of the bastards who create the problems.

Don't get me wrong, I know that the Union is powerful. But aren't you the Governator? You're supposed to strong-arm these problems, the same way you strongarmed all those women.

Anyway, you cannot put a band-aid on a gunshot wound. And that is what you are doing here. "Releasing them into different custody," or whatever the language is, is practically the same thing here. You need to push for the judges' original order of 58'000. You should be able to find just about that many first-time, non-violent offenders with only a year or so to go. Or pretty close.

I sympathize with you, Arnold. I really do. And I can agree that in a state as complicated as California there is bound to be problems. But if you are so serious about solving our problems you would do something with the prison problem, and put a few more dollars where they're needed.

And if you were really that adamant about shutting off our borders (as a voice recording some years back had proved) you'd put more energy into that as well. Instead, these problems go unnoticed...and, as always, you—along with all the other people not paying attention—have perpetuated our problems.

Mexicans immigrants, devastated by NAFTA and you're willingness to promote drug cartels, which lead to horrendous conditions, have made them come over here for a better life. Can't blame 'em. But there go the health-care costs...there go the incarceration rate...and there goes the whole fucking state.

(July 2009)

A Trickling Revolution

Or...

How I learned to Accept that Illegal Immigrants Will Never Stop Pouring Over our Walls

BE UPSET ABOUT it all you want. Hate it. Despise it, even. But in the end, you'll never be as upset as all those poor natives who were slaughtered when the Europeans first came. You couldn't have shared their despair if you lived a hundred years inside of a prison wall—ostracized from all that you know and love in this world. It's simply something you're not capable of doing...and neither am I for that matter.

But when reflecting on the historical reality, you might also begin to acquire a certain amount of sympathy as well. All

Mexicans who go through a virtual hell and virtual high water to come over to this country—land taken from them many years ago—end up picking strawberries in one-hundred-degree weather, only to go home to a cold case of Budweiser.

Now, you would think that drinking the Budweiser would be torture enough, but then, *my god*: they've crossed hundreds of miles and risked getting caught by border-vigilantes and "good-ole-boy" border patrol agents, just to work in such misery and dread. I can't bring myself to hate them for that. I have to realize the conditions that brought them here in the first place: namely, US hegemony. Starting with the imperialism that founded this country and continuing through trade agreements like NAFTA, the standard of Mexican life in their homeland is not very good these days.

These are the reasons why Hispanics are coming over here. And, again, I can't bring myself to be upset by their solution. If the shoe was on the other foot (the Red, White, and Blue boot) and the Mexican War was won by the Mexicans, we would have been equally upset about it. Because that's the leading force in the world: strong-arm and force. "Might makes Right," or so it's been said.

So at the very least, we can be happy that the Mexican people don't have the firepower to take it back from us. Instead, they've been trying a smaller revolution. A *drop-drop-drop* of reintegration back into the Land that was once theirs. And, like I already stated, this personally doesn't offend me. But from a political perspective, I couldn't exactly say whether that's the right thing to do either. After all, when they do work, it's usually *under the table*—meaning they don't pay any taxes. On top of that, the money that is paid to them is almost always split into one-third—with a third going to rent, a third going to Budweiser, and the last third going back to family members in Mexico…and, perhaps, to pay the smugglers (called coyotes) who are bringing his children over next week.

No, I can't be entirely upset with them for these efforts to survive. What I am upset about is the general behavior of their offspring. Because while the majority of illegal immigrants strive to live an honest life, it's the younger majority that feel the irresistible need to join gangs, which of course hurt people. *These* are the ones we should export back across the border. Not the ones trying to work and live.

Ah, but then what is the solution for these woes? What discussion shall we have? For starters: the firepower that *is* held by Mexicans is usually, if not always, in the hands of the drug cartels, who lobby for stricter laws on drugs so that their profit margin goes up. Eliminate the drug laws and you eliminate their power. For all the immigrants who do wish to live an honest life, we could speed up the citizenship process and bring more jobs (and more tax-revenue) for the States.

Ask yourself: if you were kicked out of your country and forced to live in poverty, wouldn't you break a few laws to make things better for yourself?

You probably would.

(July 2009)

To Mark Dice, Founder of the Christian Resistance

GREETINGS. HELLO. HOWDY. Mr. Mark Dice, sir. I am currently drunk…which is okay, because even from my intoxicated perspective, I still realize that it is within my legal rights to be so. I'll take advantage. I hope that every freedom fighter can appreciate this small feat which requires little, except paying the outrageous taxes put upon us by a corrupt government which has created so many problems. The slight headache and tinge of regret that will be with me in the morning do not change this.

I am a bit concerned, though, and I shall express my concern just as soon as I say *thank you* for your brave efforts in stopping the New World Order. I have yet to read your two books, *The Resistance Manifesto* and *Illuminati: Fact and Fiction*. Thus, I am a bit handicapped in this letter in that I am soon to offer some criticism to you and your followers without fully understanding the entirety of your objective. Apologies.

From what I heard, you are a dedicated Christian. And immediately I relate that one word to a faulty ideology, one that paves the campaign trail for all parties and candidates to tread across. Because all candidates are some sort of "Christian," devoting themselves—they say—to the work of Christ.

Recall that our current president was caught in a scandal regarding his religious affiliation. When it was discovered that he had attended the church of one Reverend Wright, and the media was unwilling, or unable, to forget the issue, Mr. Obama had to finally disown the church. He then joined...well, it might as well have been "some other church," because conviction notwithstanding, he followed the same American presidential motif. However, if one reads Obama's book *The Audacity of Hope*, you'll notice that Obama thinks back fondly to his mother's sense of spirituality, with no need for organized sects. We won't get into the issue of his Muslim heritage.

As for our past president—the incompetent, evil little toad named George W. Bush—is concerned, he was a self-proclaimed follower of the Lord, and constantly referred to Christ "opening his heart." This intervention was nonexistent. As they say, if it has all the qualities, there can be no denying it. As you certainly know, Bush was a member of the Skull and Bones at Yale University. There, he was obligated to take an oath, one unlike anything the average man has ever taken. Add to that his membership of the Bohemian Grove—that annual meeting up in the California forest, where the elites gather and either dance naked below the trees, or, more sinisterly, do ceremonies involving the blood god Molech—and Bush proves himself to be a fully-fledged hypocrite. We know these simple facts to be true. We don't need them validated by political operatives like Rush Limbaugh and Sean Hannity.

So now that I've gotten the basics out of the way, let me tell you why religious dogmatism is nothing more than cow excrement. I wish not to take all the blame for this vital blow to your conscience, so I shall refer you to a video made by the refreshingly bright journalist Cenk Uygur, titled *No One Follows the Bible*.

If we actually listen to what he says, we find ourselves agreeing with the cold reality: no one really adheres to the barbaric practices found in that holy book. One can stone their child, sell their daughter into slavery, and even kill hundreds of thousands of women and children. This can all be read for oneself—but which will never be read in any Sunday school classroom. As Penn and Teller rightly point out, the bible can be used to debunk the bible.

After all, we castigate and shun those who do attempt any literal translation of the text. All these fundamentalist sects set up in the hills: when we hear about them and what they do— child brides, a lot of the time—we, as a civilized people, condemn those practices as evil and cultish. Justifiably so! But is that not the book you're reading from? If it says to stone your grandmother for, say, cleaning dishes on the Sabbath, who then is going to gather the stones? The answer is: nobody we know.

That's the main reason I wrote this letter: We don't want a New World Order based upon central government any more than we want another order based upon religiosity. Of any sect or creed. There will be no stone grandmothers in our utopia; no specified prayer or teaching of any brand of theism; none taught to children whose parents do not wish it. We reject a Religious World Order. As David Icke aptly put it: "I don't know which I dislike more, the world controlled by the Brotherhood, or the one you want to replace it with."

Good call, David.

But I salute you, Mark. You are far more prepared than I am, and your message has reached many ears. Perhaps I'm unaware of your true intents; if you plan on destroying the New World Order only to replace it with something that I—and many others—find to be despicable, deplorable, and antithetical to Liberty.

If the Framers said it, then I shall repeat it: we demand an absolute separation of Church and State. A wall constructed of concrete, with rebar made of nothing less solid than diamonds. No neo-con or smooth-talking bible thumper will be allowed to implement that sort of legislation into our already billowing lawbooks. I wish to go even further and say that we hope that you were right, particularly on the existence of Hell, just so we could imagine Jerry Falwell burning right now as I type this final paragraph. But perhaps that's just the rage of the alcohol talking.

I enjoy my freedom.

I know you do too.

Thank you for reading.

(August 2009)

Nancy Grace, Shut Your Mouth!

YES, IT'S UNFORTUNATE that the entirety of news reporting is predicated upon the most depressing issues. Murders, rapes, and robberies are what thrives on the nightly news. That is obvious, and only requires a glance to notice. And as people sit down to watch their tube and see the latest brutality, the ratings go up at exactly the same time the paychecks do. This phenomenon is commonly referred to as *sensationalism*, and it is accepted by nearly everyone.

For this alone, I cannot blame Nancy Grace, the host of *HLN*'s syndicated nighttime show of the same name, for making an undisclosed multi-million-dollar paycheck. If she wants make money off dead babies and mutilated corpses, fine by me; it's her right to do so.

But what does disgust me about this woman is not only the endless fake tears she gives us with every "sad story" that makes its way onto the wire, nor is it her blatant humiliation of every one of her guest speakers, but what *does* truly and utterly sicken me is the combination of both of these things added with the obsessive omission of any trace of objectivity. Just watch a single episode. There will hardly be one without her shrilling voice speaking over one of her guests, who are usually there to give agreeable "expertise" on the given story. When the experts come on (the ones' she has invited) they will be constantly interrupted by the shouts of "whoa, whoa, whoa." Then she will then give her own "expert advice"—those vitriolic rants alluding to the guilt of the person whose mugshot is flashed across the screen.

So let us examine Ms. Grace's "expertise." Nobody can forget the amazing story of Elizabeth Smart. At fourteen years of age, she was taken from her home in Salt Lake City, Utah. She went missing for almost a whole year before finally being found alive. Sometime during this whole ordeal, a man named Richard Ricci was arrested and questioned about a possible role in the abduction. It was at this precise moment that Nancy Grace—who at this period was gradually gaining her nickname, Satan's Special Girl—who gave a perfect illustration of her own methodology. Ricci, she claimed, and I quote, was "guilty." With no trial, and very little evidence to support the claim, Satan's Little Girl made an absolutist statement about a suspect who was still innocent under our Constitution.

Rather strong words coming from a former prosecutor who was known to be difficult when having to cooperate with the defense. Her assertion of Ricci's guilt turned out to be untrue, and while it is sad that he died in custody and unable to get an apology from the now "Fallen" Grace, this whole scenario confirmed the method in which she operates.

This is a "point fingers first, and berate those who don't point them at all." This design can be presented in several different ways. For instance: when she was granted the privilege to interview the freed Elizabeth Smart—no doubt still enduring severe mental trauma, even after three years—Ms. Grace repeatedly pressed her to answer explicit details of her horrifying experience. After her first questions only generated a perplexed look on Elizabeth's face (a confused "of course I was scared" look), the diabolical daughter of Lucifer pressed on, despite the young woman not wanting to talk about the nightmare but instead trying to promote an upcoming sex offender registry bill.

Finally, when questioned about the burqa she was forced to wear, Elizabeth decided she had had enough. She then told 'ole Nancy that she did not appreciate having all those horrific memories being brought up. The now ashamed (or maybe it is that she has no shame at all) Ms. Grace followed up with her trademark overdramatic sympathy. I can't imagine a single viewer of her show still believing in her pathetic act.

Another demonstration of how her show is presented in the most grotesquely sensationalized manner is that of the scrolling headline that appears with every episode at the bottom of the screen. To wit, *"Breaking News" is not something we found out a week ago!* Still, she continues to roll with it—all the while lacing her commentary with "news" left unconfirmed, and emotions nobody believes to be genuine.

However, out of all of this, the most revealing illustration of her evil is in the way she selects her stories. What happened to her concern regarding the trial of "Tot Mom" Casey Anthony, or accused child murderer Melissa Huckaby when the story of Michael Jackson's death went live? Who was keeping us updated on all those high-profile cases just before the King of Pop overdosed on his favorite drugs?

The answer is as scandalous as the ratings, and only shows Nancy Grace to be a fraud. We can again confirm this as we watch the very end of the show, and see Ms. Grace give passing mention to a child found alive, or to U.S. casualties. (and only U.S.—no Iraqi child will be mentioned, for obvious warmongering reasons) To quote an old internet cliché: Nancy

Grace clearly has no Grace. Like some sort of vampire, she sucks the emotional energy out of these stories, and it might soon be that the latest sick bastard, Phillip Garrido, will be discarded when she is "finished" with him.

Now, nobody expects her to be purely objective. She doesn't pretend to be, and besides, it's the rarest of all things in this sick world. And although Grace is not the only one to use this pseudo-reporting, hers is the most exemplary. Such hyper-sensationalism deserves a new designation. For there are many institutions that make money off of war, off of laws, and off of suffering.

The subject in this essay can certainly be held in the same category. It is a syndrome, found inside the very core of human nature, which employs many a man and woman. Ultimately, it perverts the way that any civilized society should behave. It is the *Misery Industrial Complex*.

There's no need to further skewer the reputation of Nancy Grace. I'm definitely not the first person to do so. She already incurred a lawsuit, a number of insults from her own staff, and even a website appropriately titled *Nancy Grace Must Die* (it's *not* mine). The best thing we can wish for—if only for the sake of karmic justice—is that when Ms. Grace does die, she will have her death exploited in the most obscene fashion.

This will make rich the next bitch who fills her spot, and providing juicy news that the rest of us can enjoy tuning into.

(September 2009)

An Open Letter to Alex Jones Regarding his "Charlie Sheen Interview with Barack Obama"

IN A WORLD currently embroiled with lies and deception, it is not a time to alienate your allies. It is crucial that this be taken seriously by fellow freedom-fighters, realists, critical thinkers, and all others devoted to exposing the tyrannical acts that our corrupt officials inflicted upon us.

This having been said, I believe that Alex Jones made a grave error on September 8, 2009 when his website, *Infowars*, published an interview that took place between fellow "Truther" activist Charlie Sheen, and the President of the United States, Barrack H. Obama. The next headline I came across was "Alex Jones posts fake interview." I then realized that a real interview of that magnitude would have been making more waves than Hurricane Katrina.

It didn't happen at all.

This upset me. I felt betrayed. It was as if one of the leaders in the fight against tyranny was now making use of a methodology more akin to the people he's fighting. I then recalled the faked Michael Jackson video, that which "proved" the "King of Pop" was still alive. It turned out to be a deliberate fake, and instead was intended to show how conspiracies and fake news start to circulate quickly.

Unfortunately, it did just that. As journalists, activists, and researchers, we have to be completely devoted to reporting on verified information, and not drumming out some half-hearted, bogus nonsense. Because if we don't, we will end up being ignored. In short, a journalist or any other commentator is never supposed to tell fake stories. That should be obvious.

Of course, anyone can sit there and tell me that there was a disclaimer at the bottom of the transcript, and indeed there was. But that is not what I, or I'm sure many others who read that article, saw once we clicked open your popular website: a barrage of links about Charlie Sheen.

At this point, you're free to dismiss me as you like, but I implore you, from a fellow Truther and non-conformist, do not do so without taking a brief look at what is slowly happening to the Movement…because you'll realize that some people are viewing us as religious-like.

Remember—for Freedom's Sake, *remember*—that all institutions, whether private, governmental, spiritual, educational, soon become an unregulated behemoth whose only goal is to feed off of that which is most easy to exploit. Sometimes it's money, other times its power, and other times, its coercion. The fact remains that all institutions evolve into something other than what they were originally intended for.

Do not lose focus. Our goal (at least *my* goal) is regaining my Freedom. And in political terminology, that at least means transparency. Eight years have elapsed since that fateful day. And we need to continue to question our officials, if for nothing else, then for the sake of a Global Awakening. Push back against this New World Order—not with sensationalism, but with *real* information.

Again, I need to emphasize that although I am extremely disappointed with that article, I will continue to read your site daily, always doing my own work. Thank you for all your hard work.

A response is welcomed, but not expected.

(September 2009)

A War on Drugs?

A Note on Reagan-Era Policies

Drug abuse is a repudiation of everything America is.
—President Reagan

LET IT NOT be forgotten that one of Ronald Reagan's most enduring policies was an expansion of the War on Drugs. In a fit of cowboy bravado, fresh from his landslide victory, Reagan announced that the country was "taking down the surrender flag that has flown over so many drug efforts," and "raising the battle flag." And so it was that 1986 saw the passing of the Anti-Drug Abuse Act, which granted $97 million to build new prisons, $200 million for drug education, and $241 million for treatment.

His presidency also saw the creation of the organization D.A.R.E, whose mission was to prevent children from consuming illicit drugs. Remember "Just Say No"? Reagan's own drug czar, Charlton Turner, even went so far as to say he believed drug users should get the death penalty, making the ridiculous statement that "marijuana leads to homosexuality, and homosexuality leads to AIDS." Fraudulent wars of this magnitude always present themselves as noble and righteous. All presidential administrations talk about "real world" damage. But I wonder: did the "Great Communicator" really mean to vanquish drug use in this country?

I contest. The facts are much more despicable than what we've been told. There is, in fact, an incident in American history, long shrouded by neo-conservative demagoguery—the kind that looks at Reagan as the prime example of what all apple pie-eating, flag-waving Americans should aspire to be— showing him instead as the consummate hypocritical politician. This incident is the Iran-Contra Affair.

Without going into too much of a history lesson, the Contras were the remnants of a Somoza monarchy which was sponsored by the United States government. After years of brutal repression, the Sandinista rebels overthrew the government and installed a functional democracy. It was then that Reagan and his minions broke international law, putting together a quasi-army in which to oppose the new regime. This was the Contras.

One way in which this group was able to support themselves was through the sale of drugs, with cocaine being their favorite. According to Gary Webb, the Pulitzer Prize-winning reporter who broke the scandal in a series entitled Dark Alliance for the *San Jose Mercury News*, the CIA were helping the Contras to smuggle the stuff into American suburbs, with the proceeds being used to help support their atrocities. This led to the crack epidemic of the 1980's. Even more, he says, is that 'ole Reagan turned a blind eye to these operations.

These findings were later echoed by former Los Angeles narcotics officer Michael Ruppert, who has done extensive research on government drug smuggling. Recalling a 1987 CIA interrogation of Moises Nunez, a restaurant owner who dealt with the Contra narco-traffickers, Ruppert writes: "I could fill this book with excerpts from the CIA IG report." He then quotes section 490, wherein "Nunez revealed that since 1985, he has engaged in a clandestine relationship with the National Security Council." Its noteworthy to mention that the NSC operations involving the Contras were handled under the full supervision of Oliver North.

Even if there isn't concrete evidence that Reagan, or anyone close to him, had personally handled the shipments of cocaine being sent into our cities, the government finally had to admit that they knew that Adolfo "Popo" Charorro, leader of the Contras, was helping a Columbian drug lord transport drugs into the U.S., according to researcher David Icke.

With these reports, many of which came from veteran reporters and investigators, one has to wonder how sincere the "Gipper" was with all his anti-drug rhetoric. We can all imagine the conversations had between Reagan, fresh from a terrorist-funding debriefing, and his faithful wife Nancy, fresh from a D.A.R.E. fundraiser. Conversations like this would have been marvelously interesting to listen in on, but for now we can only deal with the consequences of their secret operations.

Reagan likely lied to Congress about his involvement, while at the same time tripling the prison population with mostly non-violent drug offenders. And in committing these crimes, he set the standard for other officials to come: lying, stealing, defying Congress—all justifiable because Reagan said so. It's unfortunate that future history books will bypass this part of Reagan's presidency.

(October 2009)

Truth Brigade

The Awful Effects of Tyranny and How Average People are Waking Up to the Call

Where really a New World Order can be created, it's a great opportunity.
—Henry Kissinger

A New World is emerging; it is a New World Order with significantly different and radically new challenges for the future.
—British Prime Minister Gordon Brown

WHO TODAY CAN deny that our world is accelerating into an era of unprecedented consolidation? Thirty years ago, a quiet whisper was the only way in which to speak about the concept of a global government. Today, it's spoken as any other average political agenda.

Can we not see the nations of the earth fluctuating and merging to accommodate this New World Order?

I couldn't deny it.

There would be no way for me to. And so, the other day, in an effort to alleviate these troubling thoughts, I went for a long walk. I was trying to consider all the ramifications here. Such ideals have been espoused by elites like Al Gore, the main perpetrator of Global Warming scaremongering; the House of Rockefeller, whose family ran the oil monopoly for years; and of course, one of the most power men in the world, George Herbert Walker Bush. Their idea of unilateral world governance is soon to be shoved down our throats.

To hell with democracy, I raged!

But how would the people respond to the erosion of national borders, or abiding by laws implemented by a Global Counsel? The thought made me shudder. Society continues holding on to many of its old pet peeves, some of which, like circumcision, would be seen as primitive. If we can't even deal with the negative aspects of our own culture, how can we deal with those of everybody else?

It was only when I met a homeless man at the park. His name was Bruce. After getting to know him, I was able to take comfort in the fact that the People are waking up to "what's going on?" After driving towards sanity and civility for so long, we should eventually expect at least that much.

Bruce is a 47-year-old man who lives in that Old Park that I've been going to since I arrived at this dust bowl. He's been there for two years now, living in a nicely made camp. "I've never been homeless before in my life." Being an ex-con, and living off my parents, I instantly felt an urge to remove the silver spoon from my mouth. The man was genuinely distraught. His girlfriend, who also lived with him, even offered to smoke me out with a doobie. I'm rarely one to turn down such a kind gesture.

Bruce continued, "I'm a dirt mover...we were the first ones to be effected by the Recession 3 years ago." He said 'local-something' but at this point the cannabis started to work its magic. When he started explaining the entire Global Recession, it was as if a holographic illustration was laid out before my very eyes. He had the precise mechanics down pat. "They did it deliberately," he said. "Yeah, of course...it was all planned."

Bruce was not your average homeless bum or dope fiend. "All the guys want to be here; sleeping in this fucking park all day. I don't want to be here." He had that sixth sense that had been forged by years of being done wrong in a cruel world. It happens a lot this day in age, but Bruce was a rarity: he actually paid attention to who was fucking him over.

The realization that the common people are seeing everyday corruptions was only confirmed when Bruce added one last piece of insight that was not well-regarded ten years ago: "And Obama...he's just a puppet. That's all he is." A bold statement coming from a self-described Democrat.

I shook hands with everybody, thanked them for the session. As I walked off, I looked back at the bench in which they sat, nestled underneath the overgrown trees. I saw Bruce and his girlfriend walk back to their camp, while the others lingered around or made their way to the liquor store for more booze. It was a perfect representation of what has happened to American society. Lives shattered and families broken. Sadly, many of those circumstances are the fault of only themselves...and I wondered what our species was coming to. And for some reason, maybe because of that sad portrait of life, I wasn't very hopeful.

Veteran's Day, 2009: There is, as I am happy to report, an optimistic side to this story. I usually pray for such a moment whenever I'm consumed by misery and the anger that follows.

There is a larger number of citizens who have joined the ranks of the Truth Brigades, demanding that the real promise of

Change (I was corrected: the proper term is 'Progress'). From Los Angeles to Ground Zero; from the UK to Australia; hundreds of thousands of people who were once comfortable with the standard nine-to-five, conventional, TV—programmed lifestyle, have taken to the streets in fits of anger, energized with a conviction that the evil now known, thanks to the modern era of the internet, be brought into the public eye, and that real significant change take place within our government.

You might have seen them on freeway overpasses, or on the street handing out DVD's. You might even have got one from me (or perhaps a middle finger, depending on your response). They are the We Are Change Movement. And they are the perfect complement to a generation that acknowledges such prophetic books as Orwell's *1984*, or Huxley's *Brave New World* as real-life scenarios unfolding today. As Howard Beale said in the 1976 classic *Network*, they're mad as hell, and they won't take it anymore.

I first joined the group about four months ago. For me, there wasn't much thinking required when answering the question: is there something wrong with our world? With these convictions in mind, I went to the 405 freeway on Veteran's Day, where the Los Angeles chapter of We Are Change was meeting for their monthly rendezvous.

I arrived a little early, and with nothing else to do I decided to walk around a bit, familiarizing myself with Culver City, seeing if I couldn't find where Jack FM was stationed. With no luck, and with the internal clock telling me I had been gone for hours, I decided to head back. At 2:30 PM, nobody was there yet. I began to panic, wondering if I was in the wrong spot. To relieve my aching bladder full of ice coffee, I went to the supermarket next to our meet-up street. When I emerged, I headed back to the overpass. I almost hoped that nobody would show, simply for the fear of getting too stoned and having thoughts of Men in Black positioning themselves on high buildings with high-powered telescopes.

Like an army of activist ninjas—most wearing dark T-Shirts with such color-contrasting slogans as *End the Fed* and *9/11 was an Inside Job* emblazoned on them—they had stealthily set up a base camp at the peak of the overpass.

Finally, I got to meet the troops. I had met most of them before, but this was the first time for full conversations. With no dull moments in our dialogue, topics ranged from the Federal Reserve, to the War on Drugs, the Wars in the Middle East, and, as mandatory, the Attacks of September 11th 2001.

Katy, one of two main organizers, used to describe herself as a "hardcore" liberal in favor of gun control. Then one day she began researching September 11th. Once she found out the inconsistencies with the official story, her perspective changed. "I said, 'oh, that's what the Second Amendment is for.'" I concurred and added that people nowadays have turned into ravenous beasts interested only on survival—in even if stepping on your neighbor is the way to do it.

The other organizer, Bruno, struck me as being someone who had fallen deep into the world of conspiracy. He was no doubt a regular reader of InfoWars (I'm a regular consumer myself). Every time an overly obscure subject came up—like the Moon Landing being a hoax, or the Moon being an alien space craft—you could here at least one person say "that's too far down the Rabbit Hole for me." Judging what Bruno talked about, it's fair to assume he had dived head first down that hole...and wasn't coming back.

Altogether, there was about a dozen or so people. Most, like Bob Sherman, were only more than interested in telling their story. "I'm Jewish" Bob had asserted. The blunt way he said it compelled me to offer an apology. And as I was about to offer an embarrassing retraction for my apology, he asserted another insightful morsel; "the Kabbala is a technology, not a religion. It's God's Technology."

Interesting.

I then concluded that God was, as it is becoming more and more evident today, an extraterrestrial.

When the protest was all over, we drove over to a hole-in-the-wall Indian place. As I ate my delicious multi-colored slop, I joined in a conversation about the Prison Industrial Complex, giving my own insight. Faintly, I could hear Bruno talk about how Stanley Kubrick was murdered for attempting to come clean about his involvement with the Lunar Landing. Crazy tales for a crazy world.

All in all, the event was a self-esteem booster.

I felt like I was fulfilling Chomsky's desire to see more people participate in Democracy. He wouldn't have been happy about our collective support for Gun Rights. Or our desire to end the Federal Reserve.

No, indeed, he wouldn't have been happy with those ideals any more than he would have been happy of me smoking a doobie out at the picket line.

Even still, we were out there, and together we were acknowledging that there is something wrong with our current system.

And here we have average people, you and me, from all parts of the same dystopia. But they have one unique aspect to them...a compulsory urge to get up every morning and start speaking their minds on any old gray sidewalk.

That's admirable, and anyone who castigates these people while watching a mind-numbing "reality" show or agreeing with Rush Limbaugh has little right to do so.

I might not have agreed with everything everyone said but were on the same frequency with a lot of issues. They're not demented. After all, the Fed really is a private bank which sends our money overseas; the War on Drugs is a violation of our national creed of freedom; multi-national corporations do direct policy with their influence; and our government has covered up details of 9-11. To demand reform of the institutions which affect our lives is hardly an endeavor to be shunned. We can't just sit idly by as these tyrannies run wild.

I hope Bruce would agree with me.

(November 2009)

No Surprise in the Afghan Elections

Hamid Karzai has been declared the winner in the Afghanistan elections, after his opponent, Abdullah Abdullah, pulled out of the race amidst complications of election fraud.

THIS "NEWS" IS being broadcast all over the Propaganda Wire today. So, it was declared that the White House's top choice for Afghan leadership is Hamid Karsi. For weeks, the entire world saw reports about Afghanistan's troubled presidential election. Now, the on-the-edge-of-your-seat result you've been expecting is here. Obama called for a "New Chapter" in relations with the Arab State. But the truth is, Nostradamus could have taken a nap and still predicted this one.

Gareth Porter at Infowars says that Karsai wasn't even close in the elections. Even the UN came out and declared fraud. That's unimportant when the U.S. needs the right man for the job. At a time when we're about to see a major troop increase, the United States has to make sure that everything is working properly.

It's well known that Karsai is in league with the Elites. First, we had Michael Moore pointing out that he was consultant for the oil giant Unocal back in the days when the U.S. was negotiating with their (then-partners) in the Taliban to build that massive pipeline down to the Caribbean. Despite the lie that the deal fell through due to a civil crisis, the reality is that the Clinton Administration had little choice but to renege on the deal, this because of wide scale protest from human rights activists, who seemed to be the only ones who cared that the Taliban were (and still are) regular practitioners of female genital mutilation. Our government's response to these crimes is practically null and void except to the extent in which the money starts filling their bank account.

Then, William Engdahl, also at InfoWars, wrote on a UN report that indicted a dramatic increase in opium production since the fall of the Taliban in 2001. Now, Afghanistan is once again the premier heroin provider in the world, with nearly 93% coming out in '07. It is also now said that Hamid Karzai is the Opium Godfather. He's the pimp daddy that sows a woman's vagina shut while monitoring the poppy fields.

Those goofy Popalzai tribesman!

PressTV is also saying that the opium is stockpiled at two primary sites and—*gasp*—the sites are run by joint US, UK, and Canadian forces. It's common knowledge that the elusive substance is a fundamental component of the Afghan economy. From there, it's not hard to speculate that a country with such a major imperial influence—in the form if Uncle Sam—would see a tax on such a major trade. The cost of lives and addiction are irrelevant, or so says Uncle Sam as he sends your kids over there to fight and die for the Empire.

(November 2009)

The Governator

Lame Duck, or Making a Last-Ditch Effort?

IT'S ALWAYS FUNNY seeing the portrait of Governor Schwarzenegger hanging over the main desk of my patrol office. Every time I go in, I can't help but wonder if it was up there only due to some state law, or because it's just proper in the grand political sense. The history between the C.C.P.O.A. (the California Correctional Peace Officers Association) and the Governator is a tumultuous one. They disagree over just about everything. But the portrait's there, and I like to think of it as symbolic gesture; perhaps a reconciliation of ideals, intended for the betterment of us all. But probably not.

There is a problem with the prisons in this state, as I've detailed elsewhere. And, as far back as I can look, Arnold has been talking about ways in which to fix them. Our prison system is in absolute shambles, and I suspect the public is largely in the dark. Like every other issue, the public hears that "something is wrong." Then there are some discussions, and then finally some small proposals—none of which ever solves anything. For those who have lived through it, and can diagnose the problem exactly, it seems so simple. Still, reality TV helps keep any concerns from the public quieted.

Despite becoming the Prison Question in the Golden State, the evil union would not prefer a solution. Every time someone in our congress protests, out come the threats of lawsuits or recalls; as it is, politicians easily turn yellow in the face of green or red.

There might be a silver lining coming through, as Schwarzenegger is out of office soon. So, he's got nothing to lose. At his recent State of the State address, he openly endorsed the idea of prison privatization, this as a way to save money and to allocate more funds to higher education. But wholescale privatization won't happen over here. His 2006 emergency declaration allowed for a trickle into neighboring states. It's since been struck down by the courts.

The union cries about inmate out-of-state inmate transfers, or housing them in private institutions, because money might not find its way to their coffers. Dan Morain reports on the recent developments. Three years ago, the Corrections Corps of America—a private company—signed a $20 million contract with the State of California. That came out to 900 inmates at four facilities, $63 per head per day. That deal has since evolved into 10,000 inmates, at $72 per head per day, for an overall cost of $632 million. CCPOA weeps at their losses.

Crime is a precious resource, and it is mined and refined within the facilities ran by that very same union. Those crooks take up 10% of the annual budget, housing 175,000 inmates in space originally designed for 100,000. And as they demand more and more, they do nothing to lower the embarrassingly high recidivism rate.

Their monolithic mass did not prevent them from squeezing into bed with former governor Gray Davis, who had no qualms about selling himself. Price? The union gave a $251,000 contribution—in one day! The union had some strings tied to his wrists, which were then used to sign a 37% pay increase. Finally, five private prisons were shut down.

Who can't see what's really going on here?

Where are the representatives discussing bloated budgets, corrupted officials with obvious conflicts of interest, or the general welfare of society? The question must be asked, and even if I'm the only one who has asked it, I'll continue to ask it: Where is the incentive for prison authorities—either state or private—to start working on true reform? The answer: none! For many, crime does pay. And until we realize that, there isn't much hope.

Personally, I believe that since inmates are sentenced in state courts, they should be housed in those same state prisons. Democracy would also imply a certain amount of transparency and accountability. It just doesn't happen with the C.C.P.O.A. Perhaps a temporary private hand-over would be in order, to be rescinded as soon as new guards are hired, with better oversight.

Maybe Schwarzenegger needs to read some of the editorials. After all, he is being called the new "lame duck" politician who couldn't do a damned thing for our troubled state. Maybe he'll gather some of that old courage we all saw in the theater and do something heroic.

He should get moving, before history remembers him as a pathetic onscreen he-man who couldn't' deliver in the real world.

(January 2010)

Like I Said: 9-11 *Was* an Inside Job

Simply, Politically

NINE YEARS AGO, this country was attacked. It was the first time since Pearl Harbor, that our nation was assailed on our own home soil. Four planes, allegedly hijacked by nineteen Islamic extremists, were used as missiles against government and commercial buildings—killing over 3,000 people and creating a ripple effect across the entire globe.

Nine years later, we live in the real-life Orwellian world, one where wars are waged endlessly; torturing uncharged persons is legitimized; and waging a campaign of illegal eavesdropping is considered a necessary measure in protecting against "the evildoers."

But many citizens just aren't buying it. In fact, a third of all Americans, not to mention the much larger percentage of Europeans, believe that the Government and the Bush

Administration were, in fact, complicit with September 11th. These revelations are not without their merit. For anybody willing to shed the idea that governments—including the one that controls the U.S.—are incapable of inflicting or inviting harm upon their own citizens and are willing to go the extra step in doing some independent research, they would no doubt find evidence to support the very contrary.

Jeremy Rothe-Kushel is such a researcher. Like many who witnessed the attacks, he had no inclination that the Government was involved. It was that big moment of post-attack that spurred the American population into a mood of war-time hysteria, believing that Bush was going to lead us into enemy territory and bring justice to those who dare kill our citizens.

But Jeremy wasn't duped so easily. He tells me that after attending several hip-hop concerts in Western Massachusetts where he received a "Deception Dollar," and after reading Barry Zwicker's *Towers of Deception*, he began to question the official story. I met up with him in a little hole-in-the-wall coffee shop in downtown LA, where thirty or so people were seated in a dark room out in the back, all of them huddling around a big screen projector and having conversations about the political issues of the day. He walked in soon after I got there, ordered a tuna melt and a cup of coffee, and jumped right into the fray— lending expert analysis to the given subjects being discussed. I looked on from my stool, drinking black coffee spiked with Smirnoff vodka, and wondering if the powers-that-be were aware of these groups; those that meet in secret as an effort to undermine their efforts to colonize the world.

For Jeremy, the "smoking gun" is the physical destruction of the towers. "There was a devastating force that destroyed over 1000 bodies," he tells me. "They can't find the smallest particles of them."

Another factor that he believes proves higher involvement

is the cover-up. "There were massive financial transactions taking place the day before, and the day of the Attacks. They made 'put' options on the companies that were going to lose stock," he tells me. Michael Ruppert explains this detail in his book *Crossing the Rubicon*. As for the intelligence that was gathered prior: Russian intelligence, Mossad, German, and supposedly the Saudis, were all warning or talking about impending attacks on America.

Even if one doesn't want to believe that their government would be involved, the gross number of omissions and contradictions in the official report has left the objective thinker wondering if there was another piece to this whole puzzle. For example, the official report does not mention why Flight 77 was left unmolested for almost 45 minutes before hitting the Pentagon, and nearly a half hour after Flight 175 struck the South Tower. Do we at least deserve an answer as to why our military—the one whose budget is bigger than all other nations combined—was suddenly outsmarted by guys with box cutters?

More so, why did the report tell us that Hani Hanjour had his pilot license rejected because he was a "terrible pilot" but then assure us he was the "operations most experienced pilot"— managing to fly a Boeing 757 through a 330-degree spiral dive maneuver?

Or how about the fact that the Report does not even mention—not once—the collapse of World Trade Center building number 7? For the first time in history, a steel structure was brought down by fire; never mentioned, at all, in the official report.

As for me, the clincher is in the prosecution. As it turns out, many of the 911 Commissioners, the ones who were supposed to find out what happened that Day, have publicly come out and admitted the investigation was compromised from the beginning. Max Cleland resigned from the Commission, famously stating that it was a "National Scandal." Thomas H.

Kean and Lee H. Hamilton have even coauthored a book about the deception. John Dean, former crony to Nixon during the Watergate days, has written that Bush and Cheney have stonewalled every valid attempt to find out what happened. That's true. Bush Jr. said that he refused to meet with the Commission alone or testify under Oath. This was a slap in the face to the families who lost loved ones in those buildings.

So, picture yourself sitting inside of a courthouse, where a man stands trial for murdering your daughter (or a loved one). He swears he didn't commit the crime and is refusing to take any plea deals. You see him there, sitting inside the booth, wearing jailhouse clothes; truly, you see this man as the culprit. Then, all of a sudden, the prosecution stands up and says "you know, your Honor, we just don't have any evidence against this man." What would you do? Ignore this statement? Figuring "ah, no big deal." Of course not! The compulsion, ever since your daughter was murdered, was to figure out exactly who did it, without whitewashing over facts or evidence. Why should 9-11 be any different? And why should you believe the official story, when even the Commissioners don't believe it?

This brings us back around to Taliban, who told American diplomats that they will hand over Osama Bin Laden if the U.S. is able to provide evidence. Uncle Sam refused to do so, even after telling the American people that they had hard evidence.

Through all this, and so much more, we are told to keep quiet and support whatever it is our government tells us. The roots of a totalitarian society are easily seen on the Television screen. As Glenn Beck draws on his chalkboard, coloring out communist conspiracies, he shudders at the first mention of a 9-11 government cover-up. Or when 'O Reilly shut off Jeremy Glick's microphone during an interview, just for bringing up the U.S.'s support for the radical Muslims in the 80's and 90's. It would be hard-pressed to find out if these Neo-Con commentators, the ones who are usually expressing their contempt for Big Government, are in actuality paid disinformants. Or, maybe, in a greater leap of faith—they really believe in what they're spewing from their mouths. "Hating your Country" because you question your government's actions. The defenders of the American Faith prove nothing by exercising this Right. And they try to ensure that the ones who are asking the tough questions are labeled as ridiculous and treasonous, all for demanding answers as to why our citizens had to die. The genuine fakes, as I like to refer to them.

As I sat at that table, talking to Jeremy and scribbling out notes, I remembered another aspect in this vast spectrum. History has demonstrated many times before that it is willing and able to carry out attacks against its own population. Plenty of examples are there to pick from, but the one that came to my mind was the Gulf of Tonkin incident in 1964, whereas Lyndon Johnson announced to the World that the USS Maddox had been attacked by the North Vietnamese Army. It led immediately to the Gulf of Tonkin Resolution—an acceleration of the Vietnam War. In 2005, documents released revealed that none of it ever happened.

Hitler had similar tactics. Operation Himmler was a Nazi plan to blame the Polish for the murders of German citizens. Dressing German civilians up as Polish soldiers, they would then storm towns and vandalize, steal and murder; blaming the whole thing on a country the Nazi's were eager to invade. It worked. Elementary logic then begs the question: If you were living in Nazi Germany, would it be immoral to raise a complaint?

Authoritarian power structures, like Nazi Germany, the U.S.S.R. and, yes—the United States—have no qualms about killing whoever gets in their way. How could they? The U.S. has supported murderous dictators for years; Suharto was a 40-year favorite in Indonesia; Reagan loved his Central American death squads; and Clinton cozied up with the Haitian militants,

FRAPH—leading to countless thousands who were murdered and mutilated. So why would they start caring now? With regard to 9-11, the Neo-Con think-tank, Project for the New American Century, specifically required a "New Pearl Harbor" to further implement an imperialistic agenda.

No conspiracy, folks.

As Jesse Ventura says when asked how he became a conspiracy theorist, "my government has lied to me so many times, they've lost all credibility with me."

The Truth hurts.

(February 2010)

Domestic Dissidents

Condemned as Loons, or Vindicated in Anger?

THE FEBRUARY ATTACK on a Texas IRS building in Texas left many tragic things in its passing: Two deaths (one a worker at the institution, the other a mad software engineer), a heavily damaged Federal Building, and a rapid acceleration of fear-mongering in the United States, courtesy of the usual commentary. A segment on CNN's crawling "news" bar read something like, "Some calling Joe Stack a Hero?"

It was not an inquiry; it was an assertion meant to equate such possible thinking as ludicrous or terroristic.

But does the shoe ever get put on the other foot? Can anyone remember the last commentator from the mainstream spectrum who said, "Boy, that Federal Reserve (the Brains of the IRS) really does deflate our currency with all its inflationary policies? All they do is spend our money on their rich corporate friends (the bailout)." Or how about this one?—"Amazing how that Military Industrial Complex is racking up trillions onto our foreign debt, all for a war based upon lies told by its spokespeople (various Administrations)." I'd actually like to hear it more often, with an equal amount of sensationalistic prose.

The current line of thought is little more than a constant apology for crimes committed by power structures, while those without a badge to flaunt or a flag to wave, with all their resentment boiling over from years of frustration, are to be chastised and labeled so that all the "normal" people can point their fingers and say "that's the reason we have them Patriot Acts." People who make such pronouncements are the leaders of the "Unthink" Movement—just average citizens too conditioned to push their cognitive functions beyond the nightly news.

I must believe that vindicated anger is held by a greater amount people, not just those with a pilot's license or those watching Mike Galanos. The merits of this hostility do exist; it's not a fragment of some newscaster's imagination. As for Stack's target, most historians are in basic agreement about the Federal Reserve. It was created in secret, off the coast of Georgia, circa 1910, by a cabal of big bankers. Almost one-hundred years later, it retains the complete authority over our monetary policy— printing dollars as long and as often as it feels necessary. And the clincher? It has near zero accountability to our Congress.

This endless funding also aids in America's primary function, that of empire building, making it even easier to see through our endless militarism. The driving force of geopolitics is guided by neocolonialism (economics). Corporations and Governments collude with each other (the definition of fascism) to garner greater control of resources, territory, etc. Along the way, the Imperialism (military occupation) places strategic, permanent military bases in select locations around the world.

While others will argue the timeline of this Empire, I only need since Post-World War II, when America had effectively exhausted its Oil supply. To supplement the need for a growing population, Truman and Eisenhower began the tradition of handing over vast amounts of funds to foreign dictators who were sympathetic with our ever-growing hegemony. Saudi Arabia, Iran, and Iraq have all been on the receiving end of the taxpayer's dime. Forget the regime, never mind the human right's record. With that, along with the 700-plus bases around the world, and all the money flying out the windows for these efforts, we have seen a depreciation of our currency as we've never seen before. We need not go into the perception held by other nations—the ones who speculate as to how far America's influence will go before it peaks. Again, who laments these things?

As unorganized as Stack's so-called "manifesto" is, it makes me wonder how many more people believe that *something's wrong* here at home. Ill-defined, rarely specific: but a legitimate anger, nonetheless. The next wonder is whether or not this Stack fellow should be defined as a terrorist. Why not call him a dissenter? Since 9-11, the word terror—and all its variation: "evil doers", "people who hate our freedom", etc.—have been made synonymous with even the barest of grievances. Protesting the massive health care overhaul? Well, then you're a "racist Teabagger." Don't believe the official account of September 11th? Well then, you're a "Truther Nutcase."

All of this falls under the pretenses of terroristic potentiality. The term is elastic, just as the word "communist" was before it; flexing to fit around all the people who resent Imperialism, Globalism, and Oligarchies. Ideally, this anger should be channeled more constructively; perhaps mass protests sprinkled with some criminal indictments.

The columnist Mark Ames summed it up bluntly when he regarded mainstream rhetoric about Stack's adulation as "anything to avoid seriously talking about how profound and how widely popular his suicide-dive-bombing was." Such things are never to be spoken about above a whisper. God forbid one of these mainstream commentators—the ones who would label George Washington and Ben Franklin as the same crazies—ever witness a real revolution.

They might be even more frightened to learn that 2009 had record-breaking gun sales—14 million, to be exact—more than the top 21 nations in the world.

Be not alarmed.

Or do.

(March 2010)

The Merits of Healthcare

I'M NOT IN favor of Obamacare, the new "bill" (there's always an irony with that word in the land of consumerism) just passed by our horribly abstract government. The bill is undemocratic, as it was scribbled out behind closed doors, finally coming to fruition on Sunday, March 22nd, 2010—historic day as any—and without any votes given by the Republicans.

Obama lied, saying a number of times that the discussions would be "broadcast all over C-span." I don't remember watching them either. The bill is set to revamp our healthcare industry by implementing broad regulations on the insurance companies. For instance: forbidding any sudden discharges of patients with preexisting conditions; then allocating more funds, through cuts on Medicare, to cover the projected increase in costs. Our deficit is expected to soar to anywhere between a few billion, to well over a trillion. Even without understanding all of it, it's obvious the law isn't great.

Nevertheless, reform is desperately needed. Private

institutions are a failure. There are over 47 million people in this country who are left uninsured. It's not that they can't always pay. A lot of the time it's because insurers won't cover them for fear of losing profits. Business as usual.

A relative recently gave birth to "number three," and because she was with child, she was denied coverage. Eventually she had to receive help from the state of California. She works, pays a lot in taxes, and hasn't had more than a traffic ticket her whole life. That's wrong. Worse, the "pro-life" side of politics rarely has anything to say about it. Furthermore, our Constitution declares, as ordained by God, the right to "Life, Liberty, and the Pursuit of Happiness." Did nobody tell the pro-lifers?

I think most of this is trivial. America has—or had—the resources to fix this problem long ago. Instead, over half of our federal budget goes to the Pentagon and its massive military expenditures. The cost of the two latest wars, since 2001, is almost $974 billion. At a recent antiwar protest in Los Angeles, I saw signs condemning these figures, while other signs read "What About Healthcare?"

When it comes to the matter of "coverage for all," there's plenty of people in favor of it, but are routinely shouted down by the chants of individualism. "Not a right if it relies on other people." Individualism should be constantly strived for, but it usually only goes as far as a sovereign nation allows it to. A state should not be designed in a way that protects only lone persons striving for personal wealth.

"American citizens": a popular designation that's been uttered by nearly all freedom fighters in this republic. This is a plural, democratic (a philosophy that has lost all meaning amongst slanderous terms like "communist" and "Marxist") term that grants sweeping authority to a collective voice that resides within an established nation. We frequently argue the limits of that authority. With whom? Often, pro-life, pro-war people, who become collectivists as soon as there's a new war brewing. Then, we soon hear about "we" and "us," with the urgent necessity to "fight together" against the current phantom enemy.

So. Does a business, like medicine, have the right to deny coverage? Absolutely. Do a nation's citizens have the right to put their tax dollars towards the creation of a new institution? Since we can get past taxes being the theft of "property"—it's not—we should be saying the same thing: *absolutely*.

Why don't we just go state by state and offer up a ballot measure that would allow for the creation of government-run medical institutions? Building projects and hiring doctors would offer employment. The institutions themselves could be paid for by a single-payer system, accountable only to the people, and competing with private insurers for a reduction of costs. At the same time, we could cut military spending, reestablish diplomacy, and end tons of wasteful spending (there's so much!).

Hawaii has offered universal health coverage to its population for forty years. It consistently has lower numbers of uninsured, around 8 percent averages, compared to the 15 percent found in most other states. Why not?

(March 2010)

Putting an End to the Drug Lords

FOR THOSE WHO wish to continue waging a War on Drugs, I have a suggestion for you: Go down to your local bank, get out your card, and pull out all the money you have. Just remember to save for a little in gas, because you have to drive on over to the local drug dealer—and give him every single last dime of it. In a "round-a-bout" way, that's what you're doing now if you're paying taxes! When you see the kids getting shot up at the local Jack in the Box or hear about the hitman down the street getting busted for some random murder, just know that you are the ones to blame.

This is consumerism. Americans buy far too many unnecessary commodities. So it is: provide, and demand. For those suffering from a drug addiction, the ones who do the providing are usually demented individuals who engage in those barbaric pastimes: decapitation, mutilation, sex slavery, and acid baths.

The commodities in question here are often (but not always) addictive, scarce, and dangerous. There is no doubt that many drugs have harmful qualities, and that does influence society. My concern is the apathy—or perhaps ignorance—of our politicians who create a perfect environment in which these Drug Lords can thrive, and where no one with an addiction can seek proper help.

The Drug Lord's success is predicated on the public's addiction for these drugs. In fact, they can't do without it. But drug addiction is not a crime; it is a disease. If it were the latter, then the same case would have to be made for a McDonald's hamburger. After all, many scientists are now saying that fast food could be as addictive as heroin, leading to high cholesterol and high blood pressure. Then come the high costs of medical care. Should we ban these products also?

Of course not! There is, and always has been, another way in which to deal with the problem of an unhealthy lifestyle: education. You are never going to do away with what the public demands. Not for food, not for clothes and certainly not for substances with addictive qualities. You must treat the disease itself. Instead, we spend all this money on judicial proceedings. At the end of those proceedings, we send the "offender" to either county jail, or state prison.

And until the more recent scrutiny of the prison systems, everyone had it wrong. They assumed that prison was a worthy institution in which to send these addicts so that they can receive some sort of "rehabilitation." "Rehabilitation" is a laughable misbranding. It's nothing short of an open conspiracy within a secretive institution.

How foolish. In fact, very much the obverse. Ever since Prison Guard Unions monopolized their influence, we have seen the AA, NA and job training systematically erased, while their own paychecks have doubled and tripled in size. Even more insidious is their tacit endorsement of criminal activity behind those prison walls. There, nobody can see it, and we have the inevitable outcome of criminal reproduction. With gang affiliation and racial profiling—approved and promoted by the Guards' Unions—it leads to higher recidivism rates, and thus more leverage they can then wield when it comes time to ask for more money.

My suggestion is that we take these black-marketed items, placing them under government regulation. There will be age limits, and limitations on how much you can buy. The money can then be used for adequate drug programs.

Measures like this have shown themselves to be far more effective. In 2002 Portugal became the first nation to decriminalize the possession of all drugs. Instead of jail, offenders are sent to a panel where they can receive some other form of evaluation or help. Skeptics at first believed this would lead to more drug use. A report issued by the Cato Institute shows that the number of users decreased, while persons seeking treatment doubled. It took away the criminal reproduction and replaced it with sensible treatment.

On the other hand, if you wish to continue on with criminalization, you must raise more taxes. It will be needed in order to fund the street fighting and gang wars taking place not only in our own suburbs, but also in a good part of Mexico as well. Unless you are willing to launch outright war against the cartels, you are not going to win this bogus war.

Otherwise, we must transfer the responsibility of drug distribution and regulation from the Drug Lords and place it under the watchful eye of public scrutiny.

(May 2010)

The Shirley Sherrod Debacle Jeopardized Free Speech

SO IT IS today, in the year Twenty-Ten, that we see our president, Barack Hussein Obama, as he lays the groundwork for what could be the demise of the last most essential freedom: the absolute right of free speech and expression. Obama refers to this period as "the media age"—a cryptic term that should only be described as a condemnation for the freedom that cyberspace can provide. If his idea proves to be part of this progressive government it could spell extinction for the First Amendment, as well as the internet as we know it.

"Something shows up on YouTube or a blog," Obama says with disdain, "and everybody starts scrambling." He was referring to the recent Shirley Sherrod spectacle. The 62-year-old African American woman served as the Georgia State Director of Rural Development for the United States Department of Agriculture before conservative commentator and blogger Andrew Breitbart filmed her at a meeting back in March that, supposedly, showed Sherrod referring to a racist incident 20 year ago, in which she discriminated against a white farmer. She was fired soon after it appeared on the web, igniting a firestorm of controversy across all the major media outlets. But Sherrod's troubles, as well as her angst, are but an afterthought in the much larger picture.

Enter the talking-head known as Anderson Cooper, who, like many others, acted like a snake eating its own tail. With eyes scrolling across the teleprompter at pristine pace, Cooper launched a barrage of verbal attacks against the footage, claiming it to have been "taken out of context" and lecturing on about how "real" journalists are supposed to factcheck and exercise balanced reporting whenever possible.

I've got a fact for him: Right now, there is a bill sitting in our Congress that would give the president the authority to "kill" the internet. The bill, called the Protecting Cyberspace as a National Security Act of 2010, was authored by independent senator Joe Lieberman. If it passes, it will allow the president to shut down part of the internet in the event of a cyberattack for exactly 120 days, unless Congress passes an extension, in which case it'll hold indefinitely.

Like so many instances whereby an unfortunate situation turns into an even worse form of tyranny, the termination of Ms. Sherrod can only be expected to help to draft and introduce even more despotic legislation.

Furthermore, Obama wrote in his book, *Audacity of Hope*, that he believes the Constitution is a "living document"—able to bend and to mold to accommodate the troubles of any day and age. There are philosophical differences between civil rights activists from the 50's and '60s and the strict constitutionalists making headlines today. Rand Paul, more of the latter, made a decent point when questioning the merits of the Civil Rights Act: "One reason that we have freedom is that we tolerate boorish behavior."

Exactly.

Putting these sentiments into the context of the Sherrod situation, it should be stated that the main purpose of journalism is to protect our rights, not to chastise them. The First Amendment guarantees every one of us the right to speak, organize, write, shout, yell, protest, scream, record, videotape, and—yes—keep our elected officials aligned to the values in which they espouse. So, sorry to Ms. Sherrod, but this encompasses even "bad" journalism, no matter how heavily edited the clips are.

Even if cyber security type legislation doesn't happen for another twenty years, it's still possible that it'll get passed sooner rather than later. After all, crime rates are always an easy rationale for taking away the Second Amendment, diluting it almost to the point that only criminals are in possession of firearms. Same thing with the Fourth, with "probable cause" being the only words needed for a cop to kick a door in these days. The Tenth? States rights? Only in rare cases is that amendment ever upheld, like with cat declawing or something irrelevant. Certainly not with something like drug policy, or other issues that affect the masses.

It all starts with an angry person and a small disagreement. Then the erosion of liberty accelerates, not the opposite. Rand Paul would concur. While this whole matter should have been a 30-second segment, it appears, I'm afraid, to be used as fodder for our backwards government, and the Media Machine that routinely propagates its message, to be dissected and used as a tool for further rescission of our rights.

(August 2010)

Montel Williams: An Advocate

MONTEL WILLIAMS MEANS business. He always has. His popular syndicated TV show, which ran for seventeen years, was probably the last real talk show in which he used his voice to connect real issues and real insight to an attentive public. There were no continual episodes in which loose women would plead desperately to find the father of their child, or an abundance of adulterers seen regularly on every other channel. Instead, topical, albeit somewhat sensitive issues—such as victims of warfare, abused women, people suffering complicated health issues—were at the forefront of his show, always explored with a certain depth and perspective.

Today, Montel continues his advocacy. He is widely renowned for his efforts in promoting a healthy lifestyle; for bringing awareness and charity to sufferers of multiple sclerosis; as well as being one of the most sincere and steadfast advocates in helping our society to finally recognize the medicinal properties of cannabis sativa, which has helped him manage his own MS diagnosis for over ten years. "There has been study after study after study after study that has proven marijuana's efficacy when it comes to MS and other diseases," Montel tells me during a telephone interview. He's never at a shortage of words, or facts, that showcase his conviction.

Montel Williams: ...but MS in particularly. As a matter of fact, most recently, a California state-funded study that was completed at the University of San Diego just concluded unequivocally that marijuana helps reduce neuropathic pain and helps to reduce some spasticity and pain related to neuropathy and MS. So, I'm doing what—you know, if we had just paid attention along the way to every study that the federal government has commissioned or accomplished, and paid attention to it; this illegality is a legal joke for anybody with MS or other diseases."

K.M. Patten: I see. Did you discover cannabis after your diagnosis, or how far afterwards did you...?

MW: You know, I will admit it one-hundred percent: when I was younger, I used marijuana socially and occasionally—'till I was maybe 16, 17. Then I spent 22 years in the military and I was drug tested over and over and over in the military; so I put my uses on hold throughout that time, and then after I got out of the military I was probably a casual—and by "casual" I mean less than once or twice a month—user for maybe a couple years.

Montel then explained to me how he found out about his condition. He says that his neurologic pain came on from a single episode, which he says felt like his feet came on fire.

MW: ...and they never went out. And I didn't know what to do. I immediately started taking prescription medication, some really powerful pharmaceuticals—and I'm not going to say anything negative about them; pharmaceuticals work for some people…um…this did not help me, and my usage of those pharmaceuticals went so high that I started to become afraid, and so people said that marijuana can help, especially with those twitches. And I have really extreme night tremors. My leg twitches—not that Restless Leg Syndrome. I have twitching that is neuropathic blimps that are going on in my nervous system. Marijuana helps to calm that down. Then I started to realize that, it doesn't take away my pain, but it makes it manageable, so on a scale of one-to-ten, sometimes if I'm sitting on a five and a half or a six, it can bring my pain down to a three or three and a half. [The pain] never goes away, but it makes me a contributing member of society.

KMP: That's cool (being a member of society again). Does it stagnate your condition, or does it curtal it a little bit, or is it just for pain?

MW: Marijuana has no efficacy in curing MS—let's make sure we get this straight: there are symptoms that it helps with. It helps with spasticity, with cramping; some people who have MS cramp up. I can go into a five- or ten-minute cramp while I'm sleeping, and cramp so hard that I wake up. What happens when I use marijuana—especially if I eat it before I go to sleep—that seems to give me this less-than-locking effect. If I eat it before I go to bed, I can sleep four or five hours without locking it all; if I don't, then I'm kicking my wife out of bed.

KMP: Okay, now, marijuana is not just for MS. Because I'm over here in California and I've interviewed people who…

MW: Oh no, I want to make sure we understand: there has been study after study after study that's proven its efficacy not only when it comes to MS, but a lot of other illnesses. Anything that has to do with neuropathic or single degeneration, like spinal cord injury, who have phantom pains; with AIDS patients or Wasting Disease. It also helps to settle the stomach for people who have cancer and are on chemotherapy.

KMP: Or Crohn's Disease also. I interviewed someone who suffered from Crohn's.

MW: Absolutely. As a matter of fact, eating it with Crohn's really helps a lot too. If you can get it as an oil, it can help to coat the intestinal lining, I am told. There is now proof it works with kids with A.D.H.D....even some forms of autism.

While many activists are fighting for the recreational use of marijuana, Montel is certain that the substance is a powerful medication, and that it should be treated exactly as such.

MW: Here's the problem: You have a powerful medication—and it is a medication, let us not think otherwise in any way shape or form, it is—and it should have been treated as such back in 1937 when it was made illegal. And if we researched like we have for the past 100 years, by now we would have realized that there are probably about 60,70, to 80 difference anomalies that marijuana could work with, but instead we've decided to be as ignorant as we possibly can be.

KMP: Absolutely. What do you think though—cause you're probably out there more than me—are these patients, the ones who say "yes, marijuana really does help me," are they getting the treatment they need and deserve? Or is the government really making significant strides in stopping the use of drugs?

MW: The whole issue is the most ridiculously ignorant issue that I think America has faced in the last, well, honestly since we've been a country. Let's go back for a second: marijuana has been a part of the American Fabric since this country was born. 70 percent of our forefathers grew marijuana and sold it. They grew it as hemp. This country was built with hemp. If we had not had hemp, we would not have had sails for ships, or ropes to pull those sails; or clothing in the colonial times. Hemp was one of the biggest cash crops of that time. We became so ignorant of the crop—post-the Civil War. Nobody even worried about it, and the only reason people got caught up in marijuana is because we were so caught up in Opium. It's amazing that we've come this far and haven't gone anywhere.

I soon realized that Montel really did know his stuff. He told me about the first study ever done on marijuana and encouraged me to look it up. I did: In 1944, shortly after marijuana was made illegal, a study was conducted by then-mayor of New York, Fiorello La Guardia—who was a fierce opponent of the '37 Tax Act. His study repudiated nearly everything that the Treasury Department had said about cannabis; that it did not, in fact, cause any significant harm.

MW: [Expounding on the illegality] They thought it was something that only blacks and Latinos used more than anybody else. It wasn't the fact that blacks and Latinos smoked it, it was the fact that a majority [of them] were here and were part of the work force, and not able to go into bars, not able to go and get whiskey—they were utilizing the crop off the field. Not only were they using it for the euphoria, they were using it for medical purposes also. The study continued and said that marijuana is not going to be a threat to children, it's something that's not deviant. This is back in 1944, and it said unequivocally that we should just be taxing it, and letting people use it. Now the truth is, after we've looked over the course of, now 90 years, I believe very strongly that marijuana is a drug. And we should treat it like one, without going through 30 [more] years of testing. And the federal government has already tested it for 30 years and has proven its efficacy. The federal government still dispenses marijuana.

KMP: You had said that, and I had never read about it before, that they give it out like ten times a year?

MW: No, no, no...sir: the federal government has had a program in place for 35 years, through the University of Mississippi, where every single month, they dispense canisters of marijuana to now four patients—it started off with 20 patients—the four are left because the other sixteen died. Grown by the federal government, and paid for by your tax-dollars.

Montel says that under the first Bush Regime (my words!), George Herbert Walker was hit with the introduction of the AIDS epidemic, and decided to go ahead with a program called Compassionate Use to give marijuana to these patients. After 75,000 applications, they decided to cut it off after the first 20 or so. After only four years, they realized that "Oh shit, a government that can legally do no harm, was distributing out marijuana."

MW: They were sued and were told that they couldn't stop [giving it out]. So, for thirty-five years, we've been doing it. So how ignorant is this: We have a government that grows it and sells it but locks other people up for doing the same.

KMP: Oh my god. I wanted to ask you about the Drug War entirely, but let's go back to the pharmaceutical aspect really quickly. It would seem that if there was this sort of wonder herb that helped people in all sorts of ways, then Big Pharma would lose profits from it being legal.

MW: Yeah, but they'd make the same profits off of pot. Look, let's talk about this for a second…

From here, Montel went into a horrific real-life scenario. One in which a child can walk up to any counter in any store in America, and without any identification, purchase a product that would kill him instantly. "It's one of the most deadly substances on the planet," he says, emphasizing the nightmare even more so.

MW: If you took it home, and ate about twenty of them, you'd drop dead. You know what it is?

KMP: Actually, I don't.

MW: It's called aspirin. It's made from a tree, called the willow tree. Right now, today, there is not a doctor or scientist alive that can tell you how it works. They can tell you what it does, but not how it works. If we can sell that, without knowing what it does, why can't we have a doctor prescribe marijuana? It's not the danger people have made it out to be. It's time for the federal government to do what's right. The President of the United States could change this entire insanity with the stroke of a pen. All he would have to do is change the schedule of marijuana from Schedule 1 drug, to a Schedule 2 drug—of, watch this—of heroin, of morphine, of opium. Because [those] drugs can still be prescribed by a doctor. (Sorry to correct Montel, but heroin is still a Schedule 1 drug, like marijuana—not suitable for any medical purposes under federal law).

KMP: Do you think we should just go down that route of prescription medication. Like over here, we have a historic bill on the ballot that will legalize marijuana for full recreational use.

MW: You're gonna lose it. And you're gonna lose it big, and you're going to lose it in such a way that it's gonna embarrass the entire movement. It's terrible for me to say, but I'm gonna say it; because here's the bottom line: marijuana is still illegal at the federal level. And until that law is changed...How is [the federal government] going to let one of the 50 states grow and dispense what would be an illegal substance for the other 49 states? It's not going to happen. This law, you can pass it all you want, but I guarantee the federal government will step in and shut down any usage that way.

This was depressing to hear, seeing as how close we are. He did give me a glimmer of hope when he suggested that the feds might allow it only if persons were allowed to grow and use it in their own home, and not doing in any personal sales. At the same time, Montel said that we should take away the prohibition laws of marijuana, as we did with alcohol, and control a substance that, he feels, is a controlled substance. "I don't feel this is a substance that should be sold at the 7-11 next to a bottle of beer," he added.

MW: Let's make sure we have it where someone can buy it with an ID, if you're going to try and do it that way. But for me, I need this as a medication, and I'm not going to battle with the people who want it legal [for recreational use]. But I'll tell you, I don't think the California law will pass. If the states had followed along with what they're doing in New York right now, because...the State of New York is gonna do it better than anybody.

KMP: How come?

MW: The law works this way: First of all, they're not going to let individuals grow pot. Period. If you want it, you have to go and get a prescription from a doctor, who has applied for a license at the state level, and you and the doctor will have to register. Once the prescription is written, guess where you can get your prescription filled?

KMP: Where's that?

MW: Any licensed pharmacy. Any place that has a state license to hold and manage controlled substances. Do I have to go to someone's dirty backyard? Why can I walk up to Duane Reed (a pharmacy chain on the East coast) and say, "Dude, where's my pot?" Let's take this out of the playground, and put this into the real world, and all of a sudden the whole issue goes away. When you start making it a drug, people stop playing with it as if it is.

KMP: You don't think people will still be looking for recreational pot?

MW: Well, yeah. Go ahead...

KMP: Well, that's my point, because over here, I can tell you Montel, the whole medical thing is a ruse. I walked in, paid $50 bucks, and he signed me out.

MW: You see, in New York, it's not going to be that simple. You're going to have to have a medical reason. Now, if anyone wants to have it where they can buy it at a liquor store with a license.

Montel made it rather clear that he is not a big supporter of recreational pot. While I disagreed, I respected that he was keeping it real. In fact, he says he's been trying to start a company which will operate nationwide, catering to the needs of every American patient.

MW: I'm not playing. I've, been doing this for ten years. I smoke pot every single day, several times throughout the day.

If you read General McCaffery's study, who was the drug czar back in 1999; his report came out and said it helps people with illnesses like mine. If you take a look at me in comparison with other people who have the same illness, my condition has not been in progression at the same rate as others.

The last question I asked him was about the War. He served in the U.S. Marine Corp for twenty-two years.

MW: It's a bigger question than that. We should really be asking what America's role is in the future. Every level of this government, from the judicial brand to the executive brand to the legislative branch, from the congress to the president, we can't agree on what the direction of this country is. How the hell can we set policy for the rest of the world? I'll tell you this: I will support and defend the troops to my last dying breath. Period. That doesn't mean I support the war, but I support them.

Should we bring them home?

My answer is absolutely yes.

(Unknown)

Jesse Ventura

A Second Conversation

K. M. Patten: What were your thoughts on Proposition's 19's defeat.

Jesse Ventura: Well, I was saddened by the defeat of Proposition 19, because—how stupid are they?—it would have been a new revenue source for them. The states are in such dire financial straits. Even more so, I live in Mexico and they could alleviate the problem on the border; put the Cartels out of business.

KMP: Would it surprise you if you saw troops land in Mexico, as Representative Michael McCaul is indicating he wants to do?

JV: I don't know about that, but we'd be fighting the Cartels with weapons from the U.S. But that's pretty normal 'cuz we're the biggest weapons dealers in the world.

KMP: We might have to go down there and start fighting them with pesticides and guns.

JV: It's totally ridiculous to do all that. Legalization is the simple way to take care of the problem. It's no different than the prohibition of alcohol: when you prohibit something, it makes criminals and gangsters rich. And let me add: for those who claim that the rate of usage from children would go up, stats already show that where its already legal—in Holland—less kids, percentage wise, use marijuana than do here in the U.S. where its legal.

KMP: You know, governor, over in Afghanistan we put Karzai in power even though his brother is an opium baron. If we legalized drugs, we could use that opium for patients over here, while...

JV: [Laughs] It's amazing! 90% of the world's heroin eventually comes out of Afghanistan. The Taliban shut them down. Now, look at the timing of that, to when the big international banks failed.

KMP: I don't follow.

JV: All of that money gets laundered through the big international banks. And now all those cartels are packing up and running because the banks are making a comeback. I don't know, but it seems awfully coincidental to me.

KMP: ...having a base for an anti-Taliban economy...

JV: Well, I've got a better idea: Let's bring all the troops home and end all three of these wars. We're in dire financial straits here. What business do we have fighting all these wars and putting it on the national debt?

KMP: America has its own addiction: oil.

JV: That's true. If we weren't fighting all these wars, we could take that money and put it into national health care. You could put it into alternative energy. If they want to really want to do something, then make every newly constructed home a requirement to have solar, to supplement energy.

KMP: I think we prefer the wars.

JV: Oh absolutely. We go to war when international corporations tell us to. They run the country. I made the statement that if you join the military today, you're not serving the people of America; you're just the strong arm of the corporate world. Because when people go against the corporations, then they send in the marines. It's been going on for almost a hundred years. Do you know who General Smedley Butler is?

KMP: Yes.

JV: He's the two-time Congressional Medal of Honor winner. In his memoirs, he stated that "I didn't really fight for the United States of America. I fought for the United Fruit Company." Cause whenever Central and South America wouldn't cooperate with the United Fruit Company, then they'd send in the marines.

KMP: Both of my grandfathers fought in World War Two. Back then, if they had an enemy, they'd start a draft, put a tax on it, and declare war. Now it seems like they're just leading us along to wherever it might be.

JV: What we need in this country is—and this will help stop the wars: the minute we go to war, there should be a war tax implemented. That way, everyone would feel some pain. See the problem now is, we have a volunteer military, so nobody feels any pain.

KMP: You're a former navy seal, and the Wikileaks came out and said some of our soldiers have been involved in some pretty gruesome stuff, like cutting off fingers and whatever else. Does that appall you?

JV: It doesn't bother me because you train these guys to go to war, and somehow we have a belief that war is not gruesome. And you have to remember, to go over and kill people you don't have a beef with generally, you have to train people not to have any soul or conscience. So it doesn't surprise me. There's always atrocities in war. They act like war is a damn football game. All of a sudden, we gasp and say, "Oh my goodness, how horrible." That's what war is all about. People should learn that that's why it's called war. Civilians die. That's the nature of it and that's why we should avoid it at all costs.

KMP: Do you think it could be avoided?

JV: War? Sure it could. If I became president, you know what the first is I would do? I would shut down every one of our 240-some military bases that we have throughout the world, and I would bring us all home. Because who the heck made us the policemen of the world? Having those bases all over the world, that's the same as colonization. Imagine for a minute that Hugo Chavez down in Venezuela—he's got a lot of money—imagine if he bought, say, 500 acres of land in the Palm Springs, California, and decided to move the Venezuelan Army in there. What would this country do? We wouldn't allow it.

KMP: We're more concerned about what's going on in the Middle East than what's going on right across our border.

JV: Do you know what that says to me? It says to me that some people are making big money off the illegality of drugs. Because always follow the money; the money will tell you what's happening.

KMP: What do you think we should be doing in Libya?

JV: Well, Libya is a double-edged sword too: damned if you do, damned if you don't. You certainly don't want Gaddafi slaughtering these people. Otherwise you get genocide. But you notice we never bothered in Rwanda, did we? And why? Because there was nothing to be gained in Rwanda. The corporations couldn't make a profit. Libya's got a lot of oil, so that's why Libya is more of a concern than Rwanda would ever be. It's all based upon "what can we gain from it?" What can the multinational corporations extract from the [country we're invading]? That shows where our support comes in. [If not] we'll then turn a blind eye to it.

KMP: Do you think we'll see an uprising here, like what's going on in the Middle East?

JV: I don't know. We can have a simple uprising here, and it would be bloodless. Do you know how simple that would be to do over here? Stop voting for Democrats and Republicans! Vote for anybody else. Like Ralph Nader called them: The Two-Party Dictatorship. They're been in power for all these years, so aren't they the ones responsible? And who are they blaming now? Unions. But yet not one person got busted on Wall Street. So that tells you runs the country—the Federal Reserve. These bankers. They have the money, so they run the country. It isn't our elected officials.

KMP: I agree. I think your partner Alex Jones has the right idea. It's these parasitic central banks that control the money supply. Even the Communist Manifesto says to nationalize banks. That's not exactly what Ron Paul wants to do, but why would we allow a foreign bank to control our money supply?

JV: Well, it's not a foreign bank, they're the international banks. They belong to nobody. They're just a small group of bankers that date back to when they illegally created the Federal Reserve. Because the Constitution said that [only gold and silver could be used as currency]. Then, in 1913, they ramrodded it through. And it was never fully legal because—in order to amend the Constitution—two-thirds of the states were required to vote on it. That never took place.

KMP: Right. That's why if you look at a dollar bill it says, "Federal Reserve Note." That's not a U.S. dollar. Now, I was going to ask you about how your show *Conspiracy Theory*, the episode dealing with FEMA camps, was pulled from the air.

JV: Well, apparently the United States government got so angry over the show that they put extreme pressure on AOL Time Warner, which is the parent company of TruTV. It shows that censorship is alive and well, and that the First Amendment is, you know, in big trouble. Well, read it in my book. Obama is prosecuting whistleblowers harder than Bush did. Last year alone, the U.S. government classified Top Secret 16,000,000 documents. That must be every document they put out. I'm in good company [on this issue]. Patrick Henry, 'member him? Who said, "give me liberty or give me death." Well, he had another great quote. Let me read it. The liberties of the people never were, nor ever well be secure, when the transactions of their rulers may be concealed from them." So people want to call me a traitor, but I'm in good company with Patrick Henry. And I don't think he was a traitor.

KMP: No, I don't think so, and you couldn't call it democracy when you have these small groups of people concealing all of our documents. I mean, we pay for their salaries.

JV: And that's the bottom line. We pay for the documents too. I have every right to know what my government des, because it's paid for by my tax dollars.

KMP: You have no idea why your FEMA episode was pulled?

JV: No. It came from way up top in the echelons. We must've hit a nerve. Well, we did an episode of JFK, correct? I have a full confession to the murder of JFK, and it did not receive one word of media-play. E. Howard Hunt confessed to it; he says the CIA killed him; it was called *The Big Event*; the main guys were William Harvey, who happened to be head of the CIA's Assassination Unit, and this David Sanchez Morales—and you know what he's famous for, don't ya? (Actually, I don't) Well a few years later he killed Che Guevara down in Bolivia. Took his gold Rolex watch and wore it as a trophy for the rest of his life.

KMP: You know what else happened recently that received hardly any media-play? The parole hearing of Sirhan Sirhan. He still says he doesn't remember killing Robert Kennedy. He was just up for parole and got denied.

JV: Yeah, well that always happens. They deny Manson all the time too.

KMP: Let's talk about September 11th. NIST's report (National Institute for Science and Technology) said that the towers were built with steel framing. However, I have a source over here who says that the towers were actually built with a concrete core. Do you know anything about that?

JV: We went into NIST's report on Building 7—the third building that fell, which was not hit by an airplane. In NIST's official report, they admit it was demo'ed. Well, not directly; they said it started and then went at free-fall speed. It had to be demo'ed, that's the admission. Otherwise you're defying the laws of physics. If it went at free-fall speed, that means something had to remove all the resistance.

KMP: It's been ten years since 9/11 and to this day it seems that anyone who questions it is immediately a nutcase, or a traitor, or something else.

JV: That's what the government does. That's what the mainstream media does—who are in the government's back pocket. If they can't assassinate you personally, they'll assassinate your credibility. Right away you're labeled. You're a nut. You're ridiculous. You know how I counter that? I always ask them: How much actual research have you done other than what the government told you, and what the mainstream media told you? I always tell them I've been reading and studying documents for three years. How can you call me crazy, when you're ignorant?

KMP: And even if you did accept what our government told us, fifteen of the hijackers were Saudi's! So who would have suggested that we go bomb out good friend Saudi Arabia?

JV: Exactly. Well, why did we bomb Iraq? They had nothing to do with it. And like I said, we can stop all this: just stop voting for Democrats and Republicans.

KMP: You also got a lawsuit going against the TSA. Tell me about that.

JV: Its simply the fact that I have metal in my body. When I go through a metal detector, it goes off. I could go through naked, and it's still gonna go off. It used to be that they would wand you, which was bad enough. Now they've gone to this enhanced pat-down, as well as what I call it: the microwave. Now, last summer I flew 3-4 times a week. And the government's going to tell me that going into an X-ray machine 3-4 times a week poses no threat to me? Bullcrap.

KMP: Are you still flying?

JV: No, I can't. I fly private jets. But I can't necessarily afford that all the time. And why should I? So I am suing them over the Fourth Amendment to the Constitution, which is reasonable search and seizure. I am saying that it is not reasonable to believe that Jesse Ventura—a governor, a mayor, and 6-year veteran of the United States Navy, honorably discharged—poses any threat. I've been flying for 30-years. I'm not asking for money; I'm just telling them to stop. I want a federal judge to bring an injunction to say "stop that, you're violating his Fourth Amendment Rights."

KMP: Are you going all the way with it?

JV: I'm sure the government's first thing will be for a dismissal.

And that's when it'll go in front of a judge. If he dismisses my lawsuit, then I'll know absolutely that the Bill of Rights and the Constitution are now meaningless documents. Remember, this isn't a class action. This is just for me.

KMP: Let me go back to the Drug War. In your new book, you quote Oliver North's own diary, which mentioned drugs many, many times. The fact that we have that information, that we know they were smuggling in narcotics, is it indicative of our countrymen's desire to turn a blind eye to the crimes of our elected officials and those in government?

JV: Absolutely. And not only that, you know why the CIA does it? Simple. If they get their money from Congress, then they have to report to them. But if they can get an outside income source—like dealing drugs—then they get this pot of cash, and then they can do anything they want, without anyone watching over them.

KMP: Why do you think that we continue to elect only the Two-Parties?

JV: Cause we're a bunch of lemmings. And part of it may be…the water.

KMP: You mean the fluoride.

JV: I just learned this. Do you know that fluoride—what they put in the water—is the main ingredient to? (I do. Prozac). So when you drink fluoridated water, its just like taking Prozac. And you know who came up with that, don't cha? (I know that also. The Third Reich. Nazis.) Exactly. So here we are following the Nazis again. You're a pretty good guy. You know your history pretty well, young man.

KMP: Thank you. I didn't start off with mainstream journalism, but I sort of fell into it through activism. I remember watching you on FOX News asking the anchors why no one was allowed to bring up questions concerning 9/11.

JV: Let me give you this one. We're a country that goes by the rule of law. We're ready to kill Osama bin Laden; capture him, whatever we can do, right? Well, don't we have to indict him first? We've never done that. They've had nine years for the government to go in front of the grand jury, present their evidence, bring an indictment, and then they can go get bin Laden. If he resists, I guess they'll shoot him…they'd want to kill him. He wouldn't want a trial. I think the reason we haven't done that is because I don't think we have any evidence against him. Bin Laden initially denied doing [9/11]/ To me, it all falls under a "false flag operation." Just like Operation Northwoods; just like the Reichstag Fire in Germany; the Gulf of Tonkin Incident. These are all false flag operations to put people at war.

KMP: Back to your book. Were there any documents you left out?

JV: I can't recall now. We're actually doing our next book already. We probably could've called it *A Hundred and Sixty-Three*, but we chose the best ones that really cover the gambit, and chose *Sixty-Three* because that's the year Kennedy was murdered.

KMP: Who do you think is the most persuasive propagandist in the mainstream media?

JV: You mean who's the worst of them? Fox News. Every one of them. Hannity, 'O Reilly, Beck.

KMP: The United Nations. Real fast. I was at an anti-war protest the day the Libyan conflict started. Again, Obama was down in Brazil playing golf or something, and I guess he decided to text message John Boehner—his idea of consulting congress—and just said we were going to war. How do you feel about the U.N. deciding when we go to war?

JV: The President has the ability to send the troops in—in an emergency. Then you have to bring it to the Congress.

KMP: If they're an immediate threat. Libya wasn't.

JV: [Laughs] Neither was Iraq and neither was Afghanistan. They're not threats to us.

KMP: Gotta go to war though. They love war.

JV: Oh, they love war. War makes Halliburton money. Here, I'll give you something interesting about the Gulf. About four or five weeks prior to the oil leak, all the big-shots at British Petroleum (BP) sold-off half their socks. That's good circumstantial evidence, then here's the best: three weeks before the oil spill, the biggest company that cleans up oil spills was called Boots & Coots out of Houston, Texas. Three weeks before the Gulf oil spill, they were bought by Halliburton. And it's already said that Halliburton was responsible for "bad cement" on the rig which made it happen. So, Halliburton's now getting paid on the other side to clean it up. You know what that's called? It's called Disaster Capitalism. It's where they create the disaster, and then they go clean it up. And that's what you had happen down in the Gulf.

KMP: And now they're spraying some sort of dispersant.

JV: Oh, yeah. Corexit. Thanks for reminding me. I was down there, and I said to the guy from BP, I said: How can it be good to put Corexit in there?" It has four lethal chemicals in it: cadmium, arsenic—and I forget the other two off the top of my head—and I said: "How can adding that to the water be good?" His only answer was: "Everything we did was set up by the EPA (Environmental Protection Agency). Well, get this. The company that owns Corexit is a subsidiary of British Petroleum.

KMP: They're just making money all the way around. One last bit about the Drug War. We can talk about things that are bad for us all day long. I've heard you talk about how obesity is the number one killer. Don't you think we should put some kind of regulation on what the fast-food industry is doing?

JV: You obviously saw the movie Super-Size Me. (Parts of it) Watch the whole thing. This guy eats nothing but McDonalds for every meal, and in less than thirty days he's gonna be dead. His vital organs shut down. And the doctor says if you don't change your diet, you're dead. Here's my argument: We put warnings on cigarettes, right? Well, to my knowledge, cigarettes take 20-30 years of hitting the heaters before you die. McDonalds can kill you in a month? I would think they'd put a warning on McDonalds.

KMP: Jesse, you live in Mexico for half the year. Are you thinking about getting citizenship?

JV: Yes, I am. My wife and I are contemplating it this time around.

KMP: Do you think Mexican President Calderon might be corrupted by these cartels?

JV: He's been fighting them pretty hard. If Mexico were to legalize drugs, it would put a lot of pressure on us to do the same. Over here, we believe that the Mexican government is corrupt, but we don't believe ours is. I ask myself nowadays: "Will marijuana be legalized before the Vikings win a Superbowl?"

KMP: Obama had initially said he was open to discussing the possibility of legalization. Now, he, Eric Holder, the rest, come out and say they'll be persecuting and arresting like every other administration that's come before. More indication that there's no difference between the Parties?

JV: Oh, absolutely. Both the Democrats and Republicans are totally bought and sold by the multi-national corporations. They don't want pot legalized because, after all, if it were legalized, you wouldn't have to buy a lot of pharmaceutical pills for stuff.

KMP: ...or they'd lose their Prison Industrial Complex.

JV: Exactly. And they're privatizing all the prisons. And once you do that, it becomes "for profit." It's imperative that you have a lot of prisoners. We have the most [prisoners] in the industrial world. They have to keep marijuana illegal so we can keep the prisons full.

KMP: There's this sort of national religion in this country that says we're immune from corruption.

JV: Its fascism. When I'm in Mexico, I refer to us as the Fascist States of America. It's corporations teaming up with organized religion to control the government.

KMP: I'm gonna let you get out of here, Jesse. Anything else you want to add?

JV: Let me say this: If Ron Paul were to ask me to run for president with him, I would give it serious consideration. We'd have to flip a coin though to see who would be president and who would be vice president.

KMP: What would you prefer?

JV: Probably vice. That way I could still go down to the Baja and surf.

(July 2011)

Rick Perry Speaks from Both Sides of His Mouth

HE HAS THE talk, no doubt. "And I'm just not real sure you're a bunch of right-wing extremists," the governor of the Lone Star State had told a crowd in 2009, "but if you are, I'm with 'ya!" The crowd roared, and Perry was quickly embedded inside the American psyche. Many who were paying attention saw this as his first step towards the 2012 Election.

Yet it must be said: Perry's swagger is nothing more than the same tired neo-conservative rhetoric now disguised as populist libertarianism. In fact, a closer look at Perry's record shows the same qualities as any other Washington politician. That is to say, he has a tendency to stray from his stated principles. Perry, the longest-ever serving governor of Texas, is a big fan of police states. While sleeping cozily amongst the largest concentration of private prisons in the country, and has also signed an executive order which forces young girls to receive the HPV vaccine. Parents who refuse might help to fill those prison beds.

One hundred and eleven private facilities are housed in that state, holding almost 150,000 inmates. A report earlier this month by Tim Murphy at *Mother Jones* stated that Michael Toomey, a former aide to Perry turned top corporate lobbyist now representing Corrections Corporation of America—the biggest private company in the nation—had given $20,000 for Perry's 2010 reelection big. Thomas Beasley, the founder of CCA, had given $17,000 to Perry's campaigned over the last decade.

Another private prison firm, the GEO Group, gave $15,000 to Perry's reelection campaign. Luis Gonzalez, a GEO Group lobbyist gave him another $50,000. Egregious as the cash throwing was on its face, a study by Jon Gettman at The Bulletin of Cannabis Reform, found that almost $655 million was spent arresting non-violent cannabis smokers, just in 2006. 97% of those arrests were for simple possession, leaving no question as to why, in Texas, thirty thousand people are currently incarcerated for drug offenses.

It doesn't stop there. Perry, so desperate to please the prison cartels, signed a line-item veto in 2003 which completely defunded the Texas Criminal Justice Policy Council, state agency tasked with providing "objective analysis and assessment of state criminal justice programs and initiatives."

Perry even refused to cosign a letter with other state governors who were urging a bill that would jam the signal of cell phones inside the prisons. Why would he refuse to sign that letter? According to another investigation at Local 2 News in Houston, Texas prisons are notorious for having cell phones smuggled inside the facilities. "The Texas Department of Criminal Justice says that in 2009, it found 1,110 cell phones in the possession of offenders. During 2008, TDCI says that there were 1,226 incidents of cell phones found." A marketplace of contraband thrives inside of every penitentiary, and cellphones are said to bring an easy thousand dollars to someone willing to take the risk. It's a fair guess that cell phones don't just fall out of the sky (hint: it's the guards themselves who are bringing them in).

The governor doesn't have much consistently on other subjects, either. Perry recently told a crowd that Arizona's harsh anti-immigration bill "might be right for the state of Arizona, but it ain't exactly right for the state of Texas." Then, steering off into the opposite direction, Perry expresses his unwavering support of Texas bills SB-9 and HB-12—two pieces of legislation that would effectively ban so-called "sanctuary cities" where illegal immigrants make a run to. "We believe it's even worse than Arizona's legislation," says Ana Yanez Correa of Texas Criminal Justice Coalition.

Then again, Perry has also strongly supported legislation that has been deemed "the Dream Act," which would pay the full rate of tuition for undocumented students at most state colleges. "I've been really appreciative of Governor Perry for supporting these bills," Correa says. The issue was brought up in the recently Republican debate, and Perry supported his decision.

We could keep going. Long time Texas progressive Jim Hightower has pointed out that Governor Perry rejected $555 million for social aide, while accepting $16 billion to build private roads. He was also Al Gore's Texas cheerleader in the 1980's, as well as a guest at the elitist confab, Bilderberg, in 2007. It's no wonder why his record is being thrashed onstage by other GOP candidates.

Boisterous and flippant, Rick Perry just won't do as the next president.

(September 2011)

Drugs, God, and Bush

The Work of Vincent Bugliosi

I MIGHT SAY he's the antithesis of a conspiracy researcher, an almost mythological attorney who doesn't like to see strange coincidences passed-off as empirical realities. He can quickly turn the tables on someone thinking they've got their argument made, and instead make their attestation tumble like a house of cards, leaving that person dissolute and unable to substantiate the claim much longer. Many a criminal have met such a fate at the hands of Vincent Bugliosi, the bulldoggish prosecutor best known for sending Charles Manson to prison.

Since then, he has written a panoply of best-selling indictments against various monsters of the past century, often changing the reader's mind and wondering how they could have ever thought otherwise. He destroyed the reasoning of U.S. Drug War policies; he explained to us all how O.J. Simpson got away with murder; wrote a 1,600-page tomb (which I'm still reading) on how Lee Harvey Oswald murdered JFK—*alone*; detailed the crimes of an imperial presidency in George W. Bush; and, with his latest book, *Divinity of Doubt: The God Question*, argues why agnosticism is the most reasonable position to take when it comes to the question of God's existence.

For the publication of his most recent book, Bugliosi was kind enough to talk to *Cannabis Times*. The following is both a compilation and an expansion of Bugliosi's voluminous library, including excerpts from our interview. A lot of quotations are made verbatim, and then added with my own narrative and my own reading.

"I don't want to get into that right now," Bugliosi had told me. "You can quote me out of my book...there are many of my books out there, Kevin, and you can quote me out of them, but I don't want any current statements on that." Vincent was referring to my query as to whether we should possibly legalize drugs in America. Indeed, for our interview, I had read his 1991 title *Drugs in America: The Case for Victory*. He made his statement towards the end of our phone interview, and he had answered only a few of my other questions, sticking mainly to the topic of his newest literary indictment, that against both theism and atheism.

I became interested in Bugliosi's work last year, when I picked up a used copy of *The Prosecution of George W. Bush for Murder* at a second-hand bookstore in Pasadena. Written in 2008, he makes the legal case that our 43rd president took the United States to war in Iraq under a deliberate and brazen lie— that of an immediate threat to our nation's security. It was a quick, incisive read. In it, Bugliosi summarizes startling evidence not soon to be discussed on network television.

For example, one week before Congress was set to authorize war in Iraq, in October of 2002, George Bush's administration released an unclassified version of the National Intelligence Estimate (NIE). That, a compendium of sixteen intelligence agencies evaluating Saddam Hussein's aspirations for WMD's (Weapons of Mass Destruction), was heavily edited by the Bush camp so as to insinuate that Hussein had, or was trying to obtain, said-weaponry. This version of the report came to be known as the "white paper."

The thing about this "white paper" is that it had a classified version as well, which began leaking out in '03 and '04. It was discovered then that all the dissenting criticisms put forth in the final evaluation had been completely deleted by the Bush Administration and sold-off as the last word to our Congress, including language used to indicate only an analysis or judgement instead of a confirmation. The clincher: every one of the agencies, unanimously, agreed that Hussein was not an imminent threat to the security of this nation.

October 7th 2002: One week after the affirmatory vote, Bush gave a speech in Cincinnati, where he told an unsuspecting public that Hussein was "a great danger to our nation," and that he could strike "on any given day." These warnings came on the heels of other, more dire pronouncements, which constantly led the public to believe that Hussein was "a threat" that "constituted a unique danger." Bush, so determined to take this country to war, even discussed flying U2 reconnaissance aircraft over Iraq, falsely painted in U.N. colors, hoping to "provoke a confrontation" with Hussein. This was recounted by David Manning, chief foreign policy advisor to former British Prime Minister Tony Blair.

Bugliosi does a good job outlining the lies told by the Bush Administration. That said, section two of *Bush for Murder* is entitled *Why George Bush Went to War*. It is, with respect, an undeservingly titled chapter which is more than just a bit disappointing. If it isn't already known, the true reason Bush went to war in Iraq is the same reason that we, as a privileged American collective, are inclined to forget. In two words: cheap oil. Immediately after stealing the 2000 presidential election (another topic Bugliosi deals with in his book *Betrayal of America*), Bush Jr. signed an executive order creating the U.S. National Energy Policy Development Group (NEPDG). This group was headed by Vice President Dick Cheney. Although the final report has yet to be fully disclosed, FOIA requests eventually uncovered what this "energy task force" had been studying: the remaining oil reserves in Iraq—totaling 11% of the world's petroleum. The report also included corporations considered for oil contracts.

Evidence going back even further than this are the notorious PNAC documents. That dastardly Neo-Conservative think tank, Project for the New American Century, was comprised of such real-life Dr. Evils as Cheney, Donald Rumsfeld, Paul Wolfowitz, Richard Perle, and John Bolton— all men who swam in 'lil Bush's inner circle. Its final report, "Rebuilding America's Defenses," had specified Iraq as a country in need of a new leader. This is long after having first put Saddam Hussein in power in the late 60's and nearing a decade after supporting him during our proxy war against the Iranians (which saw Hussein's near-genocide of the Kurdish tribes). Unlikely to garner support for this imperialistic venture, the 21st century Hitlerites suggested the need for a "New Pearl Harbor" in which to catalyze public opinion and shift attention towards a common goal of hegemony. This event came to fruition in New York City and the nation's capital soon afterwards.

Investigative journalist Russ Baker's meticulously detailed *Family of Secrets* provides even more evidence from a year prior. Baker quotes Texas journalist Mickey Herskowitz, who was commissioned to help write Bush's first book *A Charge to Keep*. "He [Bush] was thinking about invading Iraq in 1999," Herskowitz recounted to Baker. "My father," Bush supposedly told him during an interview, "had all this political capital built up when he drove the Iraqis out of Kuwait, and he wasted it...If I had that much capital, I'm not going to waste it." Herskowitz was subsequently fired from the writing project for failing to follow the program. Specifically, he brought up the subject of Bush's undeniable AWOL status during the Vietnam War, in which Bush disappeared from his last two years of National Guard service, evidently tired of saving Texas from the nonexistent Vietnamese invaders.

Regardless, the evidence presented by Bugliosi undeniably proves Bush as a murderer. And as much as I loved the critical, unusually controversial indictment, I was disappointed that he had omitted the petroleum motivation (which he mentioned in the work next discussed, and which I—as a damned fine conspiracy researcher eventually pointed out to him). Nonetheless, I wanted to read more of his titles, and—pray— secure that precious interview.

Around this time, I began hearing rumblings about his next title, dealing with the "god question." Wikipedia's brief entry on the man stated that Bugliosi was "an agnostic...open to the ideas of deism." That entry evolved into his most recent 338-page book that has been deemed an "agnostic's manifesto." It's a special subject for me, as I've been an agnostic since around the age of six or seven, when first posing that all important, unanswerable question to my family: Why would God create Man knowing that He was going to sentence his creation to eternal suffering? I don't think I'll ever receive a good answer to that question.

Preparing for my solicitation of Bugliosi led to a towering stack of books on my dining room table. One of them, *Drugs in America*, was a title written 20 years ago at a period when narcotics were considered to be the number one menace to society.

Dealing with another favored topic of mine, Bugliosi wrote:

The phenomenon when it comes to the drug problem,

for some unfathomable reason this nation refuses to change its policies, regardless of the failure they have proven to be. In the war on drugs, the mindset seems to be: I came, I saw, I concurred. An effort is called for to at least speculate on the dynamics behind the intellectual inertia (and hernia) which has caused our government to continue to employ an ineffective battle plan, and that will most likely cause it to refuse to employ changes recommended in this book.

And what revolutionary ideas does Mr. Bugliosi advocate? Collectively, they are known as the "Phoenix Solution." First articulating the futility of the current policies, Bugliosi writes:

When Florida's dealers and traffickers are caught and prosecuted, who represents them? Very frequently, as is the case throughout the country, former prosecutors with the U.S. Attorney's office, who, before they switched sides, had specialized in prosecuting major drug cases; IE, they are now defending the very types of drug traffickers they once vigorously prosecuted. The source of their six—and sometimes seven—figure fees that allow them to live regally in places like walled-and-gated Bay Point in Miami? Their clients' drug profits. And the game goes on.

He then outlines two different measures that, he believes, would reject this paradoxical approach and actually begin reducing the harms caused by drug use. The first, a series of "search and find missions," which would call upon the executive office to go into foreign nations that grow and distribute drugs—specifying cocaine throughout the book—and to bring them to justice. "What is meant by this," Bugliosi writes, "is the deployment of American military forces on Columbian soil for the specific and limited purpose of apprehending and bringing to the U.S. for criminal prosecution the drug kingpins who are responsible for the cocaine blitz of America." He then correctly points out that the American Empire has been launching attacks against nations that have been far less of a threat than the drug kingpins.

Sourcing from a 1952 Supreme Court case, Bugliosi documents the many American presidents who have ignored the explicit Constitutional requirement for a declaration of war, counting 125 cases since only that date in which the armed forces have been sent abroad illegally. We can add at least one more number to that total with Emperor Obama's invasion of Libya. Instead of this, Bugliosi says, we should forego any operation even resembling a military strike, and instead make it an act of law enforcement under the Posse Commitatus Act.

Meaning exactly, "The Power of the State," Posse Commitatus in the days of old allowed kings and queens to summon their citizenry to act in accordance for any and all biddings pronounced by the ruling monarchs. If one doesn't immediately view that as tyrannical, then a reading of Thomas Paine's *Common Sense* will give you a beautiful explanation as to why that policy needed to go. And even more so, the American Posse Commitatus Act of 1878 did the precise opposite: forbidding use of the military on domestic U.S. soil.

Arranging the words and numbers of the legislation as he sees appropriate, Bugliosi believes it's something entirely different when applying the law to foreign missions. "As opposed then," he writes, "to a typical military invasion, this would be a very limited search and find mission by the number of American military personal deemed necessary by the Joint Chiefs of Staff to accomplish the job"—stressing again the need to take out the drug lords of Columbia.

The second proposal is a bit more complicated. Since drug cartels have polished a near-seamless method of money laundering, Bugliosi argues that the U.S. should introduce a new form of currency into the market: One for domestic transactions, and another for transactions outside of the U.S. Comparing his proposition with a situation during the Vietnam War (and for the sake of a better explanation), I'll quote again verbatim:

> G.I.'s were selling U.S. dollars to the Vietnamese currency, because they could get more piasters (also called dong) for dollars this way than by going to an official exchange. These dollars often found their way into Communist hands, and since piasters were unacceptable to foreign manufacturers and arms merchants, the Communists would use the dollars to buy their arms and munitions. To prevent this, the U.S. military started paying G.I.'s not in dollars but in scrip called MPC's (Military Payment Certificates). The scrip had the same value as dollars but could only be used at American facilities, such as the officers' and enlisted men's clubs. Since scrip had no value outside of Vietnam, it could not be used by the Communists to buy the means of war from foreign sellers.

This would make it so that money becomes useless anywhere else. And, just to be sure, Bugliosi also argues—with his trademark prosecutorial prose—that we place IRS agents inside of banking institutions throughout the land, always to be vigilant of the potential drug launderer. Certain to upset civil libertarians everywhere, he writes that "without the money launderer, virtually all federal drug officials believe that cocaine drug trafficking in America would be dealt an incapacitating blow."

The last chapter of this book dealt with an issue very familiar to me: the legalization of narcotics. Although not listed as one of his proposals, the many pages written on the potential benefits of drug legalization left me wondering why it wasn't. Before I outline some of the reasons, a brief crash course on criminal law, taken from Latin, is in order. If, as a demonstration, someone happened to look outside their window and bear witness to a robbery, murder, or arson, there is little doubt that the immediate reaction would be one of horror. Instinctively, the basic code of human morality gives the sense that something's wrong and negates any urge to grab a philosophy or law book in hope of clarification.

On the other hand, if one were to peer outside that same window and see a person standing beside a cloud of thick, luminous smoke, one would not likely be as aghast, and might only consider the ethics involved if the observer was predisposed to the harms of smoking. Otherwise, what's the reason for concern? A "true crime," the first illustration, is wrong in itself—*malum in se*. The second example, *malum prohibitum*, becomes a crime only because it is unacceptable to the State. (Vincent would no doubt correct me and specify it as a "public welfare or regulatory offense.")

"Under certain circumstances," the legendary lawman writes, "one might feel sorry for such a person, feel him unwise, or sick, or hedonistic, or what have you, but unless you would likewise consider immoral or evil someone who is hurting himself by smoking a pack of cigarettes, drinking himself blind-drunk, or hitting his head against a wall, you would have no reason to consider the drug user or his act evil." He then says that if drug use were a "true crime," it would make all Vietnam veterans, adolescent delinquents, and previous societies, whom have dabbled in substance abuse, undistinguishable from Charles Manson himself.

The remedy proposed by Mr. Bugliosi? Instead of legalization, he says that the U.S. should only suspend the legal framework, putting a hold on current law enforcement procedures. This is a sort of puritan's vision for decriminalization. However, it is my opinion—because I'm inclined to give one—that state regulation would be needed to ensure proper facilitation. Heroin, for example, is four times as powerful as morphine, and could, as Vincent also argues, allow bone cancer patients to live the remainder of their lives pain free. But that's not to say that bags of black tar should be sold on ice-cream trucks outside of schools.

Although Vincent says that "legalization...is not a solution, only a different approach whose advantages may, or may not, outweigh the disadvantages," the recent *Report of the Global Commission on Drug Policy* adds credence to his (and my own) arguments, declaring that "the global war on drugs has failed." The 17-page report—headed by such luminaries as Richard Branson, of Virgin; former Fed chairman Paul Volcker; and three former presidents of Latin American countries—stated that "drug policies and strategies at all levels too often continue to be driven by ideological perspectives, or political convenience, and pay too little attention to the complexities of the drug market, drug use and drug addiction."

Conspiratorial as it might be, there is also a very well-chronicled legacy of secret U.S. government operations that involve narco-trafficking, which would obviously compromise any proclaimed mission of a "drug free" America. There is circumstantial evidence that Bush Sr., the namesake of which is the nemesis of my narrative, might also be indicted on these charges. Two lawyers, one representing the Columbian hit team who gunned down infamous drug runner Barry Seal (also mentioned in 'Drugs') in the middle of Baton Rouge on the night of February 19th, 1986, and another lawyer who represented Seal during a 1980's trial, substantiate this claim.

Sam Dalton, defense representative of the Medellin Cartel's hit men, told journalist Daniel Hopsicker that during preliminary hearings, he obtained a phone number found in Seal's car trunk. That number was a private line to the Office of the Vice President. Lewis Unglesby, representing Seal, said that he once called the number, and received a secretary from the office. Although only circumstantial, Bush Sr. is the former head of the CIA; he comes from a dynasty long associated with SpyCraft; while Seal has admitted to being on the CIA payroll during the height of his drug running. Sourcing from a 1998 CIA Inspector General reporter of Contra-era cocaine trafficking, the CIA admitted to "briefing" then-VP Bush on how it lied to Congress about cocaine running by its agents. A prosecutor would no doubt have his own questions about such "revisionist" history.

Vincent Bugliosi lives on the suburban outskirts of Los Angeles. That, and our mutual enemy, mark at least two things we have in common. When going on book tours, he tries to stay close to home and with his wife, Gail. When *Divinity of Doubt* was published in April, he started the same way: going to local book shops, doing telephone interviews, and lecturing on our many college campuses. This is how I found out about one of his first presentations being given, at a book fair taking place at USC.

Bringing along Clarissa, my part-time girlfriend, we went over to the campus, received our free tickets to Vincent's talk, and made our way into the auditorium, where roughly 200-plus people were sitting down waiting for the man to arrive. And then he did, and spoke of God and all the things we have wrong about Him.

Bugliosi's arguments for agnosticism reach two sturdy conclusions, at least from what I gathered. First: As a still-evolving species, we are not capable of understanding anything outside of the observable universe. Second: We are, as a still-evolving species, expected to produce mythology as a substitute for this shortcoming, even if those fairy tales have proven to be fraudulent, contradictory, hypocritical, or—as is quite often the case—downright harmful.

After the 45-minute speech was over, we all went outside and began lining up for the book signing. I hadn't purchased his new book yet, and instead brought along *Prosecution of Bush*, while Clarissa brought her copy of *Helter Skelter*. "I hope he doesn't see the other guy's signature," I remember musing aloud. It was, after all, a used copy, already once signed by Vincent.

And I am, incidentally, a useless journalist, just trying to figure some things out in this world.

(December 2011)

Gingrich Supports Government's War Against U.S. Citizens

THE FIRST OF December saw the passage of SB: 1867, the US government's official declaration of war against its own citizens.

The bill, a so-called Defense Appropriations Act, has effectively declared the homeland of the U.S. as part of the "global War on Terror." This allows for an undesired authority which sees the U.S. military having complete discretion when applying due process of law. Late night renditions could be in the near future.

Under section 1031:

> *Congress affirms that the authority of the President to use all necessary and appropriate force pursuant to the Authorization for Use of Military Forces,*

> *including the authority for the Armed Forces of the*
> *United States to detain covered persons pending*
> *disposition under the law of war.*

"Covered persons" is defined as anyone who helped terrorists carry out the 9/11 Attacks, or any person who was a "part of or substantially supported al-Qaeda, the Taliban, or associated forces that are engaged in hostilities against the United States or its coalition partners, including any person who has committed a belligerent act or has directly supported such hostilities in aid of such enemy forces." Precluded from this definition is, of course, the State—which has just put al Qaeda forces into post-Gaddafi Libya. Not precluded are "9/11 Truthers"—who believe that the Bush Jr. regime had a hand in the Attacks. Belligerent? At times, maybe, but until now, not illegal.

The Constitution, inalienable rights, government of the people—things once adored by our fellow countrymen and sanctified only with the split blood of fellow patriots—are now gone. They were flushed down some toilet in D.C. after having been used and discarded by Washington whores (not the more reputable ones found in city streets) and their multi-gazillian dollar corporate sponsors.

One such disgusting figure on this transnational level is the GOP hopeful Newt Gingrich: a treasonous man who says that "terrorists do not have the same protected rights as low-level offenders." While not addressing the recent bill directly, Newt basically supported the same neo-conservative mentality of security before liberty.

But he's much worse than he'd have you believe. In 1990, along with Senator Phil Graham, he introduced "U.S. Congressional Document H.R. 4079—an early leg of the modern-day police state. The bill was intended "to remove violent criminals from the streets and meet the extraordinary threat that is posed to the nation by the trafficking of illegal drugs. The Congress declares the existence of a National Drug and Crime Emergency."

This information comes from Jim Keith's book on *Alternative 3*. Keith writes that H.R. 4079:

> *...provides for the arrest of large numbers of people merely suspected of drug usage or dealing, and once arrested the suspected individuals would be incarcerated in one of the many forced labor camps.*

Naturally without 5th Amendment provisions.

As seen here, the Presidential "front-runner" is no stranger to acts of sedition, and in the past has done much work in getting those pesky rights taken away from not only "terrorists," but also lowly drug traffickers as well.

Important side note: Newt's partner, Senator Gramm, once attempted to challenge an amendment in the *Iraq International Law Compliance Act of 1990*.

The D'Amato amendment made it illegal for the Bush Sr. regime to sell arms to Iraq unless Saddam Hussein had promised to comply with human rights provisions. Gramm's counter amendment would have allowed Bush to veto this amendment if his administration "found that [those] sanctions against Iraq hurt US businesses and farms more than they hurt Iraq." What was that statement about politicians keeping strange bedfellows?

Whoever said it would probably be surprised at witnessing today's world of global corporate militarism, always financially supported by the Shadow Banker.

A few strange facts bring Gingrich's treason and flip-flopping closer to the topical issues. A *Huffington Post* article quotes a young Newt Gingrich who, in 1982, wrote an article for the *Journal of the American Medical Association*.

The issue? Medical marijuana. Newt's position?

Have a look:

> We believe licensed physicians are competent to
> employ marijuana, and patients have a right to
> employ marijuana legally, under medical
> supervision from a regulated source. The medical
> prohibition does not prevent seriously ill patients
> from employing marijuana; it simply deprives them
> of medical supervision and access to a regulated
> medical substance. Physicals are often forced to
> choose between their ethical responsibilities to the
> patient and their legal liabilities to federal
> bureaucrats.

Actual support for medical marijuana? For a while, it appeared so. Moreover, a year after the introduction of H.R. 4079, Gingrich introduced pro-medical marijuana legislation into the Senate. Fast forward twenty years into the future—today—and we see a campaign weary Gingrich who tells Yahoo News! that he is "prepared to say as a matter of value that it [is] better to send a clear signal on no drug use at the risk of inconveniencing some people, than it [is] to be compassionate toward a small group at the risk of telling a much larger group that it was okay to use the drug." Just like a lizard, Newt has just changed his appearance yet again.

So to recap: First, Gingrich was for the legal rights of cannabis patients. Then, he wanted to the ability to lock up every drug user and drug trafficker forever without charges. After that, he introduced legalization protecting the legal rights of cannabis patients. And just now, he has just said it is a bad idea to promote illegal drugs at the expense of dying cancer patients. "Within a year of my original support of that bill I withdrew it," Newt said of his early legislative effort.

Where does that bring us *right now*, a few weeks before

Iowa? Directly into the candidacy of one Mr. Herman Cain, who's just folded up his presidential campaign. Cain was doing remarkably well in the polls, after his much-touted "9-9-9" tax plan was given an enormous push by the media elites. Then something changed: Gingrich saw a quick and incisive surge in the polls. Why would the elites want a freshman candidate in Cain when they can have a New World Order front man leading the pack? It was time to say goodbye to Mr. Cain, and that we just did.

Constitutions don't have funerals. People do. History has provided many examples of what happens after a state has declared war against its own citizens. Hitler purged his fellow countryman who didn't agree with his program of dictatorship and genocide.

What happens now is anyone's guess.

Let's hope our military does the right thing.

(December 2011)

Jill Reed and the Twelve Visions

PRESIDENTIAL HOPEFUL JILL Reid has an objective other than just becoming the Commander-in-Chief. "We want to change the entire paradigm," she tells *Cannabis Times Magazine*. Reed is the nominee for the Twelve Visions Party, a grassroots party that originally met in Chicago in 2009. Their mission? To convince the American people that the "Prime Law" is the only way forward, insisting that no man or woman can govern anyone and that initiation of force is only morally acceptable when force is first being used against someone else. Our Constitution, Reed said, has "become eroded from what it was meant to be." Reed's fix is to pass an amendment that would legislate the Prime Law. Our hour and fifteen-minute conversation dealt with many possible ways in which this would work.

Born the daughter of a mechanic, Reed says she was taught the value of hard work, and in a way that made customers want to come back. "Find a problem in the country and then find a solution," she said, adding that believes "society suffers with rulers." Reed believes there are two main classes in life: the working class and the ruling class. Ironic as that might sound to pro-socialist types, Reed is a fervently anti-communist, pro-private property minded woman. "Look how far we've come in the computer industry," she said. "Technology has allowed it to become better, while prices have dropped." This is an example of the "Power of Consciousness" and the 10th Vision: "Have Everything You Ever Wanted"—via the free-to-soar-geniuses who help to advance super technology.

All twelve of these "visions" can be found at TVPNC.org. Many of them deal with the individual's potential to improve, bordering somewhat on the utopian. Number four, specifically, says "Slow Down Age Permanently." Reed explains this: "When Prime Law governs the people, and not small group of men or women, there is a greater production of wealth." This would lead not only to wealth but to all the resources needed for exemplary quality and advancement. "The Controllers," as she likes to call them, keep humans back. "We want to out value back in, as opposed to them who want to take value out," Reed said.

Likening the two dominant political parties to a basketball game, she says: "It doesn't matter which side wins, because we're still their basketball." From a reductionist viewpoint, Reed believes everything we deal with in society must begin with understanding the source of the problem. "With cannabis, it has properties that are both good and bad," she said. "It can deliver value, and it can also be corrupted"—believing that if the government gets involved it would most certainly become the latter, as it usually does. Reed asked: "Why regulate cannabis when it could be available?" She states that marijuana users are persecuted because they have committed a political crime, not a moral crime.

On the social externality that is drunk driving, Reed

answered again the same way: "We have to look and see if initiatory force is taken," adding that the same thing could be said about the possible harm caused by a broken tail-light. Taking this further, Reed asks: "Why do they get drunk? Maybe it starts off as recreation. But then they start feeling as if there's no hope, and they don't like what their part of." This is in line with a few other of her "visions," namely three and eight: "Feel Extraordinary Every Day," and "Have the Body You Always Envied"—respectively.

I brought up another, more immediate externality: the nuclear facility in Fukushima, which Dr. John Apsley estimates to have already killed 14,000 people in the U.S. "It would scare me to see a thousand private nuclear facilities in this country," I told her. She answered that people raised with the values of hard-work and a profit motive are not going to build a faulty nuclear reactor. "It comes down to environmental concern, doesn't it?" she said, adding that, "Children raised properly care about the environment."

I replied that, "People can't always predict when or where an earthquake will hit." Her response: "Government regulations take money away from the business, which then have less money for development and research. Regulatory agencies are another way of pitting people against businesses."

Although she has stated in other interviews that she supports the Occupy Movement for their willingness to take to the streets and discuss the main issues, they would no doubt disagree with her that "corporations are people"—a standard position within the Occupy cams. "Who owns the businesses?" She's right: people.

Another interesting topic discussed was the privatizing of law enforcement. "When my father ran his mechanics shop, he hired a nightwatchman to watch our property," Reed said. "More laws mean more crime," asserting this matter-of-factly. On the issue of the Federal Reserve, the nemesis of any freedom fighter, she says that "buying power is what's important." Seeing as the Fed has devalued the dollar by almost 98 percent since its inception in 1913, and that the 11ᵗʰ Vision promoted by Reed is, "Ride a Prosperity Wave to Riches (via falling prices and a soaring buying power)—someone is sure to be correct here.

Reed has been to all but fourteen states in the country. When our conversation was ending, she told me that she would be in Los Angeles to watch the premier of the movie Thrive, dealing with aliens and alternative energy.

Her platform sturdy, her patience enduring, Jill Reed looks to make an impact on the current political system.

Cannabis Times wishes her all the best.

(May 2012)

Dreaming of Apocalypse

I RECALL A dream I had not six months into my incarceration: me and my girlfriend at the time were in an airplane. Below us, the Apocalypse was taking place. It was just as you might have seen in theater or TV—with buildings crumbling, streets sinking into the earth, and people falling into the abyss. Death, destruction—but we survived. Vivid and frightening, I woke up with one tear in each eye. Someone who knows me might believe this to be the result of sobriety and the half-crazed illusions that follow.

My late grandfather was once hospitalized for his excessive drinking. He said he "saw" fish jumping out of his toes. He had only been sober for a few days, but had many more years of liquor concentrated in his bloodstream.

Since then, I have had a couple more dreams about the End of the World. In the last one, I remember, I was standing on the top of the world, overlooking the whole galaxy, and was trying to jump down to the surface so I could report on the massive comet that was quickly approaching. Scientifically, Nibiru hasn't a chance: thousands of amateur and professional astronomers sleep during the day and explore the galaxy at night. Reports on this mythical "12ᵗʰ Planet" are—have been—completely absent.

But the collective anxiety felt during these alleged crises is utterly tangible. Who can forget Harold Camping's assurance of the end of the world in May 2011? The most frightening thing about this was the absolutism of Camping's word. He insisted that the event would happen with no possible mishap. As he said, "there is no 'plan B.'" That night I went for a 10 mile walk with a portable crank radio, listening to George Noory on Coast-to-Coast. I met Noory once. Even as a skeptic dealing with the most bizarre topics, he has a very calming, reassuring, and empirical approach. He doesn't let bullshit pass for butter.

Sigh.

No apocalypse occurred. Camping apologized. But that entire night—as strange as it sounds—I could *feel* the anxiety. I didn't believe the world would end, but I knew that somewhere—maybe not on the dark street I was walking—there were literally tens, maybe hundreds of thousands of people glued to their TV's and radio's, waiting for their living room ceilings to get torn off, and themselves being raptured into heaven while the rest of the world met its fate. I keep telling myself that this is what had frightened me: not the part about Jesus Christ tearing up continents and residential rooftops.

This time last year I was driving back from the East Coast after a lengthy road trip (Occupying the Highways). A lone billboard in rural Alabama (I think!) asked a simple question: "2012?" Then I drove by, the sight of it disappearing behind me. We're already here, less than three weeks away from a date long-since anticipated, but never fully understood. For the record, the literature is too dense and the date too close for me to embark on a study of this magnitude.

I hadn't felt the anxiety until last night. A drunken rumble landed me in the drunk tank at the Glendora PD, there for 7 hours. Even having spent a total of one year of my life inside of a cell (added up from various times of my prison stint), I was particularly uncomfortable this time. It was the First of December. In 20 days, something was expected to occur. Other drunks had to listen to these thoughtful rants. Some researchers, like Drunvalo Melchizedek, believe it to be a cataclysm. Others, like David Wilcock, expect the emergence of a "Golden Age." Scientists have continually warned about solar flares.

At that time in the cell—being very angry and lonely—I wanted the first prediction to occur. Then when I got out, and walked in the cold, refreshing rain, I preferred the second. If neither happens, then at least I get a good suntan and a well-researched report.

Maybe then I can even work on my egotism and find out how to love something for the first time in my life.

Suppose we'll all find out in 18 days.

(December 2012)

Against the Cutter Culture

WHILE APPEARING ON William F. Buckley's Firing
Line in 1969, the already renowned linguist and anti-war critic
Noam Chomsky told a nationwide audience that there was no
longer any debate on the Vietnam War. In his view, no question
remained that the United States was the ultra-violent aggressor
against an innocent people, and that our government was
directly targeting civilian populations for the goal of total
extermination.

Even as the New Left attempted to stop an evil war, and
maybe as Voltaire and Lysander Spooner were demanding an
end to slavery, and no less than feminism attempts to stop every
last instance of rape today, so are we many "Intactivists" who are
demanding genital integrity here in America. Gender equality
will see its day, we insist. An end to hypocritical lectures by
people already protected under the law is at hand. A restoration
of sanity for us—it all is approaching.

We feel an updated report of human rights in the "freest"

country on the planet would include those 60-70 percent of baby boys that are indeed violated against their will, and then are *never told by their parents* that the Right to their Anatomy simply does not matter. This is why we say: as rape is to a rape victim, as slavery to a slave, so is circumcision for those of us several times more likely to get erectile dysfunction.

And so why would I spend three hours writing an "open letter" on Facebook addressed to my immediate and extended family? After all, I don't sleep with them. However, the forum of the Internet would also generate more thought, instead of given two lousy sentences in the living room during a commercial break, and then allowed there to be no misconception of the matter: as an address to the entirety of what I will refer to as the *Cutter Culture*.

I would now appreciate it if the dear reader would make even the slightest consideration for the following. This will be an attempt to gander into the perspective of an unhappily mutilated man. For I have a very grave concern for which I absolutely must have a resolution.

No longer regarding the differing perspectives between myself and family, and while not really intending to discuss any hypothetical children with others, I will freely admit to several recently acquired fears. In five months or so, I will have been partly responsible for bringing a little loveable creation into this world. It will get to experience a life that I have largely been unhappy with. The gender remains unknown, but I am hoping for a boy.

And yet, in the last two or so years, finally coming to realize circumcision exactly as what it is—genital mutilation, a precursor to psychopathy, and pure unmitigated evil—I also came to see how many other people were so incredibly, unbelievably cruel and hateful upon even the slightest mention of the subject.

Now the question is stuck in my head. If I do have my

desired boy, should I seriously have *any concern* that he might grow up into a community, a society, or a family where he'll be shamed and ridiculed and called an "anteater"? Maybe overhear a conversation one day that someone didn't think he was listening to, talking about how disgusting they thought he really is? Superstitiously scrubbing under his foreskin—*just because?*

The stories of shame and ridicule against the male body are numerous these days. There is much testimony of intact kids who are mocked and laughed at by callous people. At the same time, critically sorrowful men (as myself) are told to "get over it." Else, we need therapy—with the profound irony of that recommendation always lost on them.

Thanks (or no thanks) to the Internet, where I do spend too much time, these same individuals occasionally enjoy expressing their sickness by engaging chatrooms, making jokes about foreskin restoration and deformed penises. Humiliating to be sure. Yet they no doubt would act something like this at home and elsewhere.

> *Well I say, your culture and your butcherism be damned!*

Important note: It must be said that the anti-circumcision side always seems to be able to provide a fantastic amount of evidence and logic for their cause, while the Cutter Community always seems to resort to nuclear "ad hom" bombs. By that time, the calls of "penis weights" and "child rapist" appear—and yes, from even me—the "debate" is cut apart. *Why does this happen,* I think?

"We all want them to look alike."

"So he looks like his father."

"It looks nicer."

"It's cleaner."

"Better having it done at birth."

"Our religion."

"High school showers."

At no time during these boring, incorrect, anything-but-universal statements is that crucial question asked, one by me many times, ignored just as often, and that which erects the dividing wall (I believe): can cutting off fifty percent of the penis skin, what many consider the most sensitive part of the male body, not be a possible cause for permanent psychological disturbances? Those who answer in the negative take a far greater leap of faith than those who would dare take the chance.

Is there really *nobody* who thinks it possible that a nine-year-old might fully understand what was taken from him? Might he be upset at the non-answers he would inevitably receive? And perhaps even lash out aggressively at others? Leading to a spanking that could be even more harmful? All while everyone is confused about the causality? *Never once has this situation occurred?!* Parents who insist they simply won't tell their child anything about the procedure; it makes me wonder—if not this?—*what would be at the heart of ethics?*

Does nobody want to at least try for a society of lesser-aggression?

Is Stefan Molyneux not correct in his thesis that the origins of all violence are to be found in child abuse?

And is circumcision not our most obvious example of this?

Like all bigotry, the one against foreskin is based on ignorant assumptions, those that a full eighty percent of the rest of world doesn't participate in. Perhaps nobody should be worried how mutilated children could act towards others. Or maybe we all should. Since most people seem to be worried about not only their own kids, but others, and who often want to express their bigotry when they deem appropriate, every parent who sees the practice for what it is might want to make personal secession a top priority. Appearance in the locker room is nothing compared to violence on the playground or in the street.

Listening to the guilt and shame and ridicule projected onto other people (and again, even by myself) and onto their kids has become tiring for me as well. But never as tiring as hearing those many females who were not taken a knife to, who now feel qualified to tell me that it's the best thing ever. Talk about disturbed.

Nevertheless, I haven't yet seen enough people sympathetic to my perspective. So, I shall rant. Now. Scream at the top of my lungs to ensure the call for human rights only gets louder.

On the other hand, since so many of us truly are anti-social and tend to reciprocate the hate back onto others, communication might be impossible with this one.

So, since there can be no shades of grey seen between the two "camps," maybe we should all just go our separate ways.

(February 2014)

A Pleasantly Filled Dungeon:
Part One

IN EXISTENCE, NOT 30 miles from my place of residence, is a modern-day dungeon. For no mistake can be made in saying that the Los Angeles County Jail is a perfect comparison of such a thing in 21st Century America.

On the 2200 floor, where I was recently housed for just over a week, a 24-hour lockdown was in effect; there was no mentionable selection of books or literature; little of food or hygiene; absolutely none of association; with three other grown men personally sharing this small, uncomfortable pit with me (up until recently a total of eight people had occupied these three, double-manned bunked cells. Yes, the other two slept under the bunks); hundreds, if not thousands, right next to me, who, just like the anthropomorphic vendibles that they are, and with the help of California Assembly Bill: 109, experience a fate far worse than my own; and—last but never least—the primary entertainment as the endless howling and grunting and screaming that come from those many deranged minds, further lost and less hopeful than the writer's.

It should be stressed that the word "dungeon" is used not only because of these conditions, but also because they no longer house those waiting for trial, or those, like me, doing brief "county time." It is now the final place one goes after falling victim to *malum prohibitum*. "State time in the county," as it is axiomatically said.

I first discovered this dungeon eight years ago, on a much more serious crime. The misdemeanor that sent me back after this long duration has been argued by investigative journalist Radley Balko to be anachronous. That is, operating a motor vehicle with a license that has been temporarily suspended as a result of intoxicated steering. For this, the West Covina judge had given me two options: Either pay the court $1,100, or complete 154 hours of what has inappropriately been deemed "community service." I chose the latter, believing the task involved picking up trash at the local park, or sweeping off the side of the freeway, or cleaning up the cages of traditionally defined animals. Certainly it wouldn't require assisting any customers.

Although it will be said—and not argued sufficiently by one officer—that Goodwill Industries is a "nonprofit charity," and thus Mussolini's classic (perhaps misattributed) definition of fascism cannot be applied to my situation. The official response to their "status" is: "As a unique hybrid called a social enterprise, we defy traditional distinctions. Instead of a single bottom line of profit, we hold ourselves accountable to a triple bottom line of people, planet, and performance." In that case, I'm a person. On this planet. And almost always giving a considerable performance.

So, I say bollocks!

Activity that isn't done via coercion is just that, but

obeying the declarations of the statists who have sent me here still makes for a kind of fascism. Besides, nothing agreed to with the State had stipulated me having to wear a bright smile for people who paid for stuff *directly* (I always did, but that isn't the point!). The unenforceability of this would be true even if Goodwill did pay federal taxes, even if there was a public complaining about my bad habits, or even if that public didn't become customers immediately upon entry of where they shopped for secondhand merchandise.

As concerns that could never manifest alongside the 5 freeway, the lucid combination of State and Capital broke my tolerance after only one unmemorable incident. Raul: the short, aging, smug-faced proprietor, supposedly coming after working 30 years at Vons, had run his shift with a very "managerially style," as I thereafter said to him. Deciding I had not swept the floor to his satisfaction, he made a rather loud and embarrassing scene in front of the shoppers, exclaiming that he "wanted no excuses" and to "just have it done!"—a tirade one might expect to hear from an experienced manager.

Taking these kinds of orders without getting a cent?

With the only motivating factor to simply stay out of jail?

In front of people who I opened bathrooms and changing rooms for? With an inflamed forehead perfused with angry beads of sweat, I decided that I would just go to jail and serve what is widely thought to be a universal ten percent of sentenced LA county time. "If I'm going to take orders, it might as well be from the slave-master himself," I said to my concerned family.

Assuredly, I wrongly believed, with a 30-day sentence, it would be a mere seventy-two hours before I would be out.

Even then, my crime was considered so petty that the overcrowded jail didn't even want my physical presence.

Instead, it's dedicated service.

Another "choice" was given to me on the "surrender date" of Friday, April 4th: work four weekends in the visiting area, both Saturday and Sunday, for eight to ten hours, sweeping the dirty floors and cleaning the impregnable windows. After all, I could still go home at the end of the day. "Guess I'll just do that," I said to the deputy, signing onto the State for yet another month.

It was suggested that I go across the street and introduce myself, which I promptly did. "Make sure you come in at 7 AM tomorrow, sharp," said Officer Bratsworth, the tall, lanky, baby-faced white man wearing both badge and gun that were much too big for him.

Beguilement struck me the following morning. Was I to go right up to the window of this building and get their attention? Or wait outside until someone opened the glass door? Deciding to act like the civilian I still was, I waited with the patrons in the patio until such time.

Terrible mistake.

When the door eventually did swing open—ten minutes after seven—I walked in briskly, and was immediately greeted by a frustrated Officer Bratsworth, quickly putting my hands behind my back and escorting me out of the building, deciding to make an "example" of me in front of his gleaming comrades and in front of the horrified families.

"I'm not your bro," he asserted. It was anathema, something one could always throw at cops—just to hear them confirm your status with one another. Just then, I began to get loud, something never desired by fascists.

"Do you want to go back to jail?"

I said no, but the question was the final, *final* spark. "Tell you what you're going to do," he said, his voice displaying the undeniable joy he was having, "You're going to work ten hours today."

Could I really work for these psychopaths for four weekends, knowing how they just got done treating me like an animal, and right in front of people already bereaved from being here?

As I said to the other porter a half hour later, still trying to talk the rage out of me: "If I'm going to take orders, it might as well be the direct ones. You know: 'In this holding tank, down this hall, in this cell, repeat.'"

I went up to Bratsworth with the proposition.

"You want to go to jail?" he said, completely stunned. No. But yes. "Keep working, I'll let you know."

Not ten minutes later, cleaning windows, he storms in and again demands my hands behind my back.

Taking me to his police car outside, I began to spew the regular law enforcement "niceties," telling this cowardly punk that he was a member of an out-of-control Police State, and that "Stop and Frisk" was Nazism incarnate, and that he was overpaid and should be fired, and that it was a shame I had a son on the way who would eventually have to pick up the tab for it all.

"It's a family occupation," he justified.

Who cares?

During the short drive across the street, almost by mistake, Bratsworth uttered the real pleasure he took: "I don't even like working in the visiting center. I like driving around." Pulling random people over, running their names, seeing who you can arrest?

No response.

Not for the first or only time during this stint, I recommended Balko's widely praised best seller, *Rise of the Warrior Cop*, a book that I repeatedly employed for additional analysis.

(April 2014)

Note on Neo-Balkanism

AS I ATTEMPT to get this into the vernacular, I realize that dizzying levels of paranoia run through the minds of many Anti-Racist Activists (ARA's). They often hurl accusations of government authority as efforts to dispel, dissuade, or discredit a very specific lexis of differing perspectives. I take them at their word, these unabashed efforts to identify as something other than what is considered to be "white."

A menace, this social concept is determined to destroy and takeover the "History of the Entire World." And now it has found an enemy in the form of "intersectionality"—otherwise known as a collective of self-identified oppressed groups, who actively indict every single light pigmented denizen as a forebear of absolute despotism, thus as their everyday oppressor.

There is an active bewilderment from a majority of the white community, many in the Hispanic communities, and even some in the black community (including notably Charles Barkley). These people are confused as to the true definition of "racism": that "power" or "privilege" is something that every white person (no matter how well off) must own up to. They are then tasked with the personal responsibility to make it perish. If not, or if not quickly enough, condemnation and communal exile is inevitable, and oftentimes predictable.

Denied by many rich white people, this privilege is without doubt a conundrum in the minds of a growing collective of white youth, who now inherit nothing but debt, decrepitude, faux patriotism, and war; all of which are now supplanted with the zeitgeist that is a world being made aware of these injustices, this bigotry, and the unethical practices of the everyday world.

Because of a series of institutionalized racist actions against blacks, many of which clearly undertaken by "leaders" of the black community (the welfare state, Affirmative Action, the Drug War), with never enough evidence it seems to appease the ARA's of these detrimental politics, it has an intended purpose of causing a swollen tumor of shame on this class of "white citizens," who are forbade from ever discussing underlying economic reasons and methods of personal interaction.

Alas, those believed to have inherited authority from pigmentation, only capable of dissolution with some kind of "deconstruction," that with an incomprehensible "process"— specified (I think!) with a discussion, an adoption, and ending with a common projection—are then rejected from discussing or interacting with these ARA insinuators until the transformation is complete.

If this doesn't happen on a larger scale, or quicker, a polarizing effect will take place: separating the mass of the population into two or three regional groups.

One can label these things as they wish, but the work of this activism will be not integrative of the entire population, who are, on a larger than was but still not absolute scale, genuinely and sincerely without bigotry, and often very concerned for socially oppressed and economically unequal group of citizens. (Who are ravished by the expensive cost of all the beloved state allocations—cops, teachers, pen pushers, politicians, etc.)

Such scorn is a required psychosis for the ARA's; a firewall of moral absolutism if you will. (i.e. if you say otherwise, you're a "blank") Many examples could be drawn from this alone. After all, "It's not their responsibility to figure it out for you"—"but go figure out how you're oppressive and don't come back until then." An oft-repeated claim, not exaggerated by very much, it is the most straightforward renunciation of personal presence that can be witnessed.

Usually, the line comes from racially and financially privileged individuals themselves, who are insistent of their empathy for "persons of color" yet refusing to help others understand it, despite having tactical advantage for doing so. (This makes activism a bit of a redundancy)

For them, it must not be a curious mind eagerly considerate for the plight or valuation of communities, but a willing continuance of "power dynamics," via doing little more than breathing the same air or asking too many questions or speaking too often or even (gasp!) disagreeing with some of their definitions and conclusions.

The ARA's should be so bold as to have a standard rule within their community: "white person can't speak until spoken to." This would make consent of the platform much more congenial, the agreed-upon positions of audibility much more transparent.

A rebuttal to this brief analysis has been made dozens of times already, likely within the first paragraph: "white guilt."

No appending of this note could change this conclusion, and perhaps if my misanthropic worldview allowed for the occasional guilt trip, and didn't in fact witness the aforementioned (often ridiculous and child-like) denunciations and social exiling myself, or, for the very most awkward first time in my life and young "career" in journalism, not get the overwhelming sensation that I was being secretly despised, not because of my ego, listening skills, good looks, or brilliant argumentation, but solely because of my pigmentation and that alone—that I would consider "white guilt" to overshadow my curious frustration. (I don't like not knowing any more than being demanded to understand something not discussed.)

That I am seen as an oppressive predisposition—consciously observed by others in my species—is not the problem. Nor is it that the ARA's are lacking the character of Malcolm X when he had advocated for Black Nationalism and black secessionism. It is that they are not honest enough about it and are dishonestly—perhaps reflexively—making fantastic strides away from certain persons with the use of erratic and rejectionist behavior.

This raises my initial suspicion for the final time: absent some "great awakening" that makes aware a one-hundred total percentage of all ignorant white people of their presumed status as social "gods"—required to perform some function so as to dethrone themselves—that Balkanism, known in history to have occurred between religions, is likely to occur on a much larger scale here in the U.S.

This between self-identifying persons of oppressed groups, and the "others" they have strangely and persistently crowned.

(Unknown)

When the Sunshine State Said "Cut"

"THERE'S NO REASON it should not go through," Mr. Jeffrey Gillen had said.

Gillen is a judge in the 15th Division of the state of Florida. That man-in-a-magic-robe was about to swing down his papier-mâché gavel and devastate some important considerations for both autonomy and human rights. In May, he ruled in favor of a "contract" that would amputate the foreskin of young Chase Ryan Nebus-Hironimus.

The child, born on Halloween 2010, is the result of a seven-month long relationship between Heather Hironimus and Dennis Nebus; the former bravely fighting against a mutual, court-approved decision made with the insistent "father," who said he would personally handle getting it done.

That notion was forgotten for more than two years, until one day when Nebus noticed Chase urinating on his leg, soon leading to a doctor (no doubt mistakenly again) diagnosing phimosis, and thus giving a "need" to be cut. As a sympathetic note: I can almost relate.

Hironimus, by then completely regretful of her initial agreement, protested. Nebus went to the courts. Gillen made the ruling. A higher West Palm Beach court granted an emergency halt to the motion. This was so she could gain support that was at once financial and emotional, hopefully in an effort to spare her son's anatomy.

She raised $5,000 on GoFundMe and made plenty of friends from the Intactivist movement. Tragically, six months later, all final appeals have been denied, and the State, represented by Mr. Gillen, has put the final foot down: the four-year-old, eventual-man, is to undergo compulsory mutilation, for absolutely no reason at all. Hence, the judge's appropriate prefix, "Mister"—not any authority whose legitimacy should be recognized.

Walter Block, an anti-cutter, is always reminding us libertarians that there's a lot of "gray" when it comes to the age of consent. The question of maturity and the ability to decide for oneself is contained within a foggy continuum. We're never quite sure when an individual can give approval for what. Notice though that sex is usually the example discussed. Nobody argues that an 18-year-old isn't allowed to resist sexual pressure.

And except for the most perverse, nobody says that children shouldn't resist when a predator is about to molest them. Chase Hironimus—and let us give him the proper last name—provides an impeccable illustration of how young one can be and still make simple decisions for themselves, which was the reason stated by his mother. "Putting aside what they agreed to, if you're going to enforce this contract, you have to look in what is the best interest of the child," Hironimus' attorney, Taryn Sinatra, had told the *Broward Palm Beach New Times*. "The best interest of the child should always trump"—any dumb agreement.

At age four, there's no doubt young Chase is unhappy about the impending assault on his person. This has been confirmed to me by activists involved with the case, demonstrating how the contract has been made void due to his developed capacity to verbally render it so. It is not possible in any libertarian order to make a lawful negotiation negating someone else's anatomical rights; not without their unthreatened, explicit, and informed consent.

Informed? Indeed. Adding insult to injury, the man-in-the-magic-robe also stipulated that Hironimus "shall not in any way lead [Chase] to believe that she is or was opposed to his being circumcised, whether or not she accompanies [him] to the procedure"—making free speech also experience a flush down Mr. Gillen's toilet. But therein lies a brilliant depiction of the absurdity of the State: How, in God's name, does that guy think he'll prevent such a conversation from ever taking place between a boy and his mother? Maybe a round-the-clock monitoring by a member of CPS? This can't be done.

Alas, the horror of the foreskin and the "need" for infantile circumcision became a template for the American medical establishment starting in 1870, when Lewis Sayre, "America's leading orthopedic surgeon," began treating paraplegic children with a permanent, ancient excision.

True story.

Medical journals at the time repeated the claim that "diseases"—such as "nervousness" and "restless sleep" and "bad digestion"—could be cured with a "minor" operation that involved cutting off a part of the penis, that overwhelmingly sensitive bit that created within the lad so much internal hostility. The man famous for his many contraptions was not treated as a quack: when the Civil War broke out, the mayor of New York City named him as resident physician, all of this well documented in David Gollaher's "history of the world's most controversial surgery."

In 1949, soon after World War Two, when circumcision had become fully ensconced within the land of Jefferson, but was being debated on as an insurable item in Britain's new healthcare program, Douglas Gairdner, a respected English pediatrician, offered criticism in the *British Medical Journal*. Conducting research that was based on actual, randomized samplings of children (because, after all, we're not talking about quantum physics), Gairdner reported that the retraction of the foreskin had wildly differed based on the variability (race even played a factor), and that it simply depended on the young man in question.

Britain's government decided not to insure, allowing private payment instead. This data contradicted American medical literature, which insisted that any degree of non-retractable foreskin automatically meant phimosis, or the tightening of the foreskin around the glans. This is normal, if it hadn't been made clear. "If it can pee, let it be," as it goes in the circles.

But my own situation is not the same as Ms. Hironimus and her poor son's. I make no comparison to the details, and only then to the question of how we got here as an "enlightened" society. Chase is four years of age. My son is now five months. I've previously designated circumcision in America as the "Cutter Culture," admonishing everyone within the vicinity about this barbaric practice.

About the history.

The misandristic bigotry that keeps it going. How the rest of the civilized world refrains from cutting their infants. And that companies use amputated foreskins in commercial products. About the risks of psychological trauma and sexual dysfunction. How nearly every single medical institution in the world condemns it as it is: genital mutilation. I was certain I was on the same page with my son's mother.

I was wrong. I admit in one embarrassing sentence: I never changed his diaper in the half dozen times they together had visited my mother's house. I had never seen his genitals. Until one day when I did. "Did you circumcise him?" I asked plainly in a Facebook message. She admitted that she had, and this, as she said, to "keep the peace" between her and her Catholic mother.

It was the first lie of many more to discover. For, in that time, she had been letting her ex-boyfriend believe that he was the true father. A Jewish man, he had admitted to me some weeks back, during an unexpected phone call, that he wanted "his" son to be cut—not mine. As an unconfirmed note, it has been said that the Golden State is the only state in which only one parent is needed for consent. Actually, she had two, now with a name change in process.

No other interpretation of these actions should be given other than as an indirect attack *against me*, seeing as the "mother" knew how utterly and absolutely opposed to this I was, and how much I wanted to give him that choice that I was not given.

I wasn't there for her pregnancy, or his birth. I didn't much get along with her. It was only afterwards that we started becoming cordial. I had thought we would finally be able to take our son out together and become a fragmented family unit that could at least shop for clothes and go out to dinner as one; all of it now seen as the prolonged lie that it was.

Everything was thrown under the proverbial bus. Maybe other actions in the country could be witnessed as such. After all, who would cut the genitals of their protesting four-year-old son based on the grounds of "it's just normal," as the scumbag father is quoted as saying? Is this the Middle East? Are Mr. Gillen and Mr. Nebus genuine, sociopathic sadists? Or pathetically and unhappily cut men who must carry on a culture of non-consent, just so as to keep things "normal"?

Optimistically though, at least I do have a family court

judge who respects fatherhood. And I can have that longed-for relationship with my boy, albeit alone and separately away from my ex.

Such people could become enemies for life.

Not always should hate be summoned and appropriated. However, betrayal to this degree will disallow any notion of trust. It's going to be a long while. For now, one should only act civilly only as to forego the jeopardizing of their relationships with their children.

As Heather Hironimus will no doubt tell her son, as if he doesn't already know, the day will come when I will tell Porter everything about the disgusting, barbaric rape culture that is genital mutilation in America.

DEATH TO THE CUTTER CULTURE!

(January 2015)

SPECTRE: Not Scarier than the Newspapers

THE NEWEST 007 film is, all and all, a dud. Putting the summation first: It's predicable, uninspired, disjointed. It sets itself up for real potential by attempting to give the secret agent a genuine backstory, and then fails miserably without much effort. It brings in supernova-sized casting, and then wastes the talent. It teases us with a brilliant and breathtaking "pre-title" sequence, featuring Mexico's Day of the Dead festival, and then lets the rest of the action drizzle away, at times downright boringly.

But the real problem with the film—the one examined here—is that the bad guy's scheme has been completely cribbed from a Washington DC playbook, making the once-classic scenario of a "world in jeopardy" nothing more thrilling than what has already been told to us by the always enthusiastic Edward Snowden.

As Peter Suderman says in his review:

> *Every Bond film is in some sense a reflection of its time, from the Mad Men cool of the Sean Connery era to the Star Wars–inflected dorky disco vibe of the Roger Moore pictures to Timothy Dalton's chilly Cold War spy thrillers to the generic, big-budget action blockbusters starring Pierce Brosnan in the late '90s. Watching a Bond film provides a sense of a given time period's fashion sensibilities, its ideas about masculinity and power, and even its political concerns. If you wanted a sociocultural history of the United States since 1964, you could do a lot worse than watching the Bond films back to back.*

Point taken. But watching the past films, with plots so fantastic an exaggeration of world events, you easily lose yourself in a make-believe situation, one that Fleming himself, although a spy for the royal navy who once said that everything he wrote could occur in the real world, had nevertheless deliberately created in his novels. Example: In Dr. No, Bond trades "blows" with a kraken. Yes, a giant squid. (We'll come right back to the matter of tentacles in a second.)

In the movie franchise, Bond has infiltrated a secret volcano lair to prevent yet another space-hijacking; stops a diamond smuggling operation just before they're to be used for a space laser; he even goes into space himself at one point. These ventures obviously forego any serious profile of your average spy.

There were the more "realistic" plots, as in when Bond battles drug traffickers, attains secret "decoding" devices, stops further space lasers—though the villains here are menacing enough to not really notice or care. Plus, they were usually motivated by that timeless "Macguffin": revenge. After watching Javier Bardem hunt down his abandoner with the only wish to see her dead, it leaves here a feeling of absence. (Revenge was present since at least 1971, when Sean Connery returned to the role, this in a squandered entry which was set up to witness what could have been awesome vengeance for the death of Bond's wife, only to see it become the first true parody in the series.) The franchise has always toyed these angles, from the out-of-this-world to the hard-boiled spy thriller. Some worked. Others, not.

SPECTRE demonstrates neither of these dichotomies, or at least not very well. It's given straight away as something read right out of a newspaper (perhaps an "alternative" newspaper), and then lavished with the usual explosions and "Bond formula." Suderman notes: "[B]ecause the villain's plan involves secretly partnering with world governments and taking over a massive global surveillance network in order to…well, it's never quite clear, actually." Exactly. The previous, far superior film, *Skyfall*, did have a contemporary point involving computer hacking—but, to repeat, what moved it forward was the never-boring wheels of *payback*.

What returning director Sam Mendes did with that film, the wonderful use of Bond nostalgia, simply doesn't work here. The white cat and scarred face are present, but they hardly matter considering that we're never even told what SPECTRE stands for. In 1962, the first movie (Dr. No, which was the sixth of Fleming's novels), it was: "Special Executive for Counter-Intelligence, Terrorism, Revenge, and Extortion." With dastardly agendas like that, it would be *the* organization to have during the days of the Cold War. A filmmaker interested in espionage could, and did, do so much with it. As many observe nowadays, it just seems that the Bond movies have run out of ideas.

This takes us to the "Octopus" motif, what I think is the filmmakers' attempt at something new. If one wears earmuffs, so as to inoculate against Sam Smith's absolutely terrible title song, the titles themselves are actually quite enjoyable, especially if you're something of a conspiratologist like me. It features the slimy tentacles of an octopus—a favorite analogy for those who worry about a High Cabal that controls the world—wrapping itself around—well, everything, including a naked and enflamed Daniel Craig surrounded and making love to various shadow women.

In the realer world, The Octopus was being chased down by intrepid investigator Danny Casolaro, before he was found dead in a West Virginia hotel room in 1991. He had been following up on *The Inslaw Affair*, the saga of a computer software program, called PROMIS, which linked together the many databases of American law enforcement. Things got more interesting when Casolaro discovered that backdoor access had been created for the software that allowed for peeking into the files of whomever used it. After Casolaro's strange death, veteran researchers Jim Keith (who also died strangely in 1999) and Kenn Thomas followed up on his notes, leading to the publication of the aforementioned title.

"Everything is information," Bond's nemesis—a stupidly reincarnated Blofeld—says while giving the heroes a tour of his desert compound. The line is almost given with what I guess is the metaphysical, something like how this rather mundane villain might be happy that all that quantum mechanical "we're all linked together on a celestial plane" stuff could be true and would then one day reunite with the father that was once taken from him by a just-orphaned James Bond. Yet I don't think this is what's meant; which is, literally and clandestinely—*I can see you everywhere.* Earlier, Bond's chief-of staff-explains the plan: "Nine Eyes," the program that's about to merge the intelligence agencies of nine different countries, talking of the international meeting that was soon to be had, summoning both Bond's boss as well as Blofeld's very own "inside" man, and this for an "up-

or-down" vote by all involved member-parties. It was—indeed the threes words that are said—the "new world order." And by the way, horribly presented. Is it even close to being chilled? Not really; and actually, I felt more threatened by Brosnan's constant World War 3 dilemma.

Though if we were to take Suderman's advice, to view the Bond Franchise as the occasional multi-million dollar reveal of everything political and cultural and perhaps governmental, two scenes in particular could be seen as unnerving and warrant further caution. One has Blofeld, underground his desert compound, with all his computer hackers seated and heeded at random command, showing a live action video clip of an office security camera. "Is this live?" the underused Academy Award winner asks. That could prove to be daunting the next time you're out shopping for the newest tech toy.

The other is the concept of "false flag attacks." As it turns out, South Africa gives the globalized spy program a down vote. We are quickly shown a television set with what was CNN "broadcasting" the news of a major terrorist attack in one of their metropolitan cities. South Africa, as it were, changes its mind. "Who could blame them?" remarks Blofeld's government insider. Who indeed.

The first cinematic concern—a constant, round-the-clock recording of someone at work, out shopping, at certain cross streets, and maybe even at home—is mostly on time. The second—violence perpetrated by this wicked global elite—is at least 20-30 years too late, at least since the details of Operation Gladio were divulged to a shocked public. Bush Sr. might now be able to take pride in the fact that cinema has finally heeded his 1992 announcement. Maybe then we have to wonder about who comprises the new set of employees, all those state-sanctioned perverts who—as Bond muses about accurately—are mere "voyeurs" getting paid to watch tiny monitors from "9-5," their security clearance probably somewhere around level

Saturn.

At any rate. This was a movie review, not a full-blown conspiracy analysis. So it isn't to say that the film is absent of some really terrific scenes. As already stated, the opening is marvelously done, with thousands of Mexican revelers threatened by an out-of-control helicopter. Mendes was just about correct here: the biggest thing shot for a "pre-title" sequence. Daniel Craig's 007 is also given a sense of snarky, sarcastic humor. Although it's not perfect, and does rip off Dirty Harry a bit, exposing the superspy's funny bone is typically welcomed. His line, when asked about killing the husband of a woman he's about to bed, is too good not to note: "He was an assassin...he won't take it personally." Craig also has a brutal fight with former wrestler Dave Batista aboard a train, something noticeably absent from the last entry, and sure to be recognized as the updated "Bond VS. Red Grant." The promotional marketing was also new and interesting, with the IMAX poster having Bond disguised in a skull mask.

Death before Breakfast: an adage definitely appropriate for the Bond universe.

(December 2015)

The Aborted Fetus of American Fascism?

AS OF LATE April, the remnants of an enthralling legend still stand within the hills of Pacific Palisades. Down here, some seventy years ago, a potential headquarters was being constructed for the day that Adolf Hitler announced victory in World War Two. Afterwards, the Third Reich would make its way across the ocean to the shores of Los Angeles, receive some needed R&R, and only then conquer the rest of the American continent. So the storied agenda goes. As with all good legends, it's been stated and then restated with just a modicum of *fact*.

What is certain is that the City of Angeles has long wanted to tear down the dilapidated remains of Murphy Ranch. To my knowledge, aside from a novel and a general history of LA, only one thick book mentions these malevolently colorful ruins. The co-contributor of that work—Randy Young, a local historian— is cited in various articles. Therefore, for the sake of the budget, we'll go with those.

LA.Curbed probably has the best overview of this odd history. The prophecy of Nazi triumph starts with the enigmatic "Herr Schmidt," apparently an important figure in the fascistic, anti-Semitic Silver Legion of America, and whose only evidence of existence comes from a 1940 Los Angeles Times piece entitled *Trouble for Traitors*. The June report stated that he was being investigated by US Navy intelligence: "You may be sure that when he finishes, naval intelligence will know all about...." Several years before that, in 1933, the mystically endowed Schmidt was able to convince a wealthy couple to build a compound for the inevitable arrival of De Fuhrer.

Norman and Winona Stephens, the former an engineer with an interest in silver, the latter the heiress to a thumb tack manufacturing fortune—and both of them fetched by the prognostication of Mr. Schmidt—buoyantly bought some fifty acres in the Pacific Palisades. "Murphy" would be their alias. Winona, it is said, was always of the esoteric persuasion. They proceeded to spend about $4 million dollars on a vast construction project, that eventuating in the form of a 20,000-gallon fuel tank, a 500,000-gallon water tank, and a power station "large enough to support a small town." Soon there was a barn, a steel garage, a garden, and several other small-end developments—all of which now remain as the LA tourist attraction.

But they had even bigger ideas, and, quite ironically for members of the "master race," hired the renowned African American architect Paul R. Williams to draw out some plans, this in 1939. UCLA's Young Research Library houses many of the blueprints, made up from 1934 to 1941 (no, I won't be going over to check them out). Williams' own initials are absent from these, but, according to Young, the iron gate at the entrance of the compound was made from his design. Between the years of 1933-34, the operation was being supervised by the firm of Plummer, Wuderman & Becket. They eventually pictured: a four-story, twenty-two-bedroom mansion with basement, a "public floor" situated around a grand central hall, an indoor pool, and many libraries. Unfortunately for the Nazi utopians, it seems that by the late 30's, little work had been done.

Young believes that there was genuine activity in these hills: "There was a powerful presence here.... It's such a pretty place for such a stupid pursuit." He once interviewed John Vincent, the UCLA music professor who negotiated the forthcoming sale of the property, and who confirmed that it had indeed been a commune for Nazi sympathizers, complete with residential vandalism and plenty of nighttime rendezvouses. "Everything was really weird about this. The neighbors were a little freaked out about it," Young said. "Until war broke out, it was just eccentric people."

Then came Pearl Harbor. Then came war. And between those, the arrest of many. As the legend concludes, Herr Schmidt was one of them. The Stephens' would live on the property for a few more years, staying in the steel garage. In 1948, Prof. Vincent worked out a land transaction, the disappointed couple now mawkishly desirous to be rid of it. As director of the Huntington Hartford Foundation, at the behest of its owner, Huntington Harford, Vincent transformed it into an artisan's retreat.

And so it somewhat remains today, even after a fire that ripped the place apart in 1978. The city soon took control, allowing it to be used as a hiking spot.

I had heard about the Ruins a couple of years ago, never getting around to a proper visit. The city has always intended for its demolishment, making such announcements too many times to be taken seriously. But emphatic news of an impending deadline suddenly impelled me. I needed to go before I was unable to. Rumors abound that trespassing citations were being given out as gratuitously as Federal Reserve Notes on Wall St., this as an effort to begin curtailing the movement of the crowds.

Mid-February. A weekend. Glorious weather in the low 70s. I invite my longtime friend and drinking buddy. Despite promising to go without, he attempts to bring an open bottle of vodka into the car. Alas, I have a personal incentive for alcohol abstinence. No more risks, especially on a planned adventure like this. I notice his treachery even before he leaves the store (said he was buying cigarettes). I kick him out. The day is ruined. Sunday comes. My father, an embarrassed user of menthol cancer sticks, agrees to join me instead, if for no other reason but to clean out his lungs a bit. I read online that, altogether, it's about a five-mile trek. It wouldn't be quite as exciting as the third Indiana Jones movie, but it would have to do. We arrive in Pacific Palisades around noon. There are lots of hikers.

The trailhead sits below a mansion currently under construction. The dirt path is adorned with sideline shrubbery and overlooks the canyon. I guessed was that it was about a mile and a half walk before getting to the real entrance: a six-foot-high chain-link fence, with loosely attached barbed wire on top, and a big part at the bottom that is cut open. No cops to be seen. Nearly everyone goes in, while a few keep on the trail. I peel the fence apart and hold it for dad and a few others, then jump over the top. Below a quick set of concrete steps was what I assume to be the water tank. An unstable ladder is attached. I use it to climb up. Inside were the two items that never saw a shortage: beer and paint cans.

Just to the side of this tank is the declivitous drop that leads to our dual destinations—the barn and the steel garage—with the stairs probably some quarter mile downward. I look at my father and ask how he is doing, reminding him that we had to come back up. "I'm fine." And so we went. Every step has some trace of graffiti. At the bottom there is another dirt trail.

Standard hiker question: "Which way?" We'd discover that it was actually something of a circle: that going right—as we did—would take us first to the barn, then to the garage; if we kept going around, the stairway would soon reappear.

It was another half mile or so before the first ruins could be seen. Trees and overgrown grass hide the scene for only a second. The barn is also surrounded by a chain link fence. It's busy; likely a few dozen, at least. The hikers make an orbit, taking pictures and admiring the decrepitude. Another rip in the metal allows us inside. It's beautiful in how *used* it is. We go into the wooden structure. Hardly three congruent inches exist without paint. Beer cans are plentiful. A ladder takes us to the second floor. We must share with the other interested faces. Pictures. A few more.

Suddenly the thought overwhelms me: *Fascism?* Fascism! Mr. Young was right: all the lovely places of the earth that we could enjoy and explore, and we still have to contend against the forces of darkness. And tyranny! Always with the tyranny.

Let us break for some contemplation. For I have recently finished reading one of the most popular political books of recent decades, that being Jonah Goldberg's *Liberal Fascism*. Published in 2008, this is a captivating study. It's sharply argued, thoroughly referenced, wonderfully written—and somewhat deceptive in regard to a few omitted details.

Goldberg's first two chapters profile those considered as the 20th Century's original fascists: Adolf Hitler and Benito Mussolini, and he makes the case that these were dictators undoubtedly from *the Left*. Lawrence Samuels, writing at StrikeTheRoot.com, seems to have settled the matter, reporting that Mussolini—who Goldberg calls "the father of fascism"—had specified it as a doctrine of—indeed, *Leftism*.

But, as one would figure, this is ultimately a dilemma of nomenclature: what policies gravitate towards what kind of system? Hitler was a genocidal racist; El Duce had little stomach for it (Italy sheltered many Jews, and Mussolini had the support of the chief Rabbi). Both denounced bourgeois culture, simultaneously partnering with many a corporation. And both were nationalists, with Hitler believing that patriotism was the unjust premise of those who upheld established institutions, and that he was the great catalyst who would bring about much needed change. The differentiation: for their enthusiasts, the Third Reich was, of course, the third in a succession of Germanic empires; the Holy Roman Empire (962-1806 AD) came first, followed by the German Empire (1871-1918). Hitler viewed the Weimar Republic, which came after Germany's post-war revolution, as illegitimate. Thus, nationalistic, but not patriotic. For Mussolini, a dedicated socialist and intellectual, he eventually denounced a core tenet of Marxist doctrine, holding that ideologies like religion and nationalism were "opiates of the masses," and that the only true struggle was worldwide worker solidarity. "The sentiment of nationality exists and cannot be denied," he declared on page 45.

By today's political standards, socialism would invoke Leftism while nationalism would be Rightist. Corporations, to which we will return, knows no spectrum. State violence, likewise, if not always up to Hitler's insatiable bloodthirst. Reconciliation comes with a simple retort: national socialist. Goldberg uses classic libertarian vernacular: "war socialism." As El Duce said, "All within the State, nothing outside the State." Logistically, and by definition, a state needs boundaries. Paradoxically, and per usual policy, it is blind to them. Despots are always centralizers, but they are hardly indifferent to using power solely within their recognized geographical purview. No matter his intended scale of it, Hitler craved war. Mussolini was considered a traitor to his party when, in 1914, the start of the First World War, he came out in favor of Italy's involvement. Patterns are seen elsewhere, as in the American Presidencies.

Because for Goldberg, the truth is much more striking:

Before the Murphy delusion, before the Nazis, and before Mussolini, Fascism had already manifested—right here in "Freedom's Land." (As Gore Vidal would say.) Enter: the 28th President of the United States, Woodrow Wilson (1913-1921). This man worshiped the State. He wrote an 800-page tome entitled *The State*. Cheered the annexation of Puerto Rico and the Philippines. Hated Lincoln's politics but admired his centralizing prowess. "I cannot imagine power as a thing negative and not positive," Wilson wrote (page 84). According to Goldberg, he oversaw an "archipelago of agencies, commissions, and bureaus" to replace the "anti-organic, contra-evolutionary influences of the family." Wilson, the first modern adherent of "statolatry": "We were Jeffersonians…but that time has passed. America is not now and cannot in the future be a place for unrestrained individual enterprise." (Page 93)

Omission: nowhere does Goldberg mention Wilson's other fascist program, the Federal Reserve Act. Signed in December 1913, during Wilson's first year in office, and as Rothbard informs us in his essay, *Wall Street, Banks, and American Foreign Policy*, that The Fed was a pet project of powerful bankers; specifically, the Rockefellers, the Kuhn, Loebs, and the Morgans—who had bankrolled Wilson's presidential run. For now, we'll skip the details of the Monster Bank, which Ron Paul writes can provide: "Guns, butter, and everything else under the sun, including endless bailouts for failing businesses as well as foreign aid for the world…all provided courtesy of the money machine." The former congressman from Texas is quite scathing. Up for dispute is whether or not Wilson had regretted his signing of the bill, dubiously saying that he was: "[A] most unhappy man" because he had "unwittingly ruined my country" via making "a great industrial nation" now "controlled by" a "system of credit," adding that, "The growth of the nation, therefore, and all our activities" is "in the hands of a few men." (The whole quote is a Google click away)

Doesn't really sound like the man described by Goldberg. Plus, a scholar like Wilson would have had seven more years to study and critique The Fed, but didn't seem to get around to it. Elijah Johnson, YouTube investigator, discovers that the quote was a medley of different utterances, made before both Wilson's presidency and the creation of the Monster Bank. Either way, he signed the bill. And in doing so, he set forth a "coincidence"—to quote the good doctor again—"that the century of total war coincided with the century of central banking." Whether or not one describes The Fed with invective, Goldberg, who actually does have sources from Rothbard, can't be bothered with this institution.

The next chapter deals with FDR, and his "fascist New Deal." Most interesting, and damning, is Roosevelt's "Brain Trust." This was a group of special advisors which had visited and studied the experiments taking place in Moscow and Italy. Privately, FDR even acknowledged that they were doing some of the things already being done over there, "in an orderly way." (Page 122). Rexford Tugwell, important New Deal economist and pro-war hawk, wrote: "There was a new life beginning there." Both Hitler and Mussolini praised the U.S. president and his statist programs, with the former writing a letter congratulating him for his "heroic efforts in the interest of the American people." El Duce, known by FDR as "that admirable Italian gentleman," commented, in effect, "This guy is one of us." Birds of the same feather? More like snakes of the same scale.

Another important omission? I think so. There is an incident in American history that usually gets left out, likewise with Goldberg's book: the planned *coup d'état* of 1934, when Major Smedley Butler—that honorable anti-warrior—blew the whistle on what is now called the "Business Plot." Butler had claimed that a bond salesman, named Gerry MacGuire, had approached him with the offer to lead 500,000 men—

veterans—which would "be able to take over the functions of government." Working for Grayson Murphy, financier of the American Legion, MacGuire was representing some rather powerful interests: Rockefellers, Mellons, and Pews. Their goal: the removal of FDR and the installation of, according to Butler, a "fascist dictatorship." Although the press savaged any possibly of the idea, a congressional committee, taking the word of the highly-decorated Butler, eventually verified some of his testimony, concluding that it had some merit—although it probably never got past the contemplation stage.

And why would business elites want to overthrow the government? Let us turn to Professor Domhoff for some insight. Wouldn't you know: the New Deal was supported by some of the wealthiest farmers in the country? As Domhoff writes in his book, *State Autonomy or Class Dominance?* the domestic allotment program was a "key provision in the Agricultural Adjustment Act" that "provided government payments to farmers to major crops like cotton, corn, wheat, and tobacco in exchange for voluntary reductions in the number of crops they planted." This program had its "origins in private foundations and think tanks funded by wealthy business families, and the program was widely supported by leading businessmen well before Roosevelt was elected"—adding that Rockefeller foundations provided most of the financial support for plan development, as it did with Social Security. With that information, there does seems to be almost a contradiction here. FDR wasn't going against any expensive grain; he was just being challenged by another group of elites on the same class level.

Maybe.

That leads to the final criticism requiring brief exploration. Goldberg's book contains many references to that dreaded thing called *corporatism*. As left-libertarians like to remind us, corporations operate in much the same manner as states: they are dually centralist and expansionist. While boardrooms are everything, national borders mean nothing. As market anarchists who believe in business and private property and trade and travel, this wouldn't be sinister per se. However, the problem is the undeniable alliance that always seems to occur, the nexus that has been given deep study by scholars on both the left and the right. That is, when industry falls in love with the State.

Same happened all that time ago. Prescott Bush, father to Bush Senior, and grandfather to "Dubya," was on the board of directors of Brown Brothers Harriman, a firm that had many dealings with Nazi Germany, even after Hitler had seized power. They worked closely with Fritz Thyssen, a major funder of Hitler's party. In 1942, under the Trading with the Enemy Act, the Federal Government took control of their assets. I don't think there's any more dispute about this. And Goldberg's response? Ramblings from the "conspiratorial left" to propagate a "widely peddled smear." (Page 285)

In short, Jonah Goldberg's book is a treasure trove of 20th Century history. But on these questions, the contributing *National Review* editor proves to have a bias. As further example: while he doesn't come out directly as being anti-interventionist, he tells us again and again how these fascistic prototypes would use war as a mechanism for social reorganization. "Militarism in America," he writes, "as in Nazi Germany and Fascist Italy, was a means to this end, not the end itself." (Page 159) And since he's made the connection to Fascism, we're left with no other impression except that these policies *are bad*. He goes from Wilson to FDR to Kennedy to LBJ to Clinton. Obama gets notice in the new afterward. All DemoCrips. (Odes to Mr. Ventura). But ReBloodlicans? Not a single paragraph takes the hardline approach. Yet, the book was released several years after Dubya lied this nation into another bloody conflict (Goldberg: "We are in Iraq for good reasons and for reasons that were well-intentioned but wrong."), using September 11th as a sharp object to cut into the American body in order to install things like the Patriot Act; and then more than two decades after Congressman Jack Brooks asked Oliver North about the "continuity of government" program known as Rex 84. (Yes, support for Third World death squads is still quite hawkish.) In fact, Goldberg appraises the end of World War One by saying that America was "less free at home and less safe in the world." (Page 127) Whodathunkit?

I could go on a bit more. Goldberg's warns that "no police state deserves the name without an ample supply of police," then discusses Hugh "Iron Pants" Johnson and the Palmer Raids and the American Protective League and the Blue Eagle. How about something on how the Reagan Administration finally got rid of the Exclusionary Clause, thereby destroying the last arch of our once-beloved Castle Doctrine? We were classical liberals, were we not? Goldberg deems Mussolini as the progenitor of this political ideology, yet comparisons in the latter part of his book are devoted almost entirely to Hitler. Why can't there be....

...ah, but I've left you back at the Murphy Ruins. Where were we? Oh yes. We leave the barn. Utilize the standard hiker question. A young man and his girlfriend suspend their adventure to politely assure us, "It's just up ahead." Along the way we pass another concrete structure—was it used for fire?—that has been anthropomorphized. It has a fairly good dentist. The steel garage is something of a wonder. Brazenly, taggers are at work today. On the roof and inside, they collude nicely with the tourists. We go in. More pictures; a sticker of a grinning FDR: "Nice Try, Nazi Spy." I climb to the roof. Not much of a view. Dad and I go around the back, where a large dirt gully ascends to another tank. I attempt to shimmy across a tree limb to get onto it, then decide against the stunt. We go back down. Some people are having lunch, paint fumes be damned.

At the top of the stairs that lead to the garden—the last scene to be seen—there is a small plastic shot of alcoholic tea. I announce: "Excuse me...." A dozen or so faces look up. "Somebody left their shot over here." No interest except a few giggles. Then I say, less loudly, "I can't drink it right now." I put it down. Dad and I go through the garden and continue onward. As told, the steep steps soon reappear. "Ready?" I ask. He's slightly winded. Two couples pass us. But he makes it. Another short walk back to the car. Water. Home.

Final thoughts. As early as 1946, George Orwell, in his famous essay "Politics and the English Language," had observed that Fascism was coming to mean "something not desirable," thereby asking, "Since you don't know what Fascism is, how can you struggle against" it? I've tried to explore some of the terminology and report on some of those undesirable policies. My own take away? Well, I'm not a Rothbardian; not an optimist, I mean. I'm a George Carlin (Carlinian?) misanthrope. I have no stake in the outcome—which is admittedly depressing for anyone with offspring. I think people, if they can, should begin bunkering up. Flee. Burrow. Hoard. Hide. No shame in recognizing that things are bad and expecting that they could get worse.

Why? Observe.

We are in the midst of another presidential circus. On the one hand, a flamboyant and smarmy and inconsiderate nationalist—but someone who also might be the only candidate truly against World War Three. Mr. Trump. On the other, a real-life comic book villain, the criminally insane Hillary Clinton—a Hitleresque tyrant whom I thank every day is not greeted with applause by members of my generation, and, noticeably, very few from the rest. Meanwhile, there is the just-released trailer for Oliver Stone's Edward Snowden movie, which might give a fantastic, albeit dramatized depiction of how terrifyingly real Orwell's Nightmare has become. Then, closer to home, the culture wars, where college campuses are perpetually in uproar, with membership of the victim hierarchy now at an all-time high. Err…low. Somewhere in the middle is Peter Schiff's latest doom-and-gloom report. Bill Nye, deemed "the fascist guy" by social media, hovers overhead, advocating imprisonment for all "climate skeptics." Something, at some time, is bound to collide.

But I can try to be optimistic. After all, I had a great afternoon exploring the ruins of would-be fascists. I can only hope that one day soon, I'll see a similar scene at the White House, or even the many state congresses, not forgetting the Federal Reserve and its branches, or—hell, since we're fantasizing—all those thousands of child kidnapping centers and domestic terrorist stations (sometimes called police headquarters) and however more brainwashing facilities. Maybe someday they'll also become abandoned ruins of a time that needs to be forgotten: overgrown with foliage, covered in street art, and serving a much better purpose as a hiking trail and occasional playground for boozing delinquents.

And then I can finally stop pondering on that necessary question: why did we ever need those things?

(May 2016)

Trump in Anaheim

IT WAS ONLY a few weeks ago that I finally made up my mind about the candidacy of Donald J. Trump. Since a third partier would not become the 45th POTUS, I must again reconsider that dreadful thing called "lesser evilism."

This doesn't mean that I would be voting for him; sitting the election out is, as Konkin maintains, the most libertarian of all the limited choices. It just means that after insisting several caveats, I would verbalize my preference of The Donald over the DemonLord, Billary Clinton. (I intend a profile of each of them, but for now, this is just a report of the festivities.) I suggest that 60% of what comes out of his mouth is smarmy and contradictory and offensive, 30% is comedic, and 10% is actually worth listening to. I truly dislike the man. It's just that I don't despise him as much as the other.

Some weeks ago, Big Orange held a rally in Costa Mesa. Nineteen were arrested. Cop cars were set ablaze. The nationwide pattern is now almost predictable. A couple days

back, on May 24th, he was in Albuquerque. More madness. So
when he announced that he was coming back to California, this
time closer to home, in Anaheim, I decided to dust off my old
journalist bag. How come? When asked why he stays in a
country he so often criticizes, H.L. Mencken replied: "Why do
people go to the zoo?" And so, we have the 2016 presidential
election.

The rally was scheduled for the convention center, right
across from Disneyland, noon. A titillating headline from *The
Guardian* held a hopeful prospect for my story: "Donald Trump
Could Face Chaos as He Heads to 'Riot-Happy' California
City." I got there exactly at ten, parking a good mile away from
the address. As soon as I arrived in the front plaza, two Jesus
Freaks of local prominence were on their usual bull-horning
bromide, this time appended with support for The Donald. A
few minutes later, a handful of Anti-Trumpers marched
themselves and their bullhorn right up and onto them, inches
away. This is a tactic! And notice the difference: screaming
obscenities from afar is an exercise in free speech; screaming
two inches from a person's face is "activism."

I manage to ask the street evangelist if it bothers him that,
in his tower, Trump allows transgenders to use whatever
restroom they feel comfortable with. Glib response: "He'll
come around." One of the odder activists gives the baldheaded
freak a kiss via his hand, touching him gently on the face. "You
really shouldn't do that," I said to him. "Fuck you," he snarled,
with what looked to be bad case of pinkeye. I tell another
journalist that it was going to be a long, exciting day.

A cop informs me that the entrance was around the side. I
walk over. Ask another uniformed man: "Protests?" He nods. As
soon as I get there I see the first of what would become the
second of many pocket-sized conflicts. Pro-Trumpers (PT),
with their red caps and American flag apparel, and the Anti-
Trumpers (AT), mostly with "black-bloc" style dressings,

bandanas and patches and whatnot. Back and forth they went. I jump between the two main shouters, offering a seat at the table.

"Is this Mexico?" I ask the AT.

"This is not Mexico," he says loudly (well, everyone was loud). "I am an American citizen!"

To the PT: "Does it bother you that Trump has factories in Mexico?"

He evades on his bullhorn: "I wish I had a few!"

I ask to the AT: "Is it possible some cultures don't get along?"

His answer: "Yes. Some people just don't get along."

This went on for another minute or so before the PT and his son decided to take themselves to another part of the plaza. Employees of the OC Weekly are handing out printouts of a piece of artwork they used for one of their covers. It has a democratic donkey branded with the Hillary "H" bending Trump over and, I guess, raping him.

Several AT's take this and hold it for the cameras. "Are you then supporting Hillary?" I ask. "That's her logo right there." The correction is noted by the looks on their faces. One of the guys tries covering the "H" up with his finger. I stick around for a while longer, say hello to Luke Rudkowski, meet a fellow libertarian who agreeably stated that Trump was "appealing to the nativist mentality," then go inside the auditorium. Along the route, I strike up a conversation with a man named Ricky, whose theory of Trumpism was one based in "pop culture."

One whole side is packed. Many are on floor and behind the podium. I go to the third level. A black pastor is riling up the crowd. "Hillary Clinton should be in jail!" he says. Some are making their way around the place, passing out "Trump 2016" signs. I'm given about 50. Another group comes around, where I give all but one back. I reminisce about the last political rallies I was at, four long years ago, twice seeing Ron Paul. The jive isn't the same. The attendees aren't either. For one thing, there was plenty above-40-year-olds. Absent was any talk about the Fed, or the Wars, or postulations on Liberty. Just noise, with the occasional use of the noun "greatness" presented as a glum glossing. Sadness would've overwhelmed me if I didn't recognize it as the big carnival that it was, with activists on both sides displaying their favorite flavor of Hate.

About twenty minutes pass before Big Orange gets up on the stage. The crowd goes nuts. He immediately plays one of the four or five cards he holds in his hands: benevolent authority. "They said we didn't have time to do the national anthem," he says. "No, no—we have time!" More roars as the young lady is summoned. His eternal tactic is to present himself as the man who Gets Things Done. Perhaps there's some truth to that.

The tape recorder sits on my satchel, saving room for video footage on my phone. Highlights include a group of women coming up on the stage, The Donald insisting that "some women like me." One of them says cringingly, "Thank you God for sending us Donald J. Trump." His orange hair seemingly glows brighter. The first protester is revealed within five minutes. Like blood-stained arrow tips, several dozen red-capped heads point towards the offender. "The cops will get 'em out soon," says Trump.

Boos and jeers.

He calls Hillary "crooked," and that she "had some bad news today"—the Inspector General Report. "Not good. Not good." Always with the repetition of words. Now, hollers and cheers. In about 20 minutes, the first protestor is expelled. Roars. "Don't hurt him—see what I say? I say 'don't hurt him' for the television cameras...even though he's a bad person."

I picture a bully on the playground praising the teachers as they haul off another child who decided he was at last going to say something. *Bad person.* "Is there any place more fun to be at than a Trump rally?" I think of a few, but it does take a minute.

"Latinos for Trump! I love that!" he says, pointing to a group in the audience. "We're gonna do real good with the Hispanics." *The*. Funniest part is when he talks about Hillary's famous "3 AM" ad. "Whose gonna answer the call? She was asleep, folks!" invoking Benghazi. "Hundreds and hundreds of emails and phone calls...I don't sleep much." Then he talks about a few murders committed by illegal—or is it *undocumented*?—immigrants. A "build the wall" chant begins.

Another eviction comes just after the half-hour mark, the AT briefly scuffling with a PT on the floor below. Soon a couple more protesters appear on my level, on the other side, above Trump. He notices it after the redcaps make their disapproval known. A supporter comes from behind and rips the signs from their hands. Cheers. Security finally makes their way over and escorts them all downstairs.

Trump mentions his onetime friendship with Mitt Romney, mocking how he "walks like a penguin," and adding that he's "never seen people pivot like politicians." We'll see. He talks. And talks some more. When he says "in closing," I gather my stuff and head to the floor, where I take a selfie with Trump's head seen far in the background. It's over, and I rush outside to see what's happening.

Time for the real fun, as the rage of the Anti-Trumpers is augmented by the exiting attendees. We—I—have to move between a line of cops, who are decked out in commando gear. Protest signs that call of "racism" are obligatory. This is the general scene: Dozens of ATs are confronted by an equal amount of PTs.

Once again I go into the largest huddle, where the Hate is palatable. Suddenly, a man wearing a redcap (PT) is hit with an egg. I look towards the ATs and ask if these kinds of actions are going to have the accidental effect of bringing more people onto the "Trump Train." A young lady is mad: "Did we throw it? Did she?"—gesturing to anther bandana-wearing protestor, who I actually wasn't asking. Another familiar tactic: the use of anonymity coupled with solidarity. All as one, none as all. I say: "No, it was a general question to…." And she stops me: "Then why you asking her?" Another AT is more polite and we have a chat. "No racist is coming to my house"—meaning his city—"and not getting some resistance."

An intelligent Hispanic Trump supporter wearing a redcap and suit is loud and argumentative. "You're a Mestizo, aren't you?" he says to another Hispanic Anti-Trumper. He shows a picture of a wall. "The Asiaticos built this wall to protect their civilization." The other man is flipping him off and cursing. "You just don't have an argument for why you're even out here," he says.

Two more Trump supporters are pelted with eggs from cowardly assailants. One of the victims, a large man, actually saw who hit him—a teenager on a skateboard—and promptly made chase through the plaza. I follow behind, with the big man almost nearly capturing the kid several times.

An older female AT grabbed the man's arm, refusing to let go, on the grounds that "he's just a kid." *Female privilege.* I stay here for a few more minutes, then decide to go to the front of the convention center, where I'm told there is more action. When leaving, I meet a photographer named Michael Ledray, whose commentary is hilarious. "I was in Costa Mesa a couple weeks ago…we had some real angry protesters out there—not like these pussies."

I laugh and take his card.

When I get to the front, I notice that a line of police has prevented westward movement. "My car is that way," I explain. "You'll have to wait," says a cop. Two reporters pass through the line. "By what magic?!" "They're reporters with credentials," a cop says. "Oh yeah, I got mine here somewhere," I say, patting my empty breast pocket. "Can I get to it by going around the block?" I ask. They're uncertain if there are any more blockades. "I gotta try." Then go.

Light jog to the other side, where the intersection held many more contentious Pro- and Anti-Trumpers, nearly equal in number, engaged in verbal combat and hoping for it to become physical. I have a little debate with someone. He tells me that it's awful that people were attacked, but that's all they can do, since they don't have the "institutional power" to deport the however millions of undocumented immigrants.

I'm happy to finally hear someone give a justification for assault. True enough, I say, but does it bother him that Trump seems to have a number of Hispanic supporters, and that they wield the power of the vote like any white person? We go on a bit, but the raucous crowd is diverting my attention. I go further into the circle. A Hispanic AT has his shirt off, huffing and puffing and looking to fight. PT yells, "You just don't have an argument." A young man tells me that he had things thrown at him.

Yet another PT—a young black man—also testifies to being assailed. I'm losing track of the bloodless violence. I now want to help settle things down and attempt a "Kumbaya" chant. Support does not come. I'm standing there looking like an idiot. At last, a helicopter flies over us, and declares an "unlawful assembly." The crowd begins to disperse.

I linger for a while to see if there would be any more circles. There is one, but a cop prevents me from going to that corner of the sidewalk. They're doing their best to clear the intersection. After grabbing an iced tea and microwavable cheeseburger at 7-Eleven, I go back to the front of the convention center.

Anaheim's finest still have a blockade, but there is action this time.

I'm not there for a whole minute before I see the most violent scuffle of the day, between a white guy who has had his sign taken from him by a group of Hispanic ATs. At least four of them begin swinging on the PT, but he is not afraid, nor weak, and starts throwing them back, holding his own. Thirty seconds of brawling and it's over. Cops watch with aloofness, be damned their abundance of numbers and witnessing of so many confrontations. Some complaints about this.

I'm amazed at how quickly these two polarized groups reassemble after any kind of abeyance. They're like magnets towards each other, the mutual need to prove themselves correct. So it happens after the brawl. A PT pulls out a Taser, the clicking sound heard several times. I see a Hispanic Trump supporter on a bicycle and try to get a word. He says there is Hispanic support in his neighborhood, but they are afraid to come out. Another Hispanic anti-Trumper, gives me my last interview.

"So you would support Hillary over Trump?" I ask.

"No," he said. "If Bernie wins, I'll support Bernie."

"But Bernie isn't going it. The Bern has been extinguished. It's gonna be Hillary and Trump. And a third party isn't gonna get it."

"Whoever gets it, I'm voting against Trump."

"It doesn't bother you that Hillary has this 30 year track record of criminality behind her?"

"So does Trump."

"Let's see it. What has Trump done exactly?"

"He hires illegal immigrants, which he hates."

"Well, that's hypocritical, but is it criminal?"

"He tried to rape a girl."

I stumble a bit: "Wait...you're talking about his first wife?" I then mentioned Juanita Broaddrick and Kathleen Willey, two Clinton victims. "People who have actually made charges against him." We're then interrupted by a pair of Anti-Trumpers who want some attention. "We're over here having a discussion," I scold them whilst not making eye contact, "and you bring this over here? You see why people get angry, and they say 'Look, they can't even have a conversation.'" The gentleman goes back to his points, saying how if Trump had merely brought up immigration as something that needs to be worked on, it wouldn't have been like this. "Does it bother you that there are Mexicans who are supporting him?"

A Trump supporter jumps in: "Mexican right here," he says, who then brings up the fact that Cesar Chavez was vehemently opposed to illegal immigration. "He would use the word 'wetback.'" "And he was wrong there." Final question: "Let's get to the heart of the matter: Is this Mexico?" The man answers: "This is occupied Mexico." I have a hearty laugh which pretty much ends the day.

Just at three 'o clock the streets are opened, and horse-mounted police officers trek through. All the attendees decide at once that the day is over. News outlets later report a total of eleven arrests, with a couple for public urination. I walk back to my car while giving an interview to someone doing a podcast. I repeat for his audience: I really don't like the man.

This whole time the question rises and falls in my head: What if Donald Trump hadn't started off his campaign with such inflammatory language? The full quote: "When Mexico sends its people, they're not sending their best. They're not sending you. They're sending people that have lots of problems. And they're bringing those problems with us. They're bringing drugs. They're bringing crime. They're rapists...and some, I assume, are good people. But I speak to border guards and they tell us what we're getting."

He added: "It's coming from more than Mexico. It's coming from all over South and Latin America, and its coming probably from the Middle East. But we don't know, 'cause we have no protection, and we have no competence. We don't know what's happening." As political watchers will note, and many haven't, it also matters what politicians don't say—like the aforementioned factories down South.

Here, Trumpism is deduced for what it is: an appeal to nativism, to nationalism, and to benevolent authoritarianism.

He's no libertarian.

But readers of classical anarchist theorists would keep in mind that Pierre-Joseph Proudhon was most certainly a nationalist, who argued that federalism was the only answer to ending rivalrous feuds between nations, as well as dissolving empires. Closer to the 21st Century, anarcho-capitalist proponents like Hans Herman Hoppe believe that the State, wrong for stealing property via taxation, compound the severity of the crime by giving whatever stolen resources to those who manage to cross the border.

Both claim to cherish national identity, as I'm sure one would find with any three people who speak the same language, share the same pigmentation, and perhaps worship the same imaginary Sky-god.

Furthermore, the "longshoreman philosopher," Eric Hoffer, held that nationalism was the strongest collectivist impulse that we mere mortals could harbor. This is because— my thoughts—that while a religion will occasionally see lapses in one's faith, making it harder to proselytize to others, a historical record is hard to dispute.

With that, one can then claim the mantle of "their people," and, by means of extension, win World War Two, or something like this. It's a tenacious reaction in the fragile human psyche. This is why Trump can rile up so many with the slogan of, "Make America Great Again." How many trillions in debt? Are we still the world's greatest military superpower? How many crooks and murderers have there been in those offices? And then those many more darker-hued persons and workers will ask: "When was America ever great?"

But is Trump a hypocrite? If he's to be anti-violation of national borders, is he consistent with it? In fact, Zack

Beauchamp over at Vox.com thinks his "dovishness" is grossly overstated. And, as already established, he has factories in Mexico, and likely hires undocumented workers here. So, yes. He is. So, I repeat for the umpteenth time: I really, truly don't like Donald Trump. If Gary Johnson, an imperfect libertarian himself, somehow manages to get into the debates—great!

But as of right now, assuming that there are, once again, only two candidates, and if I must make an assessment—which pile of dung smells slightly less: Hillary or Trump?—I will not hesitate to give an answer, followed or preceded by many urgent provisos.

(June 2016)

The Rise of Trump

DONALD TRUMP IS a "masculine force at full tilt," may be a "benevolent authoritarian," and is someone that Ilana Mercer hopes will "continue to break things." Bold language is replete throughout this slender work, such as the man uses himself.

The general thrust of this collection from a veteran libertarian's 2016 Trump coverage is correct: he is the answer to the American electorate's culminated frustration towards a political system that is so corrupt, so wicked, and so expansive that it just absolved the career criminal named Hillary Clinton of any wrongdoing.

Thus, insists Mercer, Trump is the "quintessential post-Constitution candidate." True enough.

There's a lot to dislike about Trump. For one thing, his insistence of prosecuting American heroes—specifically Edward Snowden. In fact, he has nothing to say about a Surveillance State that watches our every move, something that Mercer criticizes in regards to the French government. A reasonable person would also speculate as to why Trump was friends with the Clintons for so many decades prior, as well as that *Washington Post* report that said that Bill had called him up just before things got underway and offered some encouraging words.

Moreover, there's recent terrible news of a possible Newt Gingrich VP slot. Also: as someone who was introduced to electoral politics with the last election, throwing my weight behind Ron Paul, I don't think it would be "feminist" of me to be surprised and dismayed if the good doctor had told a young lady that she looked good on her knees.

Yes, Mrs. Mercer, we can be both anti-feminist and gentlemanly at the same time.

But that's the phenomenon of what the author calls "the process of Trump." He's an inarticulate, swaggering, no-BS wrecking ball. The Republican Party and their prolocutors on Fox News are soaked with urine, having peed on themselves and each other.

And while I would first think, "A candidate really shouldn't imply that a woman is on her period," the immediate next impulse is that Megyn Kelly is part of a network that, four years ago, all but ignored Congressman Paul, who if it weren't for them would likely be our president today. (Maybe now Trump can finally understand why people don't get elected— something he said about Paul way back when). They're reaping what they sowed, despite one or two "polite" interviews they had afforded the good doctor.

Trump is armed with his billion-dollar bank account, sundering through with his "no apology" tour. Mercer's defense of this process, and her takedowns of those clowns, is entertaining.

Another important thing. My perspective of Trump's "dovishness" has been mired by conflicting reports. His most memorable line, as I remember, was "take the oil!" Not very dovish. But Mercer reminds us that Trump has never backpedaled on his charge that George Bush deliberately lied our nation into the bloody conflict in Iraq; not to mention (or to mention) that he'd like to see what's inside the infamous "28 Pages." This is all hearsay in Washington. Even the most liberal of Democrats don't dare make such suggestions.

Although Trump is far from the perfect libertarian candidate, his books give the unfailing impression that he genuinely cares about the future of America. It's refreshing in an era of mediocrity, when President Obama, speaking of the downgraded credit rating given by Standard & Poor, says glumly that "We'll always be number one"—sounding like he's handing out participation prizes.

Some criticism.

I don't know if it's an editorial error or her writing style, but the book has many misplaced semicolons. Example: "While voters take Donald Trump very seriously; his party's leadership does not." She also has an abundance of rhythmical-sounding words: *Federal Frankenstein—Politburo of proctologists—European Eurocracy*, to name a handful. It can be clever; other times, unnecessarily stupid.

Lastly, I resist using the word "fetishizing" when I mention Mercer's incessant lamentation of "Low-T candidates" and "the new male." She goes on and on about this. While she may or may not be correct, I don't give much credence to the idea that there's been any real biological change within the male body.

Rather, our mental condition is the collective product of enforced apathy, caused by our daily tolerance of corruption in politics, our mindlessness which is encouraged by sports and videogames, and then always hearing the constant nonstop nonsense about "racism-xenophobia-this phobia-that phobia-etc.-etc."

There's certainly a race between many a heterosexual white male to see who can become the strongest "ally" in the war against the "white-patriarchal-heteronormative-capitalist-blah-blah-blah." (These last two quotes are my own.)

It wouldn't be hard to conclude that plenty of Intersectionalist, Regressive Left-types might prefer Sharia instead of Jeffersonian Democracy.

Donald Trump simply has no time for it. Again, Mercer's thrust here is on point, if indeed she's a tad crass with it.

To understand the rise of Trump and how we as a nation came to this crescendo, pick up Mrs. Mercer's book.

(July 2016)

Clintonism, Unplugged

Yes, that is what I would have said, and because there is no cosmic point to the life that each of us perceives on this distant bit of dust at galaxy's edge, all the more reason for us to maintain in proper balance what we have here. Because there is nothing else. Nothing. This is it.

And quite enough, all in all.

—Gore Vidal, *Armageddon?*

ANYBODY GROWING UP in the late Nineties would have realized that, at the very least, the 42nd President of the United States was as good a liar as he was an adulterer. The "Mrs. Clinton" always seen on T.V. seemed nice enough, and, well, how *dare* this guy! Obvious, or perhaps not, was the fact that he was also deceiving the unduly elected Congress, along with our comically incompetent media (or was that duly complicit?), in order to salvage that charming, jazzing, indelible image.

That strange and seductive and nostalgic episode, therefore, might have made "Monica" the first political word heard by millions of ears. (I personally recall one of my earliest uses of the Internet as looking up the details of Bill Clinton's affair with Ms. Lewinski. Something about a cigar. And insertion. "Stains" and "blue dress" were also roving nouns during this time. After all, I was young, and, like many others, had far less interest in politics than I did about pornography.) Though we must note that her name arose only amidst the legal proceedings of another woman, one Paula Jones. 1991: Jones was working a conference booth in the Excelsior Hotel, Arkansas, when Governor Clinton had asked her to come and visit him in a room upstairs. There, she says, without asking permission, he ran his hands up her dress, tried kissing her, and then pulled down his pants with an offer to perform fellatio. She escaped and fled downstairs. The case settled when "Slick Willie" gave her $850,000, sans apology but with sly admittance of guilt.

Less obvious back then was the inseparability of the two: they're now known as *Billary*—the equally evil spouse that completes this political Orthrus, and who is, yet again, campaigning for that High Office. Hillary displayed those enduring oratory skills during one of her campaign stops: "I did not email any classified material to anyone on my email," she said with her usual sternness. FBI head James Comey—likely threatened—attested without revelation that these lies were just that. Not surprisingly, no indictments will be brought against members of the ruling class.

This updates the clock. And as a viewer of the infamous Clinton Chronicles documentary (perhaps the only decent thing Jerry Falwell did), or reader of stories generally thought to be on "the outside," or even a regular student of the late Christopher Hitchens, who had just finished veteran insider Roger Stone's newest timely indictment, *The Clinton's War on Women*, one would assess this nasty family much differently than what has been presented by the networks.

That would be, that they truly are: International killers who murder and slaughter without abandon (which would otherwise be called terrorism); sealers of potential loose-lips; traffickers of deadly narcotics; enhancers of a police state that prosecutes the victims the same as the pushers; long-held charges which reveal the Clintons as compulsive and professional liars—not to forget hypocritical "equality" advocates; and, making a central point of this obloquy quite clear, noting with worthy credibility *for him*—a disgusting and carnivorous woman abuser in the form of a serial rapist who "bites" his victim until she submits. *And her*, as the wife and accomplice, thereafter hiring private spooks to intimidate, harass, and discredit these women once they decide to speak out. The line that cannot be denied? She'll do anything to attain Power.

For many (yes, the following can already be seen on the Interwebz), the slogan "I'm Ready for Hillary" has always sounded like bracing for a prostate exam. The average American progressive has overwhelmingly favored Bernie Sanders, and everyone from that pool who now adopts the mantra is currently bending over, gritting their teeth and grinding their toes into the floor.

As shown by the fact that these sadistic criminals have hardly had these matters scrutinized by the talking-heads, and instead given a sort of gravitational amiability, this on a sublunary rung always held by Wall Street, the political establishment, and certain entertainment "activists" (the members of what prof. William Domhoff called "The Higher Circles" seem to have a natural attraction to one another, and so I guess the Clintons can't ever *leave*), it can be seen plainly that "Clintonistas" (nod to the author's coinage) is *still* a powerful elite organ in this Post-American Century.

Libertarian eyes and ears should alert to the reality that these people don't merely violate every last consideration of the

Non-Aggression Principle—they've also successfully convinced our entire body-politic into thinking that it hardly matters at all. This is despite a public record of state privilege shielding what would otherwise be prosecutable offenses, with their story not doing justice to the phrase "conflict of interest," including and never neglecting the heavily documented testimony relating to "Bill Cosby-style" abuse (Stone likes to capitalize on this contemporary comparison).

Because the U.S. presidency *is* a repository of violence, theft and corruption, the problem is not so much whether Hillary would make a "good" first-female president as much as whether Bill would make a *perfect* first-ever first-husband. Urgently, this election cycle shows that it is time, and—yes— *long past time*, that the juggernaut of Clintonism be unplugged once and for all.

I'll do my part.

A Memo from the Fearless, if Eccentric, Coauthor

Robert Morrow hates the Clintons. Indeed, he hates the Secret Government that seeks to control the world, which the Clintons and Bushs are part of, and as gears of extreme importance. Recently, Morrow gave up his position as the chairman of the Travis County Republican Party, a post he held to the chagrin of many, so that he might too have his try at becoming the POTUS. For this Texan is, as Stone describes his coauthor, "absolutely an eccentric character." His Facebook posts might offend a few, but he is a fearless diver into the dark waters known as "deep politics." It was he who amassed the library used for the distillation of their book. I called Morrow last year to have a chat about these grave matters. My first question was the one already mentioned: How is it possible that these criminals remain in the national spotlight?

"They're friends with people who own the media," he answers plainly. Makes sense. As his first illustration, the case of Danney Williams, a 30-year-old biracial man who is claimed, and insisted by himself, to be the long-lost neglected son of Bill. An Arkansas street hooker, named Bobbie Ann Williams, announced to the public that in 1984 she had copulated with the then-governor while he was out jogging one night, even doing the deed behind some shrubs, and thereafter totaling some 13 trysts, according to the authors. "He just looked at her and said, 'Yeah...that one right there. She looks good,'" Morrow muses in his best Clinton drawl. Bobbie Ann started alleging this in the early '90s, which steadily got louder throughout the decade. (Christopher Hitchens was asked by her to conduct an investigation. And why in Australia? Anyway, he declined.) Although the voice of this seemingly sincere woman grew loud enough to make it onto the pages of several outlets, and into the ear of billionaire independent candidate Ross Perot, it was ultimately drowned out by Clinton's many other scandals.

During Hillary's Senate run—this in 1999—the Clinton Machine propagated the story that a DNA test took place, and that it absolved Bill of any possible parentage. This fable initially ran in the yellow-stained pages of The Star, and then soon picked up by The Washington Post and TIME. Morrow says this has proved to be "very important" in maintaining the deception.

"No, no, no, Kevin," Morrow corrects me. "There was no DNA test done." He then excoriates the "pumpkinheads of that era who took that disinformation article by a tabloid owned by a best friend of the Clintons, named Roger Altman." My interviewee tells me that Howard Kurtz, who wrote up the piece for The Post, never saw that DNA test, nor did Danney Williams ever participate in one. "He's on Facebook, Twitter," Morrow says. "He's all over the place. Anybody in the world could talk to him. They just don't."

Note: Mr. Williams is on most social network platforms,

and while we were supposed to have a chat for this report, he ultimately declined.

With that assessment in mind—a culpability by major news agencies—let us continue to recognize the mis-and-non-reportage of Clinton Criminality.

What is Clintonism?

The depressing word that comes to mind is "permanence." This is not all given to the Clintons' refusal to exit the scene, but instead to what we call their "worldview"—which should be taken in a literal sense. This is the often-dismissed international policy that aims at consolidating economic and political authority. Conspiratologists will document three instances in which this ominous philosophy is hinted at.

The first comes early in Clinton's bid for the White House, when he cited as an influence Georgetown history professor Carroll Quigley. He credited Quigley again after winning the nomination. Clinton had taken the professor's class, receiving a decent "B" grade in what was supposedly a difficult course. In a system that frequently rejects the idea that skullduggery can ever be a factor, the highly respected Quigley is something of an outlier. In 1966, he published a tome entitled *Tragedy and Hope: A History of the World in Our Time,* which soon experienced efforts to have it "suppressed," so said Quigley himself.

Joseph Plummer has put a summary of the book online. It describes the existence of an "anglophile network" that seeks to bring "all the habitable portions of the world" under its jurisdiction. This group sprung up in the 1800s, in England, with Cecil Rhodes and his Round Table groups. By 1919 they had created the Royal Institute of International Affairs. Coming to America, this same cabal established the Council on Foreign Relations—the CFR—which Quigley said was a "front" for JP Morgan. (I don't wish to unweave the intricacies of the network itself. I merely want to assert that it does exist, and that those two are a part of it.)

The second instance in which Bill alluded to his allegiance came after his presidency, post-9/11, speaking at the Kennedy Center, stating that, like his predecessor, Bush senior, we needed a "New World Order." The phrase has been conjured too many times by too many movers and shakers to reject any notion of fanciful conspiracy-mongering.

The third striking example would come from Hillary. In October of 1999, iconic newscaster Walter Cronkite gave a speech to the World Federalists Association, receiving an award from them for coming out in favor of world government. Via television set, the Mrs. Clinton congratulated Cronkite for "fighting for the way it could be." Practicality? It's the word used in Pro-Trump circles: Globalism. As Justin Raimondo writes in a 1995 preface to Rothbard's pamphlet about the Power Elite:

> Giant multinational corporations, and their economic satellites, in alliance with government and the big banks, are in the process of extending their influence on a global scale: they dream of a world central bank, global planning, and an international welfare state, with American troops policing the world to guarantee their profit margins.

Sometimes politely and amorphously dubbed the "FIRE economy"—short for finance, insurance, and real estate—these institutions are internationalist in nature. Hillary has taken a lot of heat for her pandering to Wall Street, the entity that gave ample funds to the Clinton Machine.

Richard W. Behan at Counterpunch has a comprehensive article on atavistic alliance. For the Clinton family's six political races—Bill's first presidential run, his reelection, Hillary's Senate run, reelection, her first White House bid, and in the

Year of our Lord: 2016—Wall Street gave a total of $68.72 million. In what might only be a coincidence, after Bill reacquired the Oval Office, helped along with a triple dosage of campaign money (from $11.17 million in '92 to $28.37 million in '96), he signed into law the Financial Services Modernization Act of 1999, which effectively repealed the Glass-Steagall Act of 1933. Now, the financial institutions could mix commercial banking with investment banking and ended the regulation of derivatives. It has been argued that this eventually led to the "subprime swindle" that nearly wrecked the economy a few years back. Finally, the nation's Worst Family (Hitchens' coinage) routinely endures criticism for their post-'90s career choice: giving speeches to powerful bankers at a couple hundred-thousand dollars a pop.

Once again, we find a Clinton composite. We hear Shillary say something liberal and populist like, "I went to Wall St., in December of 2007, before the big crash that we had, and I basically said 'cut it out—quit foreclosing on homes,'" but then uttering that, in regards to the economic collapse, "there's plenty of blame to go around"—those homeowners who paid extra fees to "avoid documenting their income." Lest anyone might think that she's a foe of the FIRE, William D. Cohan, writing for Politico.com, thinks that: "Down on Wall St. they don't believe it for a minute. While the finance industry does genuinely hate [Elizabeth] Warren, the big bankers love Clinton, and by and large they badly want her to be president." And Warren, who once castigated Clinton on her Wall St. patronage, now loves her. Needless to say, on Wall Street, she's once again the favored pick.

Enter: Hillary's Village (on second thought, don't enter it). Jonah Goldberg opines that the *NYT* bestseller has "all the hallmarks of the fascist enterprise" folded within its pages. Right away, Hillary waxes tyrannical that, back in her youth, they "were not subjected to a daily diet of second-guessing and cynicism about the motives and actions of every leader and institution." She further admits that she "cannot say enough in support of home visits, whether the visitor is a social worker or a nurse from a program"—or, trying to stick to communitarianism and not full-blown authoritarianism—"an aunt who rides the bus on Saturday to see how her niece and the newborn are doing." What a sweetheart.

The book tries to draw a line between these dichotomies: a friendly, "we're-just-watching-out-for-the-children" call to action; and the statist, "just-do-what-we-say" prediction. I'll quote a bit throughout, but most illustrative is her chapter "Seeing is Believing." Hillary condemns television and video games as "media assault," saying that we can "look to countries such as Great Britain and Australia, which have stricter codes for violent content." She cites studies telling of the harmful effects on the developing mind, and the logic that you wouldn't let strangers tell your children stories with the same kind of content that they ingest on TV and on gaming consoles.

When combining parental vigilance, voluntary boycotts, general concern for the youth, and academic evocation—it sounds good. It becomes sour when applying Hillary's real intention: censorship. Matt Welch, Reason magazine's editor-in-chief, wrote an article for their March issue entitled Hail to the Censor. His quotations of Hillary amount as such, like in December when she talked about "denying online space" to certain groups. Moreover, she said that the cartoonists of the French satirical newspaper Charlie Hebdo had sparked their own murders. Hillary then repeatedly asserted that the attack at Benghazi was the backlash of a crudely made film, the Innocence of Muslims. At a memorial for the victims, she spoke to Charles Woods, father of the slain CIA operative Tyrone Woods. He made notes. "She said we're going to have the filmmaker arrested who was responsible for the death of my son." Patricia Smith, mother of the murdered Sean Smith, was also told that it was the fault of the video. Odiously, Welch reminds us that the Benghazi hearings unearthed a phone conversation in which Hillary admitted to the Egyptian prime minister that "the attack in Libya had nothing to do with the film." Keyboards, cameras, colored pencils, and the people who wield them: *these are the real culprits!*

That ends my throat clearing. It's enough to demonstrate that Hillary is correct when she tells her Wall St. benefactors that she has both public and private positions. For there is no sewer too low, too dark, too slimly, for the Clinton mafia to wade around in. And there's Clintonism in a nutshell: an addiction to power that is so strong that they're willing to lie, cheat, and kill to get their fix. After all, even Richard Nixon disappeared following his impeachment.

Bill Clinton: Sexual Predator

Allegations of Bill Clinton's sexual predation go back many decades, to his days as a Rhodes Scholar at Oxford. The first impulse for anybody hoping for a Clinton presidency is to home in on the word "allegation," followed by the glib but not unfair line of, Why wasn't there an arrest? The journalistic prosecutor is doomed to deal with a minor annoyance, which is the fallacy of how a majoritarian belief hardly equates with the truth; but then, nevertheless, how if all fingers and indictors point irresistibly towards someone or something, especially an object that has much influence in the public sphere, one owes it to themselves and others to give it a taste of validity. In more words, Mr. Bill has had many fingers pointed at him, and they should not be dismissed offhandedly, if only because all voters ought to know about them.

As the book notes, Bill "Clinton is one of the few Rhodes Scholars *without* a degree from Oxford." The political website CapitolHillBlue.com first published the story about then-19-

year-old Eileen Wellstone, a fellow classmate who is said to be the first woman that Bill Clinton raped, this following a meeting at a nearby pub. The authors of that piece cite a retired State Department employee who spoke with the family and filed a report with his superiors. The college, fearing a scandal, covered it up.

By far the most well-known case against Bill is made by Juanita Broaddrick. The owner of a nursing home and a volunteer for Clinton's 1978 bid for the governorship, Broaddrick was requested to have coffee with the promising predator while she was visiting Little Rock. Wanting to avoid the press, he asked if they could go up to her hotel room. She obliged. There, she claims, Clinton raped her—twice, after the accused was astonished at his ability to quickly reacquire an erection. During the assault, he bit her lip, making it gush blood. "Better get some ice on that," Bill said as he left the room.

There were witnesses to Broaddrick's condition just after the attack, five in total: Norma Kelsey (a close friend who came along for the trip), Susan Lewis, Louise Mah, Jean Darby (sister to Kelsey), and Juanita's husband-to-be, David Broaddrick. Kelsey was featured—not interviewed—in that famous *Dateline NBC* reveal. But Broaddrick still wanted to remain quiet; she wanted her good life and career to continue without any further complications. She even attended a fundraiser for her attacker a few weeks afterwards.

By the time Paula Jones' investigators got to the taciturn Broaddrick—this in 1997—her story had been circling upon whispers for nearly two decades. She repeatedly denied everything, even after Jones' team had secretly recorded a conversation in which she made no firm denial about her abuse. She simply did not want to relive that "horrible, horrible thing," saying that she would deny it all if ever subpoenaed. The next year, Kenneth Starr, lead investigator for Clinton's impeachment trial, did just that, and Broaddrick made good on her promise to remain quiet. Starr then threatened perjury, citing her own words and the word of Republican lawyer Phillip Yoakum, who she had confided in. An offer of immunity was made in exchange for the truth.

Finally, Broaddrick softened her long-held refractory stance, admitting to the world that Clinton had indeed raped her all those years before. It eventually became a footnote in the Starr Report, as she never claimed "obstruction," or received any threats, as Starr was specifically looking for. Predictably, her nursing home business was audited, and her own house broken into.

Lionheartedly, in the year 2000, Broaddrick wrote an open letter to Hillary, entitled *Do You Remember?*

After watching a Fox News interview, she felt compelled to address the "same conniving, self-serving person" that she met "22 years ago when I had the misfortune to meet you." She recalls attending a political rally that took place just a couple of weeks after the attack, in which Hillary approached her as soon as she arrived, wanting to "thank" her for "everything that you do for Bill." Broaddrick tried to pull away. Hillary held tightly: *Do you understand everything you do?* Translation: just be quiet! Yes, an authentic American horror story. Broaddrick, married and divorced three times, has recently put her home up for sale to relocate, out of fear that she might be in danger for being so vocal this election cycle. WikiLeaks reveals that Hillary's camp had anticipated Broaddrick—"Jane Doe #5" in the Jones suit—becoming part of a slimefest.

For those who notice the contradiction—that Broaddrick first said that she had not been intimidated, but then penning that letter, and coming out so loudly against Hillary today—it should be realized that a strong arm accompanied with stern but vague wording could hardly be deemed as harassment. How can an incident like that be argued after two decades had elapsed? "What happened?" "She grabbed my arm and said, 'thanks for what you do.'" Imagine the menacing subtlety. Then picture "middle-America" Broaddrick just coming out of the shadows, now in the national spotlight, saying something that she likely knew would sound foolish to the top-shot prosecutors on Capitol Hill.

There's many similarly abused women. Kathleen Willey was a volunteer at the White House in November 1993, just after Clinton secured the Oval Office. Not wasting much time in here, the red-faced bastard came alive, horns gorging through his forehead, a tail darting out from a rip in his pants. Bill then grabbed Willey, fondled her breasts, and forced her hand upon his "small twisted penis" (the quote *is* a given description). She fled the room. But still needing money, as she was in a financial bind, Willey had a lawyer send Bill requests for a paid job that wasn't in the White House. In '97, with reports of the incident coming out of *Newsweek*, Starr sent a summons. She agreed to talk.

Willey was then subjected to a vicious and sustained program of harassment. Her cats went missing. Car tires slashed. A skull placed on her porch. Most sinisterly, while out jogging, she was approached by an unfamiliar jogger, who inquired about these things. This worked: in the course of her disposition for the Jones case, her memory lapsed some 63 times. Since then, she has given many interviews, written a book, made a website dedicated to Clinton victims (which has gone defunct), and wrote the preface for Stone and Morrow. "Hillary Clinton *is* the War on Women," she urges.

Hillary again? Undeniably, the candidate who said that "every survivor of sexual assault has a right to be heard" is the same one that disparaged Bill's accusers, calling them *bimbo eruptions*. She *is* the enabler, partner, and worst-half. Let's elaborate. Melanie Morgan is a conservative activist and radio host who, in 2003, attended a writer's conference in California. There, she bumped into famed private dick Jack Palladino, a name first mentioned by the late Mr. Hitchens in an updated 2000 version of his book *No One Left to Lie To* to be one of the ghostly figures that had intimidated Ms. Willey. Morgan gained the verve to ask: "Aren't you ashamed of yourself with the business you did for Hillary Clinton? You know, come on. That stuff with Kathleen Willey was pretty outrageous. What was that? You guys ran over her cat? What was that all about?"

Palladino replied: "Well, I'm not really going to comment about that, but let me say this: The only regret that I had about the whole thing was that Hillary did not pay me in a timely fashion," adding that he "saved Hillary Clinton's ass" and that she should've been "more grateful." The disgraceful PI threatened to sue following Willey's recount of the story in her book, but in a case that could possibly prove guilt, the suit never happened.

The immediate admonishment to all this should be clear: This is all just hearsay! Baseless allegations! If it were true, Clinton would be behind bars! (Not to forget my favorite: *Bill isn't running for office*—ignoring the fact that Hillary is still married to a very likely serial woman abuser.)

First, there's a welter of accounts regarding Bill's sexual impropriety, and I hereby implore the curious Clinton voter, as well as the Clinton opponent, to read the book-in-overview for more names and stories. This is a hint for people like Cenk Uygur, who dismiss the allegations just because the author, Stone, is Trump's loudest advocate. But who cares about Stone? The women were making these statements long before his book was written. There's simply too many of them to all be false, or for me to detail here. And it's highly unlikely for any person who gets a job in the White House to dare risk their career and reputation making baseless allegations against the leader of the Less-Than-Free World.

Secondly, to illustrate the ruthlessness of the Clinton Machine, I should mention the story of Gary Johnson (no, not the libertarian candidate), the neighbor of one of Bill's consenting partners, Gennifer Flowers. This was the woman who originally brought publicity to Clinton's sexual deviances, a relationship that he had to eventually admit was—what's that evasive word?—*inappropriate*, and after years of the typical denial. Featured in the original *Clinton Chronicles* documentary, Johnson claimed to have video footage of Bill coming and going from Flowers' apartment. Disclosure could not be allowed. His consequence: thugs who kicked in his door, beat him within an inch of his life, and stole the incriminating VHS tape.

We know this because of Larry Nichols, an old friend of the Clintons. In 1988 he was fired for misconduct, and soon began speaking out about Bill and Flowers. He wasn't the only ally-turned-foe. While governor of Arkansas, Bill had something of a private gang—his State Troopers. Their side task, it is said, was to act as liaisons between the licentious Bill and his many partners.

To repeat my insisted disputation: it's highly unlikely that men of this occupation would begin making statements of the governor's criminality, especially since, if they were participants, the whole thing might backfire and they could see themselves behind bars. But these Troopers did just that. According to Morrow, two of them, Roger Perry and Larry Patterson (who recorded video interviews), would later tell Nichols that they were the ones who had burglarized and brutalized Mr. Johnson, who was also Nichols' lawyer. (All of these men are featured in *Clinton Chronicles*.) Tellingly, this means that the Clintons are willing to go to *any lengths* necessary to remain on the crest of political power.

As a third depiction of their demonic nature, the judicial case of one of Hillary's defendants while she was still a 27-year-old lawyer working in Arkansas. In 1975, Hillary became counsel to Thomas Alfred Taylor, a 41-year-old man who was charged with raping a 12-year-old girl. This case came to light a couple of years ago when WashingtonFreeBeacon released portions of an interview that was conducted with Hillary in the mid-'80s. Regarding the "interesting" and "fascinating" case, she remembers that Taylor had taken a polygraph test, which, says the cackling Clinton, "forever destroyed my faith in polygraphs."

Kathy Shelton, who spent five days in a coma and then some ten years in therapy, gave an interview to the Daily Beast, saying that Hillary "took me through hell," revealing that the witch "intentionally [lied] about her in court documents, going to extraordinary lengths to discredit evidence of the rape." This includes Hillary saying that the victim was "emotionally unstable" and had a proclivity of seeking out older men. Hillary says in the audio that Taylor got off with "time served" after spending about two months in the county jail. PolitiFact reports that Clinton had suffered a memory lapse: it was actually a year in jail and four more of probation.

It remains uncertain as to who appointed Hillary. On the tape she said it was done as a "favor"; in her book *Living History* she says she was put on the job by Washington County prosecutor Mahlon Gibson—neither of which are necessarily contradictory. Gibson told *Newsweek*, profiling the case in 2008 (which seems to be gone from the web), that Clinton emphatically tried getting herself taken off. Either way, as the late Vincent Bugliosi might have observed (who, despite all his brilliance, was another Clinton fan), even if this was her sworn duty as a public lawyer, what type of *monstrous individual* would be joking and making light of this horrendous situation, especially considering that *she* believed the perpetrator had only served a couple of months on a child rape charge? More evidence that the Clintons are devoid of any semblance of the kind of substance that we might attribute to heartfelt human beings. As written in a 1998 *Vanity Fair* article: "Feminists have, all along, muffled, disguised, excused and denied the worst aspects of the president's behavior with women."

And the same goes for Hillary.

Powdered Treason

The Secret Government is the world's largest dope peddler, or at least one of the largest. This was discovered during the fallout of the Iran-Contra days, then detailed by the investigations of the late Gary Webb. Probably the closest to a comprehensive history on the subject was written in 1998 by journalists Alexander Cockburn (RIP) and Jeffrey St. Clair, in their book *Whiteout: The CIA, Drugs, and the Press*.

The program of courting the Underworld started at the end of World War Two, when the U.S. government granted immunity to the convicted gangster Charles "Lucky" Luciano, the first of five hundred to be granted this. These gangsters would then go to Italy and conscript the recently ousted Mafia dons (done courtesy of El Duce), who would then help the Allied forces attain information.

It'll remain debated as to how much this insidious policy worked, but to quote the authors:

> *What cannot be denied is that the U.S. intelligence agencies arranged for the release from prison of the world's most preeminent drug lord, allowed him to rebuild his narcotics empire, watched the flow of drugs into the largely black ghettos of New York and Washington D.C. escalate, and then lied about what they had done.*

In 1978, the U.S. government, under President Jimmy Carter, made a last-ditch effort to preserve the Somoza monarchy that had ruled over Nicaragua for many decades. At the time, that government was in the process of being overthrown by the

Sandinista revolution. Carter hoped that by supporting Somoza's National Guard they could remain as the caretaker for "American interests." The plan failed, with the Sandinistas coming to power. With Carter's approval, Somoza's generals then formed the Contras. Through them, the U.S. government led a proxy war for nearly a decade against the new regime.

A few names are important in the California drug scene: Norwin Meneses Cantarero, a head of security for the leading Contra coalition, and Oscar Danilo Blandon, a Nicaraguan exile. In November of 1981, President Ronald Reagan signed *National Security Directive 17*, authorizing a $19 million fund for the Contras. Blandon later testified to a U.S. grand jury that more funds were needed. During a meeting with Enrique Bermudez, the CIA's handpicked man to lead the Fuerza Democratico Nicaraguense—or FDN, the main Contra organization—it was decided that cocaine sales should help out with the cause.

Meneses would get the cocaine from Mexico, coming up from Columbia, and then stash it in places throughout Southern California. Things were slow until they met a young black street hustler named "Freeway" Ricky Ross, who would distribute it widely to the inner cities. According to Cockburn and Clair, by 1983 Ross was buying over 100 kilos of cocaine a week and selling as much as $3 million worth of crack a day. By 1985 the market had extended to over a dozen U.S. cities. The Nicaraguan exiles, protected by the highest levels of U.S. Power, then sent a portion of their money back to their embattled comrades.

But there's more!

Barry Seal, a notorious name in the literature of clandestine U.S. operations, was a skilled pilot and convicted drug trafficker, who, by his own admission, flew missions for the CIA. In 1982, Seal moved his base from New Orleans to the small town of Mena, Arkansas—governed at that time by Mr.

Clinton. The Agency was anxious to hire their favorite pilot to shuttle supplies to the Contras, then stationed in Honduras and Costa Rica. Seal's fleet of planes would fly from Mena to Medellin cartel airstrips in Columbia and Venezuela, refuel in Panama and Honduras, and then return to Arkansas, where parachute-equipped packages of cocaine would be dropped onto the surrounding farmland. (Incidentally, the whole saga is now a movie starring Tom Cruise as Seal, which has just been renamed from *Mena* to *American Made*, and also pushed far back into 2017. Coincidence? Naturally!)

This is one of the stories that must be paid attention to if all compasses point irresistibly towards it. For starters, Bill's brother Roger was arrested and charged with cocaine distribution. He was subsequently pardoned. Next, according to Arkansas Attorney General Winston Bryant, who was later told to stay away from the matter, quote: "There was, in my opinion, more than enough evidence to prosecute a number of people for crimes regarding the Barry Seal case at Mena." Bryant soon reneged on a promise to convene a grand jury, despite 900 citizen signatures urging him to do so.

Utterly evidentiary is the testimony of two men. L.D. Brown was one of Clinton's state troopers, who later turned on him and wrote a book. In a 1995 court case, Brown claims that he had flown with Seal to South America to deliver packages. Coming back, he said that duffle bags were kicked out of the plane over the surrounding Mena farmland. After three such flights, he confronted Bill about it, who said "that's Lasater's deal. And your buddy [George] Bush knows about it." Dan Lasater was one of Bill's closest and most important political contributors. He was also later convicted for distributing coke.

The other man is Terry Reed, an intelligence officer who worked for the Air Force, the FBI, and the CIA. He told Alex Jones that he was recruited by Oliver North to help with the

Contra supply operation, stationing him in Mena as a pilot instructor. Stone and Morrow write that, "The first day [Reed] met Barry Seal he was in the company of Dan Lasater and Roger Clinton." After two years of walking around with "blinders," Reed stumbled upon a C-130 that was packed with cocaine. 1986, somewhere in Arkansas: Governor Clinton requested that Reed, dining with his wife at the moment, join him in the back of a security van parked outside. Bill was puffing on a cannabis cigarette and tried to calm Reed's fears about a planned trip to Mexico, saying that North was expecting him to do so. Reed went.

L.D. Brown, Bill's "favorite trooper," writing in his book, claims that he was also sent down south. His rendezvous was with Felix Rodriguez, notorious killer for the CIA, who equipped him with a 7.62 rifle. Brown's mission was to kill Reed. Upon seeing Reed in his crosshairs, Brown froze, aborted, and then dumped the gun into a roadside ditch. Reed lived to write his own testimonial book.

As further word given by respected officials, former DEA agent Celerino "Cele" Castillo, head man in Guatemala, has repeatedly recalled the time in which he confronted Vice President George Bush about Contra cocaine smuggling, who simply smiled and walked away. Castillo was later convicted for selling unlicensed firearms, spending three years in prison. He says it was retaliation.

Summation: *much* has been written, testified, and presented about U.S. government narco-trafficking. In 1995, *The Washington Post* was all set to run a lengthy investigative piece based on an archive of over 2,000 documents. It raised all the same serious questions: Mena, Seal, the Contras, local police inquiries. It then quoted Bill as saying, "I've always felt we never got the full story there," but noting that, "Clinton did not offer any further support for any inquiry." At the very last minute, the piece was squashed, with the editor calling it a "non-existent story." It was eventually published in *Penthouse*.

One paragraph stands out particularly:

> *Still, most of the larger American media have continued to ignore, if not ridicule, the Mena accusations. Finding no conspiracy in the Oachitas last July, Washington Post reporter typically scoffed at the 'alleged dark deeds,' contrasted Mena with an image as 'Clandestination, Arkansas . . . Cloak and Dagger Capital of America.' Noting that The New York Times had 'mentioned Mena primarily as the headquarters of the American Rock Garden Society,' the Columbia Journalism Review in a recent issue dismissed 'the conspiracy theories' as of 'dubious relevance.'*

Even now, someone writing about this is usually discarded, likely because of the absence of any high-level prosecution. And we can't assume that James Comey has been overseeing these cases for all this time. Nonetheless, both Menses and Blandon received convictions. Elsewhere, at other times, reporters were said to have been threatened. Prosecutors were told to lay off. Citizen watch groups finding themselves in dead-ends. So many people saying so much reveals that there must be, not just the stench of verisimilitude, but the cold hard slap of reality: elected and unelected members of our government have trafficked in drugs, and the Clintons, in all likelihood, have had their noses buried in it. At the very least one would agree with this: drug running was taking place in the state where Bill was governor, and he showed *zero interest* in helping along with the many inquiries.

This is the height of treason in a country that has half of its federally incarcerated inmates there for non-violent drug offenses, and yet touts its mantra of freedom and lawfulness. As I see it, the audaciousness of Black America's longstanding support for the Clintons is appalling and quixotic: polling data shows that it still hovers around 80-90 percent in some states. But this is par for the course. In the late '90s, after Bill's fall from grace in the eyes of many American voters, Black America maintained widespread favorability towards "America's first black president," as anointed by Toni Morrison.

Compounded by the complicity with U.S. government drug trafficking, with the subsequent result of wrecking inner-cities, Bill also helped augment a Police State that had been growing exponentially since the middle of the century, that pointy-edged device which does the killing and the arresting. Examples are as follows. He appointed retired general Barry McCaffrey to be his drug czar. He censured and then fired his surgeon general, Dr. Joycelyn Elders, in part because she had suggested drug decriminalization. He started the COPS program that saw police departments hire some 100,000 more officers. He subsidized states for hiring military-minded veterans who were returning from the battlefields overseas. He instituted "truth in sentencing" that encouraged states to make it difficult for parolees to get out early. And he instituted the "one strike and you're out" policy, which meant eviction for any person living in public housing if caught for a misdemeanor drug offense, with Clinton stating: "From now on, the rule for residents who commit crime and peddle drugs should be 'one strike and you're out.'" (For more, see Radley Balko's *Rise of the Warrior Cop*) "The first step is to take weapons off the streets and to put more police on them," writes Hillary in her manifesto. A rare moment of honesty: the State is the parent; the individual and the community are the untrustworthy children.

Some of these legislative efforts were part of that malignant 1994 crime bill, popularly passed by representatives on both sides of the aisle. It had an effect. Professor Michelle Alexander makes a few notes in her essay for *The Nation*, stating that "Bill Clinton presided over the largest increase in federal and state prison inmates of any president in American history," which saw the US having the highest incarceration rate in the world when he left office. She then writes: "Human Rights Watch reported that in seven states, African Americans constituted 80-90 percent of all drug offenders sent to prison, even though they were no more likely than whites to use or sell drugs." At the same time, Bill was slashing welfare programs with a veracity unlike any Republican. For her part, Hitlery, who "wasn't picking out the china while she was first lady" (could *not* have said it better myself), called out the *super predators* who this legislation was aimed at. And thanks to WikiLeaks, the cannabis constituency knows that her stance has evolved innumerable times: from opposing even medical pot in 2007, to being against legalization "in all senses of the word" in 2014, to now thinking the former is okay and accepting Colorado and Washington in experimenting with the latter. More of her *whatever sounds good to this person* policy.

This gets me to a rather gregarious premise, one found regularly within "Social Justice Warrior" discourse. That is, that racism is the fusion of "prejudice *plus* power." (Funny how for many Intersectionalists, *feminism* is per Webster's definition— *equality for women*—but here it means something else.) Professor Alexander opines that the 1965 Voting Rights Act was the "high water mark" of the Civil Rights movement. Was this not a grasp for *institutional power*? Surely some would concur. And yes, "power" can manifest in various ways—like directing troops from a comfortable seat in the Oval Office or pushing buttons that makes money appear. But they say that in a representative democracy, casting ballots is the same as pulling levers. As it is: in 2012, for the first time ever, Black America outvoted White America, reelecting the charming sock-puppet nicknamed Mr. Hope & Change, 66% of eligible voters to 64%, according to a government study. (I shan't mention Obama's record of warmongering and police state augmentation.)

The question must be asked: Why is this influential voting bloc once again giving support to a police state augmenter, a warmongering imperialist, and—although perhaps forgiven decades ago because of the absence of media attention, can no longer be said in the age of the Internet—an accomplice to narco-trafficking? Will it be said that this is White Supremacy brainwashing people? That such minuscule self-determinism cannot muster a reading of Professor Alexander, whose book *The New Jim Crow* also sources from Clair and Cockburn (to be fair, the book contains one paragraph on US government drug trafficking, and doesn't detail Clinton's involvement), and whose headline of that piece cited above reads, "Why Hillary Clinton Doesn't Deserve the Black Vote"? For refusing to endorse the Clintons, Prof. Alexander and Cornel West have the respect of this scribbler.

I don't mean to say that this exercise in what is at least *electoral power* necessarily ends all racial problems. Instead, it's meant as a rebuttal to a prevailing datum: that participation in the System is a repeated widespread action of Black America, which severely weakens the idea that disenfranchisement, the complete absence of voice or vote, remains as an insurmountable roadblock to the concept of "black liberation."

And as a conundrum: the difficulty of overthrowing an oppressive structure when you're helping to elect the people who actually do the oppressing. Those who say that black Americans are, once again, victims of indoctrination or fanciful politicking, evade the principle of personal responsibly. Who forces anybody to stay ignorant about Clinton criminality? Put one last way: if someone votes for Donald Trump because they believe in what he says, and that person thereafter labeled as— what?—racist and sexist (something of which might be true about many Trump supporters), does that mean that anyone voting for Hillary Clinton condones or forgives all of the horrors detailed therein? Does that make them any better or worse than the Trumpers?

Does that make one a masochist?

Again, I'd beg not.

Though it's hard to see how logic would be inapplicable, fallacious, or lacking any consideration. Surely, this energy could be refocused onto a third party. Now then, someone make a note for Shaun King and Tom Hayden.

A Maroon-Colored Ocean

War: another Clinton specialty. Here, we'll start with the "Mrs." and then move to the "Mr." A lot of information has leaked about Hillary's role regarding the turmoil in Middle Eastern countries, namely Libya and Syria. Robert Parry, founder and editor of ConsortiumNews.com, tells us "What Hillary Knew about Libya," based on 3,000 emails released by the State Department during last year's holiday season.

In 2011, amidst political strife that arose with the Tunisia Revolution, Muammar Qaddafi, leader of the state, was disposed, and then murdered without trial. Hillary, as Secretary of State, had a big part in this. Remember: "We came, we saw, he died"? Sidney Blumenthal, one of the Clinton's most conniving underlings, wrote an email to discuss the "rumors" that Qaddafi had adopted a "rape policy," in which he was supposedly giving Viagra to his troops. Although no evidence of such a thing ever emerged, Susan Rice presented it as truth before the United Nations.

In April of that same year, Blumenthal wrote an email informing Clinton that "sources close to one of Qaddafi sons were reporting that 'Qaddafi's government holds 143 tons of gold, and a similar amount in silver' and the hoard had been moved from the Libyan Central Bank in Tripoli closer to the border with Niger and Chad." It is said that the gold was "accumulated prior to the current rebellion and was intended to be used to establish a pan-African currency based on the Libyan golden Dinar"—a $7 billion dollar equivalent that was meant as an alternative to the French franc.

The email outlined the real objectives of Qaddafi's ouster: a "desire to gain a greater share of Libya oil production"; to "increase French influence in North Africa"; for French president Nicolas Sarkozy to "improve his internal political situation in France"; and then to "provide the French military with an opportunity to reassert its position in the world"; and finally to "supplant France as the dominant power in Francophone Africa." (How close these things came to fruition is not the subject of this essay, only that there were other intentions.) Qaddafi himself knew about the threat of radical Islamists, and Blumenthal stated that Sarkozy was concerned that these groups were infiltrating the rebel forces who were revolting against the Libyan leader:

> *Senior European security officials caution that AQIM is watching developments in Libya, and elements of that organization have been in touch with tribes in the southeastern part of the country. These [European] officials are concerned that in a post-Qaddafi Libya, France and other western Europen countries must move quickly to ensure that the new government does not allow AQIM and others to set up small, semi-autonomous local entities, or 'Caliphates', in the oil and gas producing regions of southeastern Libya.*

(AQIM stands for Al Qa'ida in the Islamic Maghreb, one of the "radical/terrorist" groups that the French president was "concerned" with.) Exactly as happened! Mainstream press?

The *New York Times* ran a story in July of last year on the Secretary's correspondence with Blumenthal, who was barred by Obama from working in the State Department; the advice was "unsolicited." "First, brava! This is a historic moment and you will be credited for realizing it," Blumenthal told Hillary about the chaos, adding that those in the Department "thought it might make sense for you to do an op-ed to run right after he falls, making this point." This was to be—yes, said of the serpent—the "Clinton Doctrine."

That was August, 2011. Two months later, Qaddafi was dead. And from there, the country, said to be one of the most prosperous and Western-friendly in the region, descended into hell. Paul Joseph Watson recently reported that Killary had thwarted Libyan peace negotiations due to a "personal vendetta," as Qaddafi had given his endorsement to Obama in 2008. He produces a letter from Dr. Kilari Anand Paul, an Indian peace negotiator, now naturalized US citizen, as well as a friend of Qaddafi, who was being accused of war crimes for repelling the Jihadi-minded rebels. So hopeful was the arrangement set forth that General Wesley Clark had arranged a telephone conference with Clinton, who apparently had no interest. "Had this deal gone through," Watson writes, "it would have saved countless lives that were lost in the aftermath, prevented the collapse of Libya into a failed state fought over by rival jihadist gangs and significantly alleviated the international migrant crisis that worsened dreadfully in the years that followed. It could even have contained ISIS' spread across the Middle East. The Benghazi attack would never have happened." (As stated, this was not the full reason for Qaddafi's ouster, but merely Hillary's motivation.)

Benghazi. The subject of so many headlines and congressional hearings. A year following Qaddafi's fall, in one of Libya's largest cities, an American outpost was attacked, resulting in the death of four diplomats. "Finding #1" of the Senate report states: "In the months before the attacks on September 11th, the IC provided ample strategic warning that the security situation in eastern Libya was deteriorating and that U.S. facilities and personnel were at risk in Benghazi." As constantly reminded to us by Donald Trump, this *should have been a concern* for the woman who once put out a campaign ad asking: "Who is going to answer that call at 3 in the morning?" But Hillary could give a damn less about little things like "blowback" or mass human suffering or the law she swore to uphold. Speaking of the last, Hillary *did* delete some 30,000 emails, and *after* she received a congressional subpoena. FBI director Comey admitted this in his July decision, but, as surprising to no one, the deletion was not "intentionally" an "effort to conceal them."

Now we come to the WikiLeaks data-dumps, which include "The Podesta Emails," John being the chairman of Hillary's campaign. One email was dated September 9th of 2014. Podesta stated that "we need to use our diplomatic and more traditional intelligence assets to bring pressure on the governments of Qatar and Saudi Arabia"—our great "allies" in the Middle East—*"which are providing clandestine financial and logistic support to ISIL and other radical Sunni groups in the region."* Small leap of faith to say that Obama and Co. knew more than this.

Keep history in mind.

The cozy relationship between the United States government and Saudi Arabia goes back to 1945, at the end of World War II, when FDR met with King Ibn Saud onboard the USS *Quincy*. Here, it is widely believed that the two men formed a tacit agreement: American protection for Saudi petroleum. Every President since then—Democrip and ReBloodlican (always with odes to Mr. Ventura)—has obliged this continual doctrine, making the Kingdom well-funded and heavily armed. During Bill's reign, the Department of Defense sold the Saudis some $40 billion worth of armaments, according to Michael T. Klare.

Presidentially, the Obama administration has also approved arms sales, with senators Rand Paul (R) and Chris Murphy (D) attempting to impede the freshest however-many-billion-dollar-package. Their fellow lawmakers rejected the effort, and off go more machines of death. By means of circuity, the US *did* and *does* fund ISIS. LibyaBodyCount.Org tallies almost 1,400 dead since the conflict. As ISIS spreads, the ocean fills!

Syria. It's no secret that our dear leaders are obsessed with the removal of Syrian president Bashar al-Assad. The civil war in that country has been waging for years. A quick search gives death estimates between 301,781 and 470,000. Talk of the "rebels," those fighting Assad, usually fuel the reports. We are, with our tax dollars, supporting these people.

Who are they?

Well, that's the point made by Donald Trump and others: We *don't* know who they are. But again, WikiLeaks confirms that Hillary (and, naturally, the POTUS) were aware that Saudi Arabia was—is—funding ISIS. Russia and Iran, need be noted, are two of Assad's most ardent supporters and defenders.

One of WikiLeaks' most importantly released emails is titled "New Iran and Syria," with no name on the header. There is an emphasis of protecting Israel: "The best way to help Israel deal with Iran's growing nuclear capability is to help the people of Syria overthrow the regime of Bashar Assad." It makes recommendations: "Washington should start by expressing its willingness to work with regional allies like Turkey, Saudi Arabia, and Qatar to organize, train and arm Syrian rebel forces." Required is an international coalition but laments that Russia will never go along with it; alas, "there is no point operating through the UN Security Council," concluding that: "Some argue that U.S. involvement risks a wider war with

Russia. But the Kosovo example shows otherwise. In that case, Russia had genuine ethnic and political ties to the Serbs, which don't exist between Russia and Syria, and even then, Russia did little more than complain. Russian officials have already acknowledged they won't stand in the way if intervention comes."

I wouldn't be so sure. Reports abound that Putin is readying for an all-out war. Supposedly, he's asked all students studying abroad to return to the "motherland." He canceled a recent trip to France. He talks about how "major global conflicts have been avoided in the past few decades, due to the geostrategic balance of power, which used to exist," and that, "We told them about the reactionary measures we were going to take. And this is what we did. And I assure you—that today, we have had every success in that area...I'm not going to list everything, all that matters is we have modernized our military-industrial complex and we continue to develop new generation warfare."

So Killery has one new geopolitical enemy in her crosshairs: Mr. Putin, who she repeatedly blames for hacking into her email. In one of her speeches to Goldman Sachs, she stated that Syria was a different case than Libya, adding: "They're getting more sophisticated thanks to Russian imports. To have a no-fly zone, you have to take out all of the air defense, many of which are located in populated areas. So, our missiles, even if they are standoff missiles so we're not putting our pilots at risk—you're going to kill a lot of Syrians," she said. "So all of a sudden this intervention that people talk about so glibly becomes an American and NATO involvement where you take a lot of civilians."

Fill that ocean some more:

> *Some of us thought, perhaps, we could, with a more*
> *robust, covert action trying to vet, identify, train*

and arm cadres of rebels that would at least have the firepower to be able to protect themselves against both Assad and the Al-Qaeda-related jihadist groups that have, unfortunately, been attracted to Syria...That's been complicated by the fact that the Saudis and others are shipping large amounts of weapons—and pretty indiscriminately—not at all targeted toward the people that we think would be the more moderate, least likely, to cause problems in the future, but this is another one of those very tough analytical problems.

Just call her *Hillary the Hawk*. At the third presidential debate, in defense of her stance, she said that no-fly zones would save lives. Marine Corps Gen. Joseph Dunford, chairman of the Joint Chiefs of Staff, warns correctly that this is an act of war, in which nuclear Russia could quickly be embroiled. Somehow, I can picture Hillary laughing as a blackened sun sinks below a maroon-colored ocean, charred bodies and skeleton buildings that are decorated across a static landscape.

She's dipped her claws into other pools of blood. One might have heard mentions about Hillary's support for a political coup in Honduras, NarcoNews.com reports. In 2009, their Supreme Court issued an arrest warrant for the democratically elected president Manuel Zelaya, with the military raiding his house in the middle of the night, putting him on an airplane, and flying him out to Costa Rica. The international community condemned this action. Obama and the State Department, likewise, called the coup government "illegitimate," and urged it to bring Zelaya back to finish his last few months. These talks fell apart. Obama then suspended all aid to the country.

Emails show that Hillary disobeyed her boss, using the Millennium Challenge Corporation—an institution that gives aid to countries, ran conveniently by the Secretary of State—to instead continue the funneling of funds, nearly $11 million in the first two months after the coup, and $100 million the following year. She then asked one of her cronies, lawyer Lanny Davis, who was working with the coup government to rework its image if she could meet with their new president. The cited website quotes an email from a State Department legal advisor: "The action memo will require the Secretary to decide whether Honduras is a country without a 'specified legal prohibition' or whether such a prohibition has in fact attached." No prohibition was ever made by Hillary, who shunned those demanding that the coup be recognized as such. Experts say this left catastrophic results, with Honduras having the highest murder rate in the world by 2014.

Let's not also forget that, although today she says that the Iraq War was a "mistake," she did indeed vote for it as a senator. But that, neither, was her foray into militancy. For she is married to someone who Edward S. Herman once called "The World's Leading Active War Criminal." His reasons include: Continuing support for the genocidal Indonesian dictator Suharto, a long-held client of the U.S. government, saying that he was "our kind of guy"; bombing Baghdad in June of 1993, killing eight and wounding 13, and this as retaliation for Saddam's assassination plot that targeted Clinton's political "opponent," Bush Sr.; his support for Turkey's declaration of war against the indigenous Kurdish population; his bombing of a Sudanese pharmaceutical plant, justified as a suspicion that it was a front for Osama bin Laden; weekly missile attacks upon Iraq; and then, of course, presiding over the "sanctions of mass destruction" imposed on that country, which left a reported one million civilian casualties.

As remarked by Chip Gibbons at *Jacobin*, this was "war by other means," reporting that, "It not only banned weapons of battle, but technologies that ostensibly had military and civilian uses—like pencils, which the sanctions regime said could be fashioned into bullets." Bill, cheerfully surfing on the waves of a maroon-colored ocean, simply denied the figures.

The last one should be placed into a contemporary context. The sanctions began in August 1990, four days after Saddam's invasion of Kuwait, lasting until he was removed from power, in March 2003. Two respected international diplomats, Denis Halliday and Hans von Sponeck, who administered the UN oil-for-food program in Iraq, resigned from their posts in protest, saying that the sanctions were strengthening the dictator while at the same time leaving so many dead. Campaigning for Hillary this election cycle is Madeleine Albright, former Secretary of State and Ambassador to the UN. In 1996, appearing on *60 Minutes*, Albright was asked about the embargo that left half a million children dead. Her infamous, obdurate, icy-cold response: "We think the price is worth it." Albright has now said that "there's a special place in hell" for women who don't help Hillary. More laughter as they sail on the top of a body of blood, skulls and corpses sinking to the bottom. No big deal. Elect the first female president.

But then what do you expect from a family that is friends with Henry Kissinger? Or from a man who pardons international criminals? Or from a woman that might very well have ordered the siege on a compound in Texas that left 82 dead? Nothing...except the proper designation: *killers*.

No wonder Hillary has the support of so many neoconservatives.

Nailing the Coffins and Boarding the Closets

Evil, while not objective, cannot be entirely *subjective*. Those who live by separate sets of standards should be put on the list. If someone signs laws that criminalize drug users while once trafficking in drugs, that means something profound. If one proclaims themselves to be the champion of female and child victimhood, and yet laughs at the comments of somebody who approves of the death of children, while also neglecting to leave their psychotically abusive partner, that too means something small. Because of this dual presentation of their true character, added with the inexhaustible evidence of their criminality, the Clintons would have to meet every single criteria for any hard definitions explored here. To quote the silly but solidly-antiwar conspiracy theorist David Icke: "I would call Hillary Clinton evil, except that I would expect to be sued for defamation of character...by Evil."

Corny, yet accurate.

I began this project reading Stone and Morrow's book, then Hitchens', chatted with Morrow, watched a couple documentaries, noting from several other titles in my library, and at the same time going through a stack of articles. I then found myself squirming through Hillary's *It Takes a Village*. It's difficult to contrast one's newly found education about high crimes with that of the loving, tender warmth of "What about the children?" rhetoric. For instance, vomit nearly came out of my mouth when reading of Hillary's experience in breastfeeding her daughter Chelsea, who was "taking in [her] milk." It's just not the kind of thing you'd envision these demons doing; instead, maybe feeding Chelsea a warm bottle of freshly extracted goat's blood or dropping the infant child into a vat of poisonous toxins. Certainly not an act as natural and healthy as *breastfeeding*. Quite macabre!

My other intention was to castigate all those who endorse the Clintons. Despite their ensorcellment long having worn off the vast number of American citizens, they still have in their corner: the black vote, the Hispanic vote, "Big Brainwash," Wall St., neoconservative hawks, the Libertarian Party ticket, and many Hollywood champagne liberals. Take Matt Damon, one of the worst actors in the business, who thinks that Hillary Clinton cares about clean water: "She understands it from a number of different angles—as a national security issue, as a human rights issue, and, obviously, its impact on women and girls. This is not a partisan issue, which is one really good thing about it." She's concerned with human rights, Matt. We've made that clear here.

Liberal—icon?—well, figure and filmmaker, Michael Moore, could also hardly wait to go shilling. The day after the second debate, Moore tweeted: "Trump's comment that Hillary's 'heart is filled with hate' was one of his biggest lies. Say what u will, I think her heart is full of love." Did you get that warm, fuzzy feeling? On the other side is Glenn Beck, a handsome reploid, who has said everything from "Hillary would've been a better President than John McCain," to writing that she should be "behind bars," and today suggesting that electing her over Trump is a "moral, ethical choice."

Unlike these buffoons, Hillary does have intelligent apologists. Montel Williams—that is, Shill'iams—comes to mind. He's a "Never Trump" guy, also helping to sharpen the devil's pitchfork. A man who has counseled so many abused women, has interviewed Gary Webb, apparently can't become a "down with the Two-Party Dictatorship" guy. Too bad. Noam Chomsky is another, who says to "hold your nose" and vote for Hillary over Trump, if only because of her stance on Global Warming.

Of course, I was expecting the day when the liberals at *Huffington Post* and the talking-heads at MSNBC would, in reference to Clinton's accusers, use adjectives like "unsubstantiated," and quip that "Bill's not running for President." I did not expect those same grave robbers to offer the women a place on their shows. Chris Hayes, one of the whiniest reploids, had time to bring on Jill Harth, a woman who is suing Trump for sexual assault. But what about Clinton's victims, who have been around for much longer? Those over at the major networks, proved by WikiLeaks to live in the back-pocket of Hillary, suggested that they were merely paid agents of The Donald. This is all happening, or not happening, in the final weeks of what is perhaps the most important presidential race of our lifetime. You'd have to be deaf and blind not to notice the slanted coverage. Now that *does* give me a warm, fuzzy feeling: all the phony "equality" activists, who are not just condemning Trump, nor advancing a Third-Party nominee, nor discussing the recent comments by Putin ally Vladimir Zhirinovsky, but taking the lowest and most dangerous road in the world.

Maybe that's a good reason to support Hillary: this idea of "institutional power" can finally come full circle. The Left—for all its talk about the rights of women and minorities—can at last have their radioactive cake and eat it too. Hypocrisy be damned! If she's sitting in the Oval Office, the reason why should never be allowed to reach oblivion, which it probably will. In the same interview, VP Joe Biden called Trump a "sexual predator"; he then announced eerily that the U.S. would "send a message" to Russia. The women coming out now, oddly in the very last month before the election, claiming that Trump assaulted them, can take comfort knowing that they are helping to elect a bloodthirsty warmonger. Justice will come when nuclear fire engulfs planet Earth, with Hillary and her elite friends sheltering deep underground, as prayers are uttered silently that a mushroom cloud reaches The Donald. During their final moments, at least they'll be able to proudly retort: "We didn't elect a sexist-racist-xenophobe-etc."

Sure, it's tragic that our political system really presents us with *two choices*. So, by mathematical deduction, the following question is given as a rebuttal: *Do you really want Trump as President?* The answer is: no, I don't. I suppose I'd still prefer Gary Johnson or Jill Stein over the two of them. I truly dislike

The Donald and have even considered those commentators who suggest that he's trying, with all his bombast and stupidity, to "throw" the election so as to give it to her (Actually, Morrow has taken this stance.

But lest I instigate a personal feud between the two authors, I'm not going to touch that here). Insulting people's wives is not something I would have heard from Ron Paul, not to mention the comments about grabbing, kissing, and groping women at random.

It should be said then that Trump, for all his lewdness and lawsuits and hyperbole, does not seem to have created a maroon-colored ocean with a tide that washes up to his ankles every single evening. Truly, aside from his belated criticism of the Clintons, the only thing I genuinely like about him is his suggestion that two nuclear superpowers should get along. As Stein said, "All of what Trump has said is not as bad as what Hillary has done." I concur and cannot in good conscience support those blood drinkers whose thirst is unquenchable. My "hashtag" has always been "Reluctantly Trump." After all, there is more to this debate than sexual abuse claims. (Naturally, as a libertarian against representative democracy, I would never criticize someone who "voted their conscience" by voting for a third party or sitting the election out completely. We aren't responsible for what these people do.)

This was the same dilemma back in 1992. Hunter S. Thompson, the late, brilliant-but-mad journalist, had decided to endorse Bill over Bush: "We still have a problem explaining why I feel very strongly about voting for Bill Clinton on November 3—except that four more years of the Reagan-Bush band will mean the death of hope and the loss of any sense of possibility in politics for a whole generation that desperately needs that fix and will wither on the vine without it." Murray Rothbard, the late libertarian sage, went with Bush over Bill: "A vote for Bill Clinton is a vote to destroy the last vestige of parental control and responsibility in America. A victory for Bush will—at least partly—hold back the hordes for another four years."

These very different writers might have missed the beat, for Bill and Bush are one in the same, and in fact great friends. Both are globalists, elitists, warmongers, drug traffickers—and each forego opportunities to entertain actual wrongdoings. Examples: Bush Sr. was told about Bill's sexual misconduct way back when, and Stone and Morrow point out that he had personally declined to bring it up. Clinton, in turn, has thrashed people who question the attacks of September 11. And both are chummy with the Saudi Royal Family, who have a habit of violating the basic rights of women and those identifying as LGBTQ. (Though perhaps it's odd that while "lil" Bush's veep, Mr. Cheney, has endorsed Trump, the Bushes themselves have been conspicuously silent on their endorsement, which wouldn't be surprising if one were to look at Trump's constant berating of Jeb on the campaign trail.)

This is why I still have respect for Governor Jesse Ventura, the loudest voice for a viable third option: "I vote *for* somebody, not *against* somebody." I think that, for minarchists and "small L" libertarians, it's admirable considering our constricted political system.

Can we get lucky? Is the door closing on the Clintons? Well, I'm sure I acted like most good Americans when seeing Hillary being dragged into an SUV—laughing hysterically and replaying the clip several dozen times, each play giving me more and more mirthful satisfaction. The reports have made her health an issue. While denials are obligatory, the DailyMail.UK reports that Dr. Drew was fired specifically for raising the same concerns. Personally, I say that it would be tragic if Hillary was stricken with Parkinson's or Alzheimer's: she shouldn't be so fortunate to forget the crimes she has committed in this life; all too convenient for her to pass away without always being reminded of them. Whatever her condition, the Elites would probably just prop her up on a pole and present her to the masses as good as new; the talking-heads gleefully pretending that nothing was wrong. They've already done this on every other front, including ignoring the subversion of Bernie Sanders' campaign, which saw three DNC officials step down. As well, investigator James O'Keefe just presented video evidence that the Democratic Party was using the services of groups that initiated violence at Trump rallies, along with organizing voter fraud. One of these cretins is Bob Creamer, a convicted felon that set up Democracy Partners—a "consulting firm"—and who visits the White House regularly, meeting with the President on many occasions. "My fear is that someone would decide that this is a big voter fraud scheme," Creamer admits in the clip. The extent of this, of course, won't be dug into by the likes of MSNBC and CNN. *The system is rigged*, something that prominent Democrats have been saying for years, and the reaction now is either silence or shrieking, depending on where one is positioned.

I asked Mr. Morrow if he had ever been personally threatened. He said he had not. But there are enough dead bodies that surround the Clintons to warrant a legitimate fear. The mythologized "Clinton Body Count" has not yet been mentioned in this work. This is because it's too big an investigation for my small operation, and also because I wanted to stick to the corpses that are most rotted.

And I should hope that my name won't be getting on that list. Though there's one final anecdote to end this report. On June 7th, 2013, Bill Clinton made a trip to Los Angeles to bid farewell to exiting mayor Antonio Villaraigosa. I went with activist intentions in mind. I'd mention Broaddrick, and Mena, and the Iraqi sanctions. As I remember, security wasn't so tight. The elites were up on the steps; the rest of us—several hundred—standing out on Spring St. and sitting on the Grand Park lawn, directly across.

I met up with some friends and fellow Occupiers.

We sat and talked for a while before Bill got up on the microphone. The crowd cheered, but not so loudly. The swagger and the drawl were on full display. "Look, we're friends, Hillary and I love him, he's been good to us," the ex-prez said about the outgoing official.

As he's talking, I notice the appearance of another veteran activist of the Occupy LA scene, a lady named Mary, who likes to be referred to as *Mama*, what with her age and regularity. Mary always has this cart that she rolls around. Equipped on it, a TV screen, used for watching educational material, and one particular nuisance-making toy: a loudspeaker.

I am puzzled as to how she got this past the iron gates which we all had to go through. But there it is. And I am rather certain that she would have let me jump on it, and shout a few unfriendly facts, if only so that Bill *could know* that there was at one person out here *who knew*.

Despite how easily this could have happened, the 20 or 30 seconds that I would've had before security took me to the ground, an overwhelming sense of fear overcame me.

The rebellious feat did not happen.

Ever since that day, whenever reading of the Clintons, seeing them on TV, I've wanted the opportunity to properly express this unvented vituperation. I've become envious of the many brave protesters across the land who've interrupted Clinton rallies.

So yes, it is somewhat personal.

They've done a lot of harm, and since they're once again on that Grand Stage, the future must be considered. Yet I have no desire to die at the hands of this family.

Like they no doubt wish of their many opponents, I just want them to go away, to take their fortune to some island far from here. The remotest possibility is that the Clintons gain some form of conscience, to come clean, to disappear, and so there's really no point in hoping for any of this.

Therefore, the only reasonable option is to hope that Clinton and her cohorts are not elected on Nov. 8.

(October 2016)

RIP, Intactivist

Suicide was my biggest weapon. The thought of it gave me some peace; the thought that the cage was not entirely closed actually gave me some small strength to linger within the cage.
—Charles Bukowski

LAST YEAR, OUR asinine American society lost a brave crusader. On May 9th, Jonathon Conte, a prominent Bay-area Intactivist, took his life. He was thirty-four.

The tragic news was delivered by Marilyn Milos, the original conscious objector of circumcision, who posted on Facebook. Tributes poured out from the community. They remembered his smile, infectious and without pretentiousness. The sincerity of his friendship, those who had the privilege of earning it. His dedication to the cause, the protests and the daily bike-rides he took through the city and the parks, always with his "info-cart" in tow.

And the testimony he told of his own mutilation, that

which no doubt led to this moment. Ever the meticulous planner, Conte acquired pure helium—supposedly hard to come by—and his death likely happened quickly with less pain than his infantile abuse.

In recordings and public statements, a crestfallen Mr. Conte recalled that at the age of fourteen he saw a video on the internet of an intact penis, leading to the quick realization that a piece of him "had been cut away." This was the beginning of a lifelong feeling of "incompleteness, both physically and sexually," admitting something that he likely knew far too few American men ever would: "I battled depression, particularly whenever I had to see my penis." For him, activism became a form of therapy, and he was soon one of the main signature-gatherers for the doomed 2012 San Francisco bill that attempted to ban the operation for anyone under 18. It's said that he also designed the "blood-stained" jumpsuit that now makes its appearance in cities across the land.

I met Jonathon once, during the San Francisco ACOG (The American Congress of Obstetricians and Gynecologists) meeting, May 2015. He disappeared for a moment, and when he returned, he had donned a menacing alter ego: a "blood"-splattered lab coat and rubber Zombie mask. "Cock cutters for sale!" he snarled at the exiting doctors. While demasked, Conte was known to "meet people where they are," talking candidly about the horror.

My well-received response to his suicide, said in Facebook groups, was that we should pushback against the inevitable: that his final act will be seen as martyrdom. But this was not preventable. Although Conte did not explicitly state his mutilation as the cause for his final action (as far as I know, he made no suicide note), his mental state was clearly sullied by it. Blamelessly, one can't help but to interpret his death as the outcome of what he had realized way back when.

The secondary group, with their mendacious eyes rolling

along the online obituaries, had offended me much more—
those that would say that Conte had "other problems" and
rhetorically ask how anybody could kill themselves over such a
silly thing. Any psychologist worth their salt can agree that a
person's suicide is nearly impossible for another to grasp.

As any Intactivist will testify, men who recognize
unnecessary scars on their manhood can become obsessively
troubled by them. And as Cesare Pavese pointed out, nobody
who takes their own life lacks the rationalization for doing so.

Here in America, the majority of males—at least up until
the last couple decades—are born to an awaiting sharp tool. A
few years later, almost everyone else is ushered into a
brainwashing center, sometimes called "public schooling." If
you're less fortunate, a religiously inclined relative will inform
that eternal damnation awaits if you reject certain ancient
doctrines, showing even death to be an unviable escape hatch.
Meanwhile, participation is often reinforced via corporal
punishment and psychotropic drugs. You'll then soon be told
that working and giving up half your paycheck are life's only real
choices, thereby making cocktails and sex and occasional
vacations as the ventures that allows one to subsist. As it is, good
justifications can be pinpointed—any combination of which
could result in the next helium exit. Inflammatorily, plenty will
ignore the appallingly high rates of suicide amongst the young
and instead insist that these are but The Best Things.

And so why not place the late Mr. Conte—who attempted
to end at least two of these six items (I'm sure he was opposed
to corporal punishment as well; nearly all Intactivists are)—
alongside Alexander Berkman and Aaron Swartz and however
more self-immolating Buddhists? What cannot be honestly
asserted is that we'd all be better off if we simply killed
ourselves, for the cultures of violence would merely snicker and
carry forth. What is not mistaken is observing how, subsequent
of one setting themselves on fire, people seem to notice the

severity of the crimes they were trying to bring attention to. From this loss will arise observation, motivation, and determination.

Incidentally, a few months after Conte passed, another person died that was involved in this nonquestion—one Edgar Schoen, a pediatrician and longtime advocate for circumcision who was put in charge of the 1989 AAP "task force" meant to evaluate the subject.

Two years prior, Schoen wrote an "Ode to the Circumcised Male," with the lines:

> *Don't rue that you suffered a rape of your phallus.*
> *Just hope that one day you can say with a smile*
> *That your glans ain't passe; it will rise up in style.*

He then effectively reversed the AAP's 1975 position, which was that "a program of education to continuing good personal hygiene would offer all the advantages of routine circumcision without the attendant surgical risk. Therefore, circumcision of the male neonate cannot be considered an essential component of adequate total health care." Schoen's report stated all the usual nonsense: prevention of phimosis, cancer, urinary tract infections, HPV. Now the procedure had "potential medical benefits and advantages as well as disadvantages and risks." Unlike Conte, Edgar Schoen will always be remembered for being a malicious fraud and likely pervert.

The efforts of the late Jonathon Conte, and those of the entire Intactivist movement, can already be demonstrated: nearly every week an article appears decrying the dropping rates of MGM. As was once said of Women's Suffrage, "We have no choice but to win." The cause is so obviously just; it's the stubborn, prickly thorns of bigotry (oftentimes from females who needs their "pretty penises") and willful ignorance that makes it so frustrating. Incurred from an act not of his choosing, this became Mr. Conte's calling in life; one might believe that he could hardly escape it.

Perhaps the rest of us can take comfort in a slight modification of Desmond Morris' commentary:

> *The continuance of such practices in the twentieth century against a background of modern enlightenment is clearly going to puzzle historians of the distant future.*

He meant, *not too distant.*

Then let us forego deathly nihilism, come together in what we believe and are willing to fight for, and thus finally force a smile upon the face of Sisyphus.

(January 2017)

About Anonymous Alcoholism

Notes on the Cultocracy

LEST I BE accused of throwing every problematic drinker under the bus, let's get the boringly obvious out of the way: there's no doubt that the institution of Alcoholics Anonymous has helped a few people overcome their addiction.

But I find it refreshing that after decades of monopolistic influence on the courts and rehabs, AA is finally facing the opprobrium that it very rightly deserves. Jack Trimpey, founder of Rational Recovery, and one of the original malcontents, described AA as (however unoriginally) a *Cultocracy*.

It is, that annoying word, systemic, and so Charles Manson and Jim Jones would have their competition cut out for them. AA could further be defined as an Open Source Cult: you can either be the vulnerable drone, the convenient torchbearer, or the high priest who bashes you over the head with "how many days" he has, looking knightly for the young ladies and saintly for the hapless dregs.

But this is mainly for those who are here *voluntarily*.

If you will, consider an erroneous comparison. Between what? The near-universally mandated 12 Step attendance with your mother forcing you to eat broccoli. Is broccoli coercive? In this vein, neither is the gun that you know will be unholstered for refusing to file your taxes, nor the car that takes you to the jail, or the building in which you'll be housed. Just the people who do the coercing.

Technically, your mother is acting coercively, and while vegetables are good for you—and she's your mother!—being threatened with jail else you attend a religious meeting, this for merely walking down the street intoxicated, is harmful to the individual. If we do get into the libertarian semantics—who owns the sidewalks: private companies or sovereign municipalities?—I think it's fair to ask about the federally-worshipped institution that enjoys a tax-exempt status while also receiving thousands of drunks who are quick to throw a dollar around. If they must pay nothing for helping boozers, why should I have to pay the State for being a boozer?

Suppose that Lockheed Martin is completely absolved of collusion with the State, despite negotiating billion-dollar contracts to sell off their armaments. Perhaps the best analogy: Would I be a voluntarist if that same State ordered someone to come and wash my car? Could I look them in their eyes and insist that I'm respecting their volition, even after I said, "you missed a spot"?

I venture, no.

Therefore, if the cheerleaders of the Cultocracy want to defend the notion of a "100% voluntary organization," they'd agree with me, and demand that AA make *some sort* of statement about their reluctance to sign those damn court cards. This can't be done—maybe seeing as they "have no opinion on outside matters" (10th Tradition) and that "every group is autonomous" or whatever other cowardly datum is at hand. Alas, the very strong mixture of Church and State will still likely be served regularly.

Cult! It's usually a stupid verbal missile that gets thrown overhead without validity. In this case, AA actually does have its genesis in a Christian cult—named the Oxford Group, which during the mid-30's was its parent organization. Ken Ragge, another early critic, wrote an excellent expose in 1998, first titled *More Revealed* and later republished as *The Real AA*. My mangled copy still draws a strange history.

The story starts in 1919, with a man named Frank Buchman, who was holding a series of meetings in China called "house parties." Buchman was "attempting to bring about a revival of what he perceived to be the first century Christianity, hence his group's first name: First Century Christian Fellowship," writes Ragge. He then "capitalized on perceived but nonexistent ties to the internationally prestigious Oxford University after the name 'Oxford Group' was reportedly coined by a South African baggage handler and adopted by the group in 1921." The only relation to the famous college, according to the Wikipedia page, was that several of its students were members and held some parties here. (The organization brought in many thousands, and parties were held everywhere.)

The Oxford Group had the modest goal of taking over the world, this through "God-Control," which, Ragge quotes straight from Buchman, "make[s] God-Controlled nationalities. This is the aim of the Oxford Group. The true patriot gives his life to bring his nation under…" we got it. (Browse Wiki for all this repeated.) Those who were "too insane" to join on their own were given special techniques to assist them, these deemed "the five C's"—Confidence, Confession, Conviction, Conversion, and Continuance.

Ragge continues: "The Oxford Group was most concerned with bringing rich, famous and powerful figures under God-

Control so their influence could be used to sway the public."

One such person was the son of rubber baron Harvey Firestone, the former with a hostile drinking habit. An Oxford member who had discovered the man took him to a conference in Denver, where they joined up with God, who supposedly told Firestone to knock his shit off. January 1933: The senior, very impressed, invited Buchman and a team of sixty to come to Akron, Ohio, to "conduct a ten-day campaign," gathering in the house T. Henry Williams. Among them was the local surgeon, Dr. Bob Smith, now credited as one of the two founders of Alcoholics Anonymous.

The other founder resided in New York City. The name and subject of so many hagiographies is Bill Wilson, a Wall St. stockbroker as well as a vicious drinker. Hospitalized numerous times for his habit, he soon met Dr. William Silkworth, who "impressed on him the hopelessness of alcoholism." Silkworth's theory was that he had "an allergy combined with a mental obsession." As told by the Big Book—AA's text from heaven— Wilson was visited by a friend who had also met up with God. What the Book doesn't say (at least not my "fourth edition") is that the man's name was Ebby Thacher, a member of the Oxford Group, which by now had a side chapter for those with drinking problems.

Wilson, along with his wife Lois, began attending these meetings, becoming a regular by 1935. Taking up the fifth "C"—"Continuance"—the inaugural alcoholic saint realized that, "If he did not work he would surely drink again, and if he drank, he would surely die." For six months, he was a total failure at this game, not saving a single drunk. Despite being dazzled by the Oxford Group, Wilson was taking issue with the group's methodology. Dr. Silkworth advised him to try a different approach, to "deflate these people first. Pour it right into them about the obsession that condemns them to drink..." That is, fear. This was quite the obverse from the Oxford

Group's tactic of arousing guilt.

In May of 1935, Wilson made a business trip to Akron, Ohio. Feeling and fearing himself close to drink, he had a revelation that would become a cornerstone of AA: "You need another alcoholic just as much as he needs you." Phone calls were frantically placed. After talking to a few local groupers, he came into contact with "Dr. Bob." Fireworks without the cocktails. The pair quickly teamed together and began obtaining new members for the burgeoning theocratic sect.

Elsewhere, schisms widened. For one thing, Buchman was an open supporter of Hitler's regime, and the public was getting tired of these political sympathies. (I've never seen any evidence that Wilson shared these politics.) Ragge notes, "Another major issue was that the alcoholics preferred to remain anonymous, which was contrary to the Oxford Group methods of public witness." More, "Bill W.'s" new means of recruitment was aggravating the NY chapter of the Oxford Group. By 1937, in the Big Apple, the two had separated. A year later, Wilson was hard at work synthesizing material for the Big Book, released in 1939 (which I'll be selecting from). As an aside, demonstrating the program's utter silliness, Wilson decided to pick the number "12" (for the steps) simply because Jesus Christ had twelve apostles, thus why it's hardly surprising that the steps seem repetitious.

Returning to our delineation, the most significant indications of AA's "cult status," in my humble assessment, is the dogmatically relied upon "disease model," which refuses to accept other theories; nor does the Cultocracy allow disagreement of their "non-opinionated policy"; and then the members who avoid the pesky noun leftover by the Big Book's main authors: "Creator"—a clear definition of what kind of god they had in mine. So long for, "Your Higher Power can be a doorknob." The next person who tells you that should be put, not in rehab, but an asylum.

All three of these are intertwined, but let's try to untangle them separately, in careful turn.

Of course, it will be said that the whole program is one big "suggestion"—textbook AA terminology—and then why can't I suggest that AA operates cultishly? Suspend the language for just a second. Keep in mind that the doctrine is predicated on the "disease model"—you are powerless because alcoholism is a verifiable disease, and even questioning it is your "stink'n think'n." A perfect failsafe! (As well as sounding like something that a statist would tell their subject.) Absolute abstinence is everything, and your last sip is the equivalent of your birthday— literally. Therein belies any "suggestion." Grimly, this disease is "progressive," and you will die from it if not for our grace. Right! Exactly what we tell kids in a cancer ward: "You're powerless. Give up on this idea of self will and inner strength and permit that only through faith in the doctors do you have a chance."

Aside from the sardonicism, the "science" of Disease Theorem has been much studied and debated. The best thing that the State and the Rehab Industry has going for it is knowing that the layman can't be an expert in neuroscience and biology. Me neither. But we can defer to more qualified minds. The one that has faced some recent ire belongs to Dr. Lance Dodes, an addiction expert who has written three books on the topic. His latest, *The Sober Truth*, was released in 2014.

One of Dodes' most interesting findings is this: in its earliest days, AA was viewed as nothing short of quackery, with the American Medical Association calling it "a curious combination of organizing propaganda and religious exhortation." *The Journal of Nervous and Mental Diseases* was even more scathing: a "regressive mass psychological method" and a "rambling sort of camp-meeting confession of experiences." Ouch.

AA then hit a series of lucky strikes, starting with two

articles in popular journals. The first was written in '39 by Morris Markey, published in *Liberty*, a magazine run by Fulton Oursler, who was an Oxford Group member that would later serve as a trustee of the Alcoholic Foundation, AA's governing body. The article tells us that the alcoholic is "genuinely sick" with a "specific illness of body and mind." But, as a miracle, working with AA, they would experience a "psychic change. Their 'compulsion neurosis' was being altered-transferred from liquor to something else." That was, a "psychological necessity to rescue their fellow victims from the plight that made themselves so miserable." Sounds liberating!

The second piece came in the *Saturday Evening Post*, which at the time was probably the most widely read magazine in the country. Written in 1941 by one Jack Alexander, the long piece tells how a skeptic came to be swayed into believing the good that AA was doing. Disingenuously, Alexander informs that "the rate of success is exceptionally high." No citation needed except for AA's self-reportage—and self-promotion. One chapter claimed that 87% were saved; and that 50% "recover immediately." Reification was on its way. (We'll come right back to the topic of success.)

From there, AA teamed up with Marty Mann, a wealthy Chicago woman and one of the first females to join the club; and then with E.M. Jellinek, called the originator of Disease Theorem. The former soon formed the National Council on Alcoholism and Drug Dependence, still in operation today, then testified many times for the medical community. In 1946, the latter, Jellinek, produced a legendary paper that would become bedrock for AA. His research? A questionnaire mailed out to sixteen-hundred of its own members, this through their magazine, *Grapevine*. Of the 158 returned, 60 were "thrown out either for being incomplete, from women, or for having multiple responses," writes Ragge. "Progressive"—"denial"—"intense physical craving": the usual claptrap at its nucleus.

Jellinek is said to have distanced himself from this work, urging AA not to interfere with new medical discoveries. (Also, it's rumored that the idea of addiction as a disease was foreign to early AA congregations, as addiction was supposed to be a "spiritual sickness," not a medical ailment.)

But by now the wind was already in AA's favor. Dodes reports the following. In 1951, AA was honored with the Lasker Award, "given by the American Public Health Association for outstanding achievement in the fields of medical research or public health administration." In the 60's, AA "won a landmark decision" when "two decisions from federal appeals court upheld the disease concept of alcoholism." Lyndon Baines Johnson—monster of a man, JFK's likely killer (just to throw that in there), and a heavy consumer of Cutty Sark scotch—proclaimed to the nation that "the alcoholic suffers from a disease which will yield eventually to scientific research and adequate treatment."

In 1970, Congress passed the *Comprehensive Alcohol Abuse and Alcoholism Prevention Treatment and Rehabilitation Act*, which also established the National Institute on Alcohol Abuse and Alcoholism. Yes, Marty Mann and Mr. Wilson spoke before our dear leaders. In '73, President Nixon was presented with the millionth copy of the Big Book. The clincher: Dodes cites a 2009 paper that examined state-sanctioned physician health groups, finding that 95% of all programs were—are—based on the 12 Steps. Journalist Gabrielle Glaser, writing for *The Atlantic*, citing another work, says that there are 13,000 rehab facilities in the U.S., and that 70-80% subscribe to the One True Path laid out by a narcissistic louse. Enrollment in these centers can cost thousands of dollars.

Regarding addiction, there are, of course, several theories. However, as many have pointed out, the irony is striking: if we're dealing with a disease—ala cancer or diabetes or high blood pressure—why do we treat it with...faith? Glaser recognizes the contradiction. She writes about certain medications used to curtail problematic drinking, with only three brands approved by the FDA. Although these pills are not outright forbidden by AA, personal stories indicate that usage is largely frowned upon by their membership.

Naturally, anybody will look stupid when speaking about such technical subjects without a doctoral degree hanging above their heads. So it's best to quote the experts. A neuroscientist named Marc Lewis took up the study so as to understand what he suffered from in his youth. His 2015 book, *The Biology of Desire*, is subtitled *Why Addiction is Not a Disease*.

"The brain disease model," Lewis writes, "is supported by two pillars that have proven rather difficult to crack. First is the corpus of evidence that the brain really does change with addiction." The other is the "control issue. Addicts really do seem to have lost control." But Lewis goes on to explain that behavior is strengthened every time an action is repeated. "The kind of brain changes seen in addiction also show up when people become absorbed in a sport, join a political movement, or become obsessed with their sweetheart or their kids." He then describes the brain's function of a "feedback loop": the more we humans do something, the more likely it is that we'll do it again; the synapses grow stronger. "Addiction," he writes, "may be a frightful, devastating, and insidious process of change in our habits and our synaptic patterning. But that doesn't make it a disease."

For Dr. Dodes, addiction is tightly linked to compulsiveness; Dr. Lewis, similarly, believes that it must return to its place as the bedfellow of psychology and personal experience. So far so good. And then the unexplainable: Why is it that American Vietnam vets, hooked on heroin in the oversea swamps, instantly stopped after coming back home—some 90% of them? Same with cigarettes: when the Surgeon General required warning labels on packs of smokes—1970 and 1985—

smoking decreased dramatically. Again with hospital patients on a daily diet of morphine: they never seek the stuff out upon being discharged. If the disease is permanent, unmalleable, and indeed progressive—why does this happen? With alcohol, many studies show that the bulk of people who drink excessively can and do regress into moderate consumption, as stated by every source I've listed here.

That gets us back to Alcoholics Anonymous, the "12 Steps," and Dr. Dodes, who appeared on Tom Woods's radio show to discuss. Dodes, better at crunching numbers than I'll ever be, ascertains that the amount of people who attend AA and stay sober remains within 5-10%. Not that great. As anyone who looks at AA will tell you, it's extremely difficult to investigate a place that keeps no names, no numbers, and guesses no measure of accomplishment. Retyping the key word: anonymous. As well, the definition of success is a conundrum; one can often hear it said as "I'm not drunk today" and/or "prolonged sobriety." Doesn't help much either. Finally, Glaser reports that *The Handbook of Alcoholism Treatment Approaches* ranks AA as 38th out of 48 methods. At the top were those that encourage—imagine this—*motivational enhancement*, IE: empowerment.

At this point I should confirm the reader's guess: I have been arrested for breaking the drinking laws, afterwards coerced into AA. Moreover, a recent episode (I won't detail here) in my life saw me not just inside the meetings, but also another drug treatment flock, to whom I was to bring said signatures to.

Surely it has been seen that scores of AA goers who, when the meeting is over, dart to the table that holds their court cards, snatch them up and bolt for the exit. This scene is pathetic in its mechanicalness, labeled for what it really is: obedience training. The people-in-the-magic-black-robes don't give a damn about you, your drinking habits, or how many dumpsters you piss on whilst making your way home. They want to watch the poodle jump, and then come back for a second or third round. This is why I theorize (and it's a theory without evidence) that the State knows that AA is a failure—similar to "rehabilitative" prisons— and thereafter sends you onto a hamster wheel so they can watch you fall off and on again all while cashing their checks. Likewise with the Rehab Industry, that, like a friendly casino, wants you to come back and blow another $30,000.

Nevertheless, the circular self-assurance is heard everywhere: "You're obviously in here for some reason." The thinking goes, if one faces the wrath of the law, even for something minor, it is still evidence of a disease, and thus justly warrants AA attendance. This is facile reasoning, a presumption that all laws are righteous by their mere existence, or that AA is the only dignified place to be.

Interestingly, if this line is pursued, we would immediately notice parallels with Mr. Wilson's case: when it was discovered that Wilson was experimenting with LSD, the AA board of directors felt themselves "violently opposed" to it. As a result, he removed himself from his position. That's not much different than getting in trouble with your mother: someone of authority has figured that you have broken a rule, and punishments follow. (It's unclear what might have been the outcome if Wilson refused, but with you and me, fellow drinker, things are more predictable.)

Drudging through the meetings, I twice had unexpected encounters with admitted pedophiles (they kind of blurted it out, and I'll forego recollection of the details). This is when I engaged in some Googling, book-collecting, note-taking. I came across a project by Monica Richardson, a Los Angeles activist and longtime AA member, who had become disillusioned after learning about the amount of crime taking place between and beyond those walls. The name of her film-in-development was *The 13th Step*, a euphemism for the process in which seasoned members prey and take advantage of newer, younger, usually female attendees. Monica and I had a phone chat, and she promised to invite me when the documentary debuted at the Beverly Hills Film Festival in April of last year.

Her investigation is horrifying. The stories, heartbreaking. The numbers, staggering. And the absence of accountability—consternating. Monica once told me that she's received calls and letters from "hundreds" who've attested to sexual assault and other forms of abuse. Dual revelations are revealed when reviewing her work. 1): The State, all states, are sending violent criminals—as well as convicted sex offenders—into these rooms. (I haven't seen a number for how many, but Monica's petition claims that 150,000 people—altogether—are sentenced every year.) And 2): Every time AA is sued as a part of a subsequent crime, a judge dismisses them as counter-defendant.

Compare this to the judgement just made by a Colorado court, ruling that four victims of the Aurora mass shooting owe Cinemark, owner of the theater where the massacre happened, $700,000 dollars. Why: they tried going ahead with a lawsuit, but the judge had already determined that there was no way the cinema could have possibly known that a psychotic gunman was coming to do what he did. Costs are now authorized for reimbursement.

How can this be said of Alcoholics Anonymous, which must know that the State is sequestering predators inside their rooms? If AA is so beneficial and voluntary, why aren't their groups ejecting these people? Does voluntarism not entail the authority to regulate "their own" and maintain a safe setting? (It's upsetting that libertarians typically grant a positively charged definition, coming together, instead of the negatively charged, going apart.) I haven't heard of a single occurrence. (Though I'm sure I'll hear someone tell me about the time they...)

The scum who preys on women—and men—who are at their weakest are as despicable as those who let it go on unchallenged. And the logic follows that, since addiction is a "disease," and drinking could be the same as touching kids or preying on the downtrodden, they can all be equally summarized as symptoms of Disease Theorem. After all, "It's not my fault…I'm powerless against the disease." Personal responsibility sold separately. Though again, "everybody is welcome."

As the Big Book says: "We want to stay out of this controversy. We do not want to be the arbiter of anyone's sex conduct. We all have sex problems. We'd hardly be human if we didn't. What can we do about them?" (I'll apologize for lumping child molestation together with what I think is inappropriate womanizing…they're not equal in their immorality. The point is that the courts are sentencing all kinds of abusers, and it's hard to know who is who.)

What else to expect from a program that has as its "4th Step" a requirement to make a "fearless moral inventory"— which translates into divulging everything personal to someone who is not a professional, not beholden to any legal repercussions, and could very well be a deranged psychopath? "But," warns the holy text, "they had not learned enough of humility, fearlessness and honesty, in the sense we find it necessary, until they told someone all their life story." The emphasis is Mr. Wilson's.

Speaking of whom, our favorite drunken saint likely set the standard, as he was the original "13th Stepper." Taking advantage of his newfound veneration, Wilson became a "compulsive womanizer" who was "imaginably adulterous." It wouldn't be difficult to find one of these druids, immersed in this interesting literature, getting the hint that following in such big footsteps leads one to the top of even bigger mountains (if you know what I mean). When will AA become opinionated on this controversy? Seems tricky, as another "A" is always important in this debate: amorphousness, which is all the more reason for the courts to change direction. Although it's vital to read the "Ninth Tradition" in full: "AA, as such, ought never be organized; but we may create service boards or committees directly responsible to those they serve."

Directly responsible.

There, grounds for solicitude.

(Monica ends her film by listing several alternative treatment programs: SMART Recovery; HAMS: Harm Reduction for Alcohol; LifeRing Secular Recovery; SOS: Secular Organization for Sobriety; Women for Sobriety; Moderation.org. To the extent that these programs are recognized by the courts, I am unsure.)

An additional grievance came to mind during my stretch with the Cultocracy: mandatory lying. When someone who disbelieves in Alcoholics Anonymous is ordered there regardless, and also told to secure a "sponsor," it should be realized that a lie must be given to that prospect, convincing others of a commitment that won't be sincere. As successfully argued in a Shasta County courtroom, Barry Hazle is correct: A.A. is a religious gathering, and for the State to force someone to abide is for the State to violate their First Amendment rights. As a secularist before a libertarian, I am hereby utterly appalled.

We can't all be Zeligs, thank you kindly.

The word *God* is replete throughout the Big Book, along with descriptions like "Spirt of the Universe" and "Father of Light" and "Creative Intelligence." This theistic language isn't necessarily foolish. I am an agnostic, not an atheist (it's a big universe out there.) If troubled individuals get strength in the belief of a "higher power," it seldom perturbs me. When it does, however, is after insisting that I, or anyone else, must also hold a faith, in direct violation of my belief that I needn't hold any such thing. Mr. Hazle is one of a number of rewarded plaintiffs who feel the same way. In 2006, paroled on a meth charge, this combative atheist was sent back to prison for refusing to attend 12 Step meetings. He then sued, contending that his First Amendment rights were violated. He's now a happy millionaire. (Other courts in the nation are waking up to this too.)

Wait! "It's spiritual, not religious." More of the elastic locution. A basic definition of religion is: "A specific fundamental set of beliefs and practices generally agreed upon by a number of persons or sects." This fits tightly with AA and its adherence to the 12 Steps, the doctrine that disavows the idea that a "real alcoholic" can ever become a moderate drinker. It is a faith in the conduit to "God"—the group, which is the only thing that can save you. Precisely why the fourth chapter of the Big Book is "We Agnostics." Bill Wilson had the foresight to know there would be disbelievers: "Actually we were fooling ourselves, for deep down in every man, woman, and child, is the fundamental idea of God." Religious? Cultish? Aren't they often said the same: religious cult? A clue is provided by the divine writ: "It is seldom wise to approach an individual, who still smarts from our injustice to him, and announce that we have gone *religious*." Emphasis mine, but unneeded to determine whether or not this program is secular.

Anyway, I was made to frequent a number of meetings a week, then show those signatures at my substance abuse class. Sure. No worries. Besides, the homeless population is more than willing to give a scribble in exchange for pocket change. I'd then have to tell the facilitators that I had that "sponsor," and was in regular contact with him. But this can't happen with honesty: any frank criticism of the Cultocracy would impede such a compact (not to mention wasting everybody's time). As they say in AA, "fake it until you make it." Accordingly, this produces an imperious falsity, at least via omission of one's true thoughts.

Some members probably endorse other programs, but as a monolith that has a headquarters in New York, they don't advocate for it; they simply hold no position on the matter, exactly as their mantra proscribes. Glaser asked the General Service Office, AA's administrative HQ, their stance on this. The reply: "Alcoholics Anonymous neither endorses nor opposes other approaches, and we cooperate widely with the medical profession." As already detailed, the last part is a redundancy, seeing as "12-Step" programs are part and parcel of America's medical monstrosity. If we want the courts to recognize alternative treatments, it is up to us to protest and sue until these things are granted.

This mobilized pushback against the Cultocracy has upset a few people. (For more muckraking, check out Orange-Papers.org, a longtime compiler of anti-AA articles; Stinkin-Thinkin.com; and LeavingAA.com, Mrs. Richardson's blog). Truth is, it's hard to be anodyne when criticizing AA, because it is a faith, and faiths—especially communitarian types that provide friends and lovers and free coffee and occasionally seeks to remedy a serious condition—hits the next person right in the liver. Still, this has to be done. AA is hardly as magnanimous as they would like it to be. Every time the institution is challenged, an AA devotee screams: "What about those who are getting a benefit from it!?" A guess: they're afraid that their skills of proselytization—the 12th Step—lack refinement. Thus, the State needs to be involved. It's devastating to admit that your faith is incorrect, let alone harmful. But these are the same charlatans who would say, "It doesn't work for everyone," and then five minutes later, seeing a drunk on the street, ask him: "Wanna go to a meeting?" It's not a one-size-fits-all. Except when it is.

Nearly lastly. Although this is a bit heavy-handed, I don't mean to say that AA is full of cult members who're there for dumb or egregious reasons. Certainly there's decent people just trying to get help and to help others. In fact, I want to stress that AA is in no way comparable to bureaucratic cults like Scientology, with its central authorities and black-sites and "specialized knowledge" and the fear that apostates have of going public. If one were to "fall down the rabbit hole" with AA, they likely wouldn't go a foot below the surface. It's the function of the program, which mimics or acts cultishly, usually amateurishly but always dogmatically—that is the concern. Indeed, I'm not even saying that it's necessarily wrong to use AA as a dating site.

No. My venom disgorges from the anger of having to violate my own principles, namely deceiving people who want to hear me confess to "what step I'm on," knowing that my heart isn't in it, but doing so for the sake of severe consequences. It comes from befriending Mrs. Richardson, moved by her film, and concluding that "anonymity" is extremely dangerous when combined with the inordinate amount of sex offenders made to go inside those rooms. And then the bad science of Disease Theorem, taken as gospel throughout the land. Yes, when technology and medicine become outdated, *we do* replace them. Kind of like the world that is free of reinforced religiosity. That too will be coming.

Sure enough, the best thing that can be said about this institution is that you don't have to "work it." If your only intention is to jerk off the judge, then AA is the perfect place for you. Find a big meeting, sit in the back, put the headphones in, drink coffee—perhaps spiked—and zone-out.

And yet Alcoholics Anonymous, with its Siamese twin, the 12 Steps (you really can't separate the two; they were both created in the same 1939 book), is in great need of reform, and we activists don't require any permission to document and bring that to the attention of others.

However, as I just repeated for a thousandth time, now appended with an actual justification for AA's continued existence, I don't wish to close down all the rooms or convince everyone that they're always detrimental. I simply request that, if we are going to have courts that send people to rehab, and if rehab centers want to be brought into the 21st century, other programs and better science ought to be accepted.

We're getting there, slowly.

In the meantime, people can continue to "volunteer" where they wish, maintain sobriety, and take comfort in knowing that so many in the State and Rehab Industry have milked the sacred dead cow for so long.

(January 2017)

Intersectionalist Inconsistencies

AMID THE RECENT upheavals, in which conservative superstars Milo Yiannopoulos and Ann Coulter had to pull their speaking events at Berkeley University, a few brave liberals were surprised to find themselves jolted upwards and condemning the evacuations. How many of those who emerged from when the culture wars kicked off—circa 1960's—would today condone the violent actions of AntiFa and BAMN and other "activists" of that ilk?

Since the Free Speech Movement, synonyms of much lesser value have been attached to the word liberalism: crassness, irascibility, and derangement. Here, the aptly dubbed *Triggly Puff* and *AIDs Skrillex* provide two particularly freakish examples.

Due to such bastardizations, I think "liberalism" is a spurious term for describing the felonious thugs seen daily on college campuses, blocking roads, and perhaps even sitting in the first-class section, where a progressive-minded bourgeoisie can comfortably make excuses for this behavior, saying things like "you have no right to an audience." These aren't the prodigy of Rawls or Galbraith or MLK, which confirms all required exordiums (IE, classical) to the word.

Therefore, critics oughtn't use their methods of rebellion—hurling unfounded accusations of "racism," "fascism," and "phobia"—and thus deem them what they are not. For there is a preferred term for those who, although they share a taste for certain state policies, deride liberals as too soft and not radical enough.

This is, Intersectionalism.

Patrick R. Grzanka, a professor of psychology, edits a "reader" of this postmodern prattle. To prepare accordingly, one should bring their favorite salad dressing, as the work is filled with jargon and invented words.

Gander upon this gem:

> It would appear that the current moment would require us to think also about how the deployment of sexuality subtends and is anchored by the contemporary capitalist mode of production.

The masterpiece is sprinkled with illuminating salt like, "White-capitalist-heteronormative-patriarchy." It implores us to consider new modes of "knowledge production," as knowledge is always linked with power. This is an idea that the late, sagacious Michel Foucault came up with, who once said that he wished his books were to act as "Molotov cocktails or minefields; I would like them to self-destruct after use, like fireworks."

I remain convinced that the aforementioned lightweight terrorists adhere to this sort of scholarship.

I've made further observations. Intersectionalists, including their dandy apologists, are the type of people who, in the event of a terrorist attack or mass shooting, will say, "You can't generalize all Muslims," but then turn around and pronounce that, "White people must account for this."

Who will look at a single case of white-on-black homicide, ala Dylan Roof, and make it exemplary of White Supremacy, but then ignore the six-to-one ratio of black-on-white crime. Who will praise a football player for exercising his First Amendment, but demand that anyone else be boycotted or fired for daring to criticize their avocation. Who will decry the "cultural appropriation" of dreadlocks and Native American headbands but ask what the problem is with a black James Bond.

Who will gripe about using pronouns properly when discussing a transgender person but insist that colorblindness is impossible because their race is what you'll instantly recognize. Who will say that the male sex oppresses the female sex but won't see anything untoward if a man identifying as a woman goes into a locker-room labeled: "Ladies." Who will criticize those that slut-shame Miley Cyrus after she asks if people want to touch her vagina, but then damn men who say "hello, beautiful" to a woman on the street. Who will call for "equal rights," but then say "there's no reason to ever hit a woman"— even if that woman had initiated violence against a man.

Likewise with musicians and companies who will boycott a state for not respecting LGBTQ "rights," but then play in a country that forbids, via brutal death, said lifestyles. That will sympathize with "democracy," but, when seeing the wrong person voting or running for office, insist that "he's not my representative!" Who will call themselves anarchists while aggrandizing a larger entitlement state.

Plainly, consistency has never been a consideration of these finger-wagging "activists." Suggesting this all, again, is merely an act of "racism" or "sexism" or "guilt" or "derailment"—IE, mental off-switches that save people the trouble of having to use logic.

But they should be pleased of the progress they've made. After all, there does seems to be a race among white Intersectionalists to find out who is strongest "ally" in the war against female and minority oppression. For men, this is usually demonstrated with acts of effeminateness, speaking in decibels not of their own natural voice. For women, complaining about "fake allies!" And for both, by screaming at the first Straight White Male who doesn't recognize his godhood.

This celebration of self-flagellation is meant to dissolve themselves of any such privilege and power. Unable to rip the skin off their bones, it's the only option they have. That must count for something. In a word, the rantings of these prigs amount to little more than *therapy*, an item that Eric Hoffer left out when writing about "the nature of mass movements." It begs questions. Does that make a therapist out of those who are unfortunate enough to listen to their madness? Finally, how does one visualize the "victory"?

Common ground? Intersectionalists scream about the need for "tolerance," "diversity," and "inclusion." This is what I have dubbed Kumbaya Theorem. Discounting the reality, it is urgent that, in a pluralistic society, no conflicts can possibly exist.

As can be seen, Intersectionalists also advocate for separation, this when they keep away from white people who don't acknowledge their "privilege." (Rather than, say, someone who endorses Sharia Law but who also organizes a "women's march" on the nation's capital.) One can also see this with "safe spaces" and separated dorms on college campuses.

Most insidiously, since they know who the Enemy is, many unwitting participants are conscripted into the Cause. What they believe in or how they behave: irrelevant. Black and Hispanic Trump supporters are traitors. The end. This is the Mission of Dethronement, the tactics of weaponized delirium, the likes of which unseen outside the walls of a psyche ward.

(May 2017)

Gun Grabber Logic: 101

IT'S A QUIET evening. A homeowner, his wife, and their two kids sit on the couch and watch T.V. Outside and down the street, a squadron of government agents are about to execute their plan. For it turns out that this homeowner is also a gunowner, and it seems that he has refused to relinquish his firearms.

"We're ready," says the commanding officer. The door is kicked open. "Everybody down on the ground!" The wife and one of the kids obey, thus spared. The husband is in the kitchen, getting more popcorn. He's hysterical, not able to see his wife and children, knowing that one of the kids is in the upstairs bathroom. "Down-down-down!" the agents screamed. He wants to see his family alive, stays standing, and is then shot dead for noncompliance. The agents go upstairs; a weeping child is scared to open the bathroom door. It is then kicked in and the child riddled with more bullets.

The agents search the house and are rewarded for their

violent act: a closet holds several "assault weapons" recently put on the list of those prohibited. Elsewhere, people with proudly displayed credentials congratulate themselves for putting down this terroristic black American family, one of many that have stockpiled since the 2016 Election.

The next day, a raid occurs at one of the nation's many gun-expos, where weapons are sold free of background checks. The coroner's office is suddenly given a large workload. The goal, after all, is to prevent more death.

The commentariat gleam. They have finally witnessed the measure that will make a real difference, that of preventing schoolyards from turning into shooting ranges. But they enjoy reveling in their lies. A month prior, Rachel Maddow was still assuring us that, "nobody wants to take your guns!"

Although it might appear that I have erected a man of straw, I have not. The inescapable fact is that guns will not be taken away without the use of force, and even if that force yields results, a black-market will quickly spring into action. The Grabbers must grapple with this.

For these are the days in which people scream "I am the resistance!" while simultaneously trying to disarm the population. But then again, reason is merely a tool of the oppressor, or so I'm told. Even so, for those who still attempt to reason — however shoddily — they should be kind enough to do away with the pretense: We all know that the real goal of those who go on and on about "sensible" gun control *is disarmament*. "Why do you need one?" they endlessly whine, implying real intentions. With that single agenda perfervidly in mind, these Grabbers can ignore the bigger killers — handguns and knives — and then obsess on those sinister "assault" thingamajiggers. Neither do they talk about obesity or the sickening increase in the rates of suicide — the biggest killers of young people. It's "death-by-scary-gun" — and that's the end of it. This is strange, seeing as school shootings have actually dropped since the 1990's. Still, every time there is a school shooting, it becomes painfully clearer to me that we should ban public schools.

Somehow, the massacre at Parkland High School presented an opportunity to state the real objective more candidly than in times' past. Retired Justice Stevens penned an Op-Ed arguing a full-on repeal of the Second Amendment. On Facebook, faux rebel Michael Moore laid out an entire rewording of said Amendment, the dictatorial items too numerous to list. (No more sales of semi-autos, can't own a clip that holds more than 6 rounds, all owners must be fingerprinted and licensed, etc., etc.) Delany Tarr, Parkland shooting survivor-turned celebrity victim, was the most forthright: "When they give us that inch, that bump-stock ban, we will take a mile. We are not here for breadcrumbs; we are here for real change." In February, the Democratic Party's reliably demented bulldog, Tim Wise, tweeted this:

> *Everyone has fantasies. Some of mine involve ripping guns from the hands of pathetic bubbas who think firepower=manhood. I want to rip their guns from them in front of their children while they scream and wail about their "freedoms" and the evil "gubmint." Sorry not sorry.*

Wise, a critic of government power when it suits his "anti-racist" activism, and conversely so when it does not, quickly deleted that tweet. Apparently, he has no problem redirecting state force *away* from persons of color and *towards* white gun owners. Similar flirtations with violence can be seen in a viral video of hopeful Sheriff of Buncombe County, Daryl Fisher, who said that he would be happy to oblige the late Charlton Heston's famous warning. "You've heard people say...to pry my gun from my cold dead hands." Fisher shrugs: "Okay."

On social media, the memes practically create themselves. Dwayne Johnson, as a driver, turns around and asks the young female passenger: "Are we still protesting police this week?" She answers: "No, now we're saying that only police should be allowed to have guns." Gasp. Another has someone holding a gun to a man's face. "You idiot…you can't threaten me with that…this is a gun free zone." Reductionist, perhaps, but the practicality is still with those who favor individual gun ownership.

Although I'm no longer much of a fan, Canadian commentator Stefan Molyneux sums it up perfectly with this oft-quoted aphorism:

> If you are for gun control, then you are not against guns, because the guns will be needed to disarm the people. So it's not that you are anti-gun. You'll need the police's guns to take away other people's guns. So you are very pro-gun. You just believe that the government—which is of course so reliable, honest, moral, and virtuous—should be allowed to have guns. There is no such thing as gun control. There is only centralizing gun ownership in the hands of a small, political elite and their minions.

The scores of dishonest people who promise not to take guns away while advocating policies that forbid the purchase and sale of scary machines are drawing an increasingly visible picture, one that shows us all who the more violent group is. These Grabbers are optimistic: they are hopeful that the "March for Our Lives" kids will hold their breath until the age of eighteen, whereby they can run to the voting booths and elect the most despotic politician on the ballot.

The evidence of this is in the use of such brazen Orwellian doublespeak ("no, we don't want to take your guns away…but yes, we do want to take some guns away.") Children trapped inside of public schools are already made to regurgitate lies, and it's not hard to imagine "extra credit" being offered to those who show up with a boring sign that reads: *How Many More?* Which sounds entirely sane at first, until one considers the measures and sacrifices needed to achieve it. It seems then that only Ms. Tarr was given the correct speech to read from.

Some will say "this is only for the future," thus letting slide those who already possess scary weaponry. The numbers are inexact; we don't know how many Americans own what exactly. Jacob Sullum over at Reason reports that about 15 million AR-15-style rifles are held privately, with semiautomatics estimated at 310 million. A. Barton Hinkle writes that 73 million Americans own a firearm, with 5 million possessing AK-style machines. Justin Peters at Slate.com tells us that a 2012 congressional report found: "114 million handguns, 110 million rifles, and 86 million shotguns." Adding that data with research done by the NRA (reporting that 1,626,525 "AR-style rifles" were produced domestically and not exported between 1986 to 2007), as well as other reports, and Peters' best estimation is that there are probably some 3,750,000 "AR-style" rifles floating around in the US of A.

Gleefully, the Grabbers assure us that, even with all the numbers above, only about 3 percent of Americans own assault weapons. Those people are said to have some sort of "fetish" for these arms. Indeed, a 1992 book titled *Arming America* argued that, prior to the Civil War, gun ownership was relatively low amongst the average citizenry. "The Civil War thus transformed America from a country with a few thousand guns into one with millions of them," notes *The Economist* in its review. Interestingly, the bibliographical section of that article notes contrary evidence, with some historians finding that half of the households in 1774 owned guns.

So then: maybe or maybe not. But what cannot be denied

is the debates and jeremiads that were produced after the Revolutionary War that centered on the concept of Power. These were the grave concerns about "standing armies" and how the State has historically held firmly to monopolies of both "purse and sword." A corollary of this was, obviously, firepower. It wasn't some abstract question that happened to come up during the course of an unfortunate war, or engendered with the help of a crafty gun salesman named Samuel Colt (who once convinced a court to let him demonstrate the effectiveness of his newly made weapon...after convicting his brother for murdering someone with an axe!) — even if that event and that person had blasted the issue to the forefront.

If one has the patience to read old-style English (I won't claim it's easy), they can learn this easily enough by picking up copies of the Federalist and Anti-Federalist. "Who meant what back then?" is largely irrelevant to the main fact that the principle was being discussed right from the very beginning.

I offer commentary on the following quotations given by those who helped form the government of the United States. Alexander Hamilton, the most vocal Federalist in favor of the drafted Constitution, made his arguments in Number 29 of the Papers:

> The project of disciplining all the militia of the United States is as futile as it would be injurious, if it were capable of being carried into execution. A tolerable expertness in military movements is a business that requires time and practice. It is not a day, or even a week, that will suffice for the attainment of it. To oblige the great body of the yeomanry, and of the other classes of the citizens, to be under arms for the purpose of going through military exercises and evolutions, as often as might

be necessary to acquire the degree of perfection which would entitle them to the character of a well-regulated militia, would be a real grievance to the people, and a serious public inconvenience and loss. It would form an annual deduction from the productive labor of the country, to an amount which, calculating upon the present numbers of the people, would not fall far short of the whole expense of the civil establishments of all the States. To attempt a thing which would abridge the mass of labor and industry to so considerable an extent, would be unwise: and the experiment, if made, could not succeed, because it would not long be endured. Little more can reasonably be aimed at, with respect to the people at large, than to have them properly armed and equipped; and in order to see that this be not neglected, it will be necessary to assemble them once or twice in the course of a year.

But though the scheme of disciplining the whole nation must be abandoned as mischievous or impracticable; yet it is a matter of the utmost importance that a well-digested plan should, as soon as possible, be adopted for the proper establishment of the militia. The attention of the government ought particularly to be directed to the formation of a select corps of moderate extent, upon such principles as will really fit them for service in case of need. By thus circumscribing the plan, it will be possible to have an excellent body of well-trained militia, ready to take the field whenever the defense of the State shall require it. This will not only lessen the call for military establishments, but if circumstances should at any time oblige the government to form an army of any magnitude that

> *army can never be formidable to the liberties of the
> people while there is a large body of citizens, little,
> if at all, inferior to them in discipline and the use of
> arms, who stand ready to defend their own rights
> and those of their fellow-citizens. This appears to
> me the only substitute that can be devised for a
> standing army, and the best possible security against
> it, if it should exist.*

At first, Hamilton acknowledges the futility of trying to train the citizenry to the point that they would become experts in military matters. Nonetheless, Hamilton's argument in favor of local mobilization is clear, as it would serve as a bulwark against the frightening prospect of a "standing army" erected by those in Washington.

This, a group of trained citizens, could be summoned for the "defense of the State"—that is, the individual state. And if the central government ever found the right circumstances in which to raise such an army, that army ought never be so great that it would supersede the power of the state militia.

The Federalists had faced fierce opposition from large segments of the population, resulting in the Anti-Federalist Papers. Even a cursory look at Herbert Storing's edited volume shows an almost totalized fear of government overreach. Some of them disagreed with each other. For example, "The Impartial Examiner" argues in favor of a militia that needed superlative discipline. The people of Pennsylvania, the first to raise complaints against the drafted Constitution, felt otherwise. Addressing the "Reasons of Dissent," the "minority of the Convention of Pennsylvania" outlined their own propositions.

Number 7 on the list reads:

> *That the people have a right to bear arms for the*

> *defense of themselves and their state, or the United*
> *States, or for the purpose of killing game; and no*
> *law shall be passed for disarming the people or any*
> *of them, unless for crimes committed, or real danger*
> *of public injury from individuals; and as standing*
> *armies in the time of peace are dangerous to liberty,*
> *they ought not be kept up: and that the military*
> *shall be kept under strict subordination to and be*
> *governed by civil powers.*

Who won the debate? Both groups did, actually. The ratification of the Constitution was a win for the Federalists, while the Bill of Rights, argued as a necessary addendum by the Anti-Federalists, was codified a year or so later.

"Well regulated!" the Grabbers yell. But the judicial interpretation? St. George Tucker offered the first "extended analysis" of the Constitution in 1803. A veteran of the Revolutionary War and friend of James Madison, Tucker witnessed the constitutional debates as they unfolded. His *View of the Constitution of the United State*s made clear that the right to bear arms was intended for "nonmilitary" persons. His commentary was cited in the famous 2009 Supreme Court ruling *District of Columbia V. Heller*, which reaffirmed individual gun ownership. "This may be considered as the true palladium of liberty," Tucker wrote of the Second Amendment.

These historical facts will appear shocking to those who think that Wayne Pierre and the NRA board of directors had traveled back in time to help draft the Constitution. As it is, the NRA is only a nominal defender of the Second Amendment. In the 1930's, the NRA helped President Roosevelt draft the first federal restrictions, placing heavy taxes and regulations on machine guns, shotguns, and silencers. In the aftermath of the JFK Assassination, the organization supported the 1968 Gun Control Act, which extended gun bans on felons and the mentally ill. (Thanks a lot, assholes.)

Regarding that last point, it's hard to know exactly when and where Grabbers will move along the spectrum. Some days it's "ban the assault weapons!" and on other days it's the somewhat more reasonable proposal to keep *all* weapons out of the hands of the mentally deranged. I say "somewhat" because, as the late psychologist David Rosenhan discovered, it's not always easy to know who is and who isn't a crazy person. A grim prospect follows. What if the Grabbers get legislation passed that forbids firearm sales to someone who has a history of taking psychotropic medication? If such a bill comes to pass, it would immediately exclude millions of Americans, and by no fault of their own. "The number of atypical antipsychotic prescriptions to children under age 18 in the United States doubled from about 2.2 million in 2003 to 4.4 in 2006," writes Robert Whitaker. A 2014 government study found that 1 in 13 underage children were on psychiatric medication.

I'll go out on a limb and say that the Grabbers don't care about the mass-drugging of children. How could it be otherwise? Pills and chemicals are healthy. For these are the days in which it is entirely reasonable to argue that "race is a social construct" while also castigating a white person who lived and worked as a black person, but then quickly accept a middle-aged man's insistence that he's just as much a female as your grade-schooler who recently endured menarche. Experimental puberty blockers are just part of the agenda, and you're a bigot for daring to question that. These are the sort of lunatics who believe that health screening is necessary for firearm acquisition, and it could just as well be a projection of their own illness.

The Grabbers read all this and still they act with puerility: *"So we should do nothing?!"* But, as is the main thrust of this report, how do they achieve their aims without empowering the State even more so? The Aussie illustration is soon invoked. "Australia made it happen!" Port Arthur, Tasmania, April of

1996: a shooter kills 35 people and wounds 24 more. His weapon of choice was an AR-10 semi-automatic. The Australian government then set out to extract these weapons from the public. Their plan is a mandatory "buy-back" program, whereby they would pay money to those who relinquished peacefully. According to most reports, nearly 650,000 guns were handed over to the authorities. The anonymous administer of a site called GunsAndCrime.org writes:

> Although most jurisdictions released no details, Victoria did; their proportions should be close to typical. Although "military style" centerfire semiauto rifles were the firearms that were supposedly of primary concern to the gun control advocates, those types having been used in the massacres, only 3.2% of the firearms Victoria bought were centerfire (probably semiautos), other than shotguns. 47.5% were .22 rimfire rifles ("pea shooters") and 47.8% were pump or semiauto shotguns.

The study also informs that this was only about 1/3 of the 1.5 million prohibited guns that were expected—hoped—to be handed over, and this out of 3.5 million from the total number of firearms in the country. I won't pretend that I've done the research into Australia's gun culture. However, it's well known that every time a mass shooting happens in America, gun sales skyrocket. I take this to mean, very obviously, and despite polls showing that 2/3 of Americans want stricter laws, that many will refuse to hand them over peacefully. Keep in mind, too, that we live in the age of Instant Information. Even if only 3 percent of Americans are in possession of the heavy stuff, nearly everyone is in possession of cameras. If the scenario I described at the beginning ever does happen, it will likely be recorded and then broadcast to the entirety of the country. That's sure to set fire under many a patriot's arse. Furthermore, if the numbers are to be accepted, one will notice that America has *far* more guns than Australia ever did. In other words: *it's too late*. We have many guns, and so any attempt at confiscation will surely end up in mass bloodshed.

Rather than Australia, a better country to look at is America's southern neighbor. A recent international study found that Mexico was the second most violent country in the world in 2016, only after Syria. Surely not by guns— because Mexico also has but one single gun store, and its run by the government! "Mexico has some of the toughest gun control laws in the world," reports William Booth.

Edwin Mora adds that the murder rate in Mexico is more than twice of that in America, where the population is 3 times as big. Tweak and play with the numbers all you want (I am basically illiterate in mathematics), but the real question remains: *Why would these numbers be comparable at all?* The Grabbers have assured us that gun regulation must necessarily mean fewer gun deaths.

And how can that be? It will then be said that this is only because Mexico gets most of its guns from the U.S. and its many manufacturers—which might be true, but only underscores two simple facts, one dismal and the other happily repeated. Again: the time has long since passed whereby a benevolent State could melt all the guns into little hearts and roses with our Social Security numbers inscribed on them. And two: that *people* are responsible for killing; not machines, and not lobbying groups. It's the culture, stupid, that intangible item that no state can correct for. Random mass shootings did not occur more often during the first half of the 20th century—unlike racial violence, which was corrected not by any state policy, but general shifts in morality (with perhaps the pendulum now having swung to the other side).

Now we only get the smug face of celebrity victim David Hogg, lecturing on and on about what we're allowed to own while he and all the others ignore the underlying reasons of what causes violence in the first place. As Larry Correria said:

> People get hung up on the tool because they want something easy to blame. They want an easy solution. And there is no one, easy solution. And plus, banning guns in America is fundamentally, logistically impossible at this point. And the way technology is going with 3D printing and home machining, it's even more impossible.

Unlike some, I'm willing to be a Utopist. I want to understand why violence happens, the culture that reinforces it, and how we can change that. None of us can know everything — and I will sound like an idiot if I try to make it seem like I do — but I won't accept that human nature is always and forever immutable. Or that humankind can never come to a consensus on what is right and what is wrong. That's the whole point of libertarian advocacy!

As Butler Shaffer wrote:

> If conflict and violence are indeed a part of our genetic chemistry—which I doubt—then we had best learn not to control or suppress our nature, but to rise above it. For along with whatever other attributes we have been provided, we humans also possess minds capable of transcending the present limitations of our conscious thought process. Evolution, after all, is a continuing process in which we are active participants, not simply end products.

We are a learning and developing species. It's our superpower.

Even if it takes several more decades to achieve, I think that one day most of us will come to accept the premise that murdering people is *wrong*. For such an elementary thing still needs to be insisted to people that do not murder but like to make excuses for those who do.

Why do these massacres happen? What causes the murderous psychosis? Research continues from the 20th century when studies of the brain became routine and commonplace. Instead of advocating a civil war with the average American gun owner, I'd be willing to examine any combination of factors that led to the development of a mass murderer's brain. One such factor has already been mentioned here: We come to wonder why so many of these shooters seem to have been on a cocktail of psychotropic medications. As it is, many countries have issued warnings about these drugs. There are more considerations. Ronald Goldman has speculated on what long-term effects male genital mutilation (euphemistically called "circumcision) might have on the larger society, while Peter Gray has argued that the decline of childhood play has led to more cases of psychopathy. Alas, Grabbers prefer the easier route of condemning inanimate objects rather than scrutinize the brains that turn them deadly. That's easier to do, after all.

A single combinatorial factor will, of course, remain tentative. But at least they attempt to dig at the root of the problem, rather than just blaming "toxic masculinity" or the "loss of their white privilege" or whatever other stupid thing it is. In the meantime, we should argue for more armed guards in schools and shopping malls. Another viable option is something called a Gun Violence Restraining Order (GVRO). Rather than collectivize punishment, GVRO's would abdicate gun rights only to individuals who are shown to exhibit violent behavior.

Alas, solutions won't put smiles on the Grabber's faces.

They prefer their CNN invitations.

(June 2018)

To Help, or to Hurt, the Homeless

The Johnny Bobbitt Situation

THE FOLLOWING STORY, having already made "international headlines," should serve as an everlasting lesson for all those looking to help the homeless. In 2017, 29-year-old Kate McClure ran out of gas while driving on Interstate 95 in Philadelphia. Coming to her rescue was a genteel homeless man, 35-year-old Johnny Bobbitt, who used his last $20 to put in her tank so she could make it home. Thereafter, McClure returned several times to the streets where Bobbitt roamed, giving him sandwiches and water. This should have been reimbursement enough. Apparently for her, it was not.

McClure and her 39-year-old boyfriend, Mark D'Amico, then set up a fundraiser on the crowdsourcing site GoFundMe. Headlined as "Paying it Forward," the intention was for "first and last month's rent at an apartment, a reliable vehicle, and 4-

6 months' worth of expenses." The page tells its potential donors that Johnny is "very interested" in finding employment.

Reading the original text, one thing is clear: the donations were not intended for either heroin habits, or to let seemingly benevolent people live out their sumptuous lifestyle. The fundraiser mentions neither needles nor vacations. Donors knew exactly what they were giving for—to help Johnny get that "one little break." That's what it says.

A jackpot!—as D'Amico later said to Megyn Kelly. Too true. Far surpassing the $10,000 the couple had hoped to raise, fourteen thousand people donated to what eventually amounted to over $400,000. Six eyes, and the question of how many which saw those dollar signs as well-deserved remuneration.

Now we see a maelstrom of misusage, greed, and old-fashioned lying. Bobbitt is suing the couple, charging that they had refused to hand him over the money, instead using it on themselves. He claims that the couple used the money not only to travel, but also on a new BMW and other expensive purchases. He also says that D'Amico is a gambler, and there went some more of it.

D'Amico certainly is a gambler. In that same interview with Kelly, he admitted that he had politely requested a mere $500 dollars, to be used for his own habit, but which was quickly given back. But he's also gambling with his reputation, assuring us that the money was not misspent, and that it's all there—or here, or somewhere. The courts have launched an investigation, and D'Amico is betting on those investigators clearing his good name. The reason for withholding the funds from Bobbitt, the couple says, was because Bobbitt has a drug habit—blowing some $25,000 in two weeks—and therefore could not be trusted with it. Coming out of a courtroom for an unrelated charge, D'Amico says that answers will soon become "crystal clear."

The one-sidedness here is appalling. The confounding

consensus is: "Couple, bad; Johnny, good." Homeless people, goodhearted as they might be, are irreproachable. Every comment section and Twitter feed agrees that Johnny Bobbitt is an innocent victim, and rather that the couple are guilty of the lowest form of chicanery. Even if Bobbitt did use the money on drugs, they say, *oh well.* That's nobody's business but his. One editorialist in Philadelphia wrote this exactly: "People spend money in ways that some might disapprove of all the time." To hell with the donors who thought they were helping him out.

Evidence that the couple has used the donated money for their own splurging is, so far, inconclusive; there is more than just reports of Bobbitt's drug use: his own lawyer, Chris Fallon, has admitted that his client is a drug addict. And while Fallon is quoted as saying that "it's not heroin but another problem," journalist Thom Nickels recalls getting to know Bobbitt while he was begging for change outside of a Dollar Tree in the Port Richmond Shopping Center. Writing for the *Huffington Post*, Nickels reports meeting some of Bobbitt's friends, who contradicted the latter's claim of being addicted to pharmaceuticals. Of course, if he wasn't a lawyer, that would make Fallon a liar.

As for the couple, their lawyer has said that he won't be representing them for much longer, because one or both are likely to face criminal indictments. On top of that, their house was raided by investigators, with footage of the BMW getting towed going viral. None of this looks good for the couple.

But my contention still stands: It's entirely possible that *both* parties misused the purpose of the donations. Speaking to Kelly, the couple said that Bobbitt rejected the idea of owning a house or renting an apartment, instead asking for a motorhome so he could travel the country. This is something that he got, one that he picked out himself. Barbara Boyer, reporting for the *Philadelphia Inquirer*, quotes Bobbitt as saying that he wants to "experience life. That's why I bought the camper—so I could go hunting and fishing," adding that his "dream is to be on a little piece of land somewhere."

For a while, that piece of land was owned by the couple, where he parked his RV outside their home. The couple says that he would rack up his Uber account taking trips to the shadier parts of town, there to get his dope. (Bobbitt says that the couple wouldn't even give him the keys to the truck that he had also picked out, but which didn't run that well.) I'm hoping that criminal charges do come about, that way the power of perjury and subpoena will show whether or not I am correct.

Personal responsibility? Bobbitt's sympathizers believe that, since he is grown man, he can make his own decisions. "At some point, people have to put trust in me," Boyer quotes him as saying. Boyer. I can't be the only one who can picture the three of them sitting around the table, discussing how all that money is going to be spent: the couple holds onto the funds in their own bank account, promising that whatever they use will be reimbursed, and all while they turn their head to Bobbitt's little errands downtown.

If—and right now, is an *if*—that's true, then two statements will be heard. The first, said by everyone else, is that the couple was exploiting the addiction of a noble man who had helped them out. And the second—likely only said by me—is that Bobbitt is complicit in the misapplication of the funds.

Friends of Bobbitt can't have it both ways: they can't say that he is responsible for his own actions and then turn around and say that his decision-making capacities are rendered null because of addiction. And again, this does not absolve the couple of responsibility. They probably are swindlers who tried to find a way to spend that money on themselves. After all, they really should have given the funds to a third-party trustee. "We're doing that now," D'Amico tells us. He'll forgive us for being a bit skeptical, especially considering the reports saying they were ordered to turn over the funds—something they never did.

Meanwhile, GoFundMe representatives have promised that Bobbitt will get everything he is owed. "When there is a dispute, we work with all parties involved to ensure funds go to the right place," their statement read. Misuse, they add, is very rare. Since returning the money to the donors, the real victims here, is out of the question—which it should not be—then rehab would be the next best thing.

As it is, the couple say they already gave Bobbitt $200,000 of the raised funds. Bobbitt says it was only $75,000, including the vehicles; his lawyer shocks us by informing us that the rest of the money is gone. Did I mention how anxious I am to get the results of that investigation?

I'm not saying that it's always wrong for people to give to the homeless even when it's assumed that it will be used on drugs or alcohol. Usually, if I'm asked for change, and I have some, I'll give it without question. Bums like beer. If it eases the daily pain, good. Other times, if only armed with credit, I'll offer to buy a sandwich. They do need to eat, too. Obviously, the case here is much different. Forty cents will receive less attention than $400,000.

But benefactors to the downtrodden must have some sense as to what they're giving for, and those who concern themselves with where their donated money goes should not be shamed. It's OK to want to give for food or shelter instead of drugs or alcohol. However, the next person who insists that Bobbitt receive his huge chunk of cash, and who one day sees him spending a quarter million dollars on smack, should tell him directly: "Good job, Johnny. At least you're no longer being taken advantage of." And how wonderful is it that so many see it this way!

Would these same people shrug upon discovering that the Red Cross was using donated money to help support the vodka habits of their office employees? Probably not. Would the couple still be seen as monsters if they had set up the fundraiser with the headline: "Help Johnny get himself some dope"? Probably, yes. The public mind is schizophrenic like that.

Let the image of a handcuffed Mark D'Amico or an overdosed Johnny Bobbitt serve as a lesson, then. If one truly cares about *helping* these folks, maybe they would consider donating to a church or charity, or bringing them a gift package, or a nonrefundable coupon at a place that sells only food.

Don't give to GoFundMe, where the money can disappear into either bruised veins or the pockets of covetous couples claiming to want to help, not hurt, the homeless.

(October 2018)

Regarding Racism and Inevitable Second Civil War

ETHNIC EXTREMISTS ABOUND! In the one corner, some Alt-Rightists are wishing for a new Hitler to soon come to power, only to begin the mass deportation of every single last person who is not of 100% European descent. Tens of millions of blacks and Asians and Latinos—even if they came legally, just peacefully working or raising their families—must be disappeared, somewhere far away from the United States.

Even worse, these people forget that the ends are always influenced by the means: that a state big enough to do that can then do things like mass sterilization-via-vaccination (something very much discussed in our corrupt agencies). Then comes genetic testing so we can kick out the mutts—people like my son. "My god," someone says, "that person is one-sixth Jewish...they're not to be trusted." They're cursed to act as one might expect a wind-up toy, never able to rise above who came before them. *It's in their blood. They can't help it.* We cannot let these hybrid toddlers go running around. A part of them might rebel against the other part—or perhaps even rebel against you! The generalizations come swift and easily now: "They-They-They...Them-Them-Them." *We* must populate every single last inch of this vast continent. For liberty? Hardly. For blood. And, hopefully, a Swastika-clad Christ will be the one who signs it into law. Brown-skinned Christians don't stand a chance against white-skinned Jesus.

Moreover, what else to be gained from an ethno-state aside from the preservation of genetic purity? We can look across the ocean and notice that a lot of nations with homogeneous populations are ruled by tyrants. And so not only do we need genetic purity, but we must also have moral purity—complete with an established state church that requires tribute, either in the form of taxes or attendance. Then came anti-miscegenation laws and the prohibition of pornography. All of these measures will be for the sake of The Race, and I can imagine them easily coming into place.

In the other corner, there are those salivating for the day in which the *New York Times* declares: "White Minority in America!" For solid evidence, read Tim Wise and Steve Phillips, both mainstays on the liberal circuit. Or just type some interesting words into the Twitter search bar, where you'll soon find all kinds of anti-white hatred. "What's the matter?" they'll say sinisterly, "*Is there something wrong with being a minority in America?*"

Plus, they mean to add, *We believe in democracy.* You see, your rights are contingent upon our vote. Now add gun control and tax rates without limits. Worse things than that go through their heads, one can be sure. Just pull the lever, and viola— disarmament, while still having to pay those federal extortion fees. But, oh well, there's nothing you can do about it: "Multicultural democracy," "you're on stolen land anyway," "you have this coming."

This side is also faith-based. They're members of the Church of Intersectionality. Much more than merely respecting different ethnicities, we must now accept absurd premises, such as the following: "Islam is a Religion of Peace," or "Women can have penises." Finally, they have their own apostates: if a darker skinned American believes in the Bill of Rights or would like to see the southern border made secure, they are a traitor to their race. You *must* be on our side; what's in your heart and mind are irrelevant. Sensing the impending alienation for daring to entertain such a treasonous thought, more wind-up toys go marching on.

A white person might've once thought that they have no social or psychological investment in either their heritage or their pigmentation. They might've heard something like: "Whiteness and race are social constructs" — then immediately told that, despite that metaphysical fact, you still have to be punished for it. Metaphysics matter only insofar as they mean both nothing, and everything, at the same time. Contradictions be damned! Soon the realization is upon them: that even if you have no such investment in the way you were born, many other people have already made a deposit in your name. Those who are "white-passing" or "not white passing" are likewise ensnarled into an obsessive identitarianism.

Scroll some more on your social media feeds. *"Muh people, muh people, muh people."* We're nothing more than a branch growing out of a tree. How can someone possibly have that much affection for people who they don't even know simply because they happened to be born with the same skin color or raised with the same language? There are many who don't know how to think without using their blood.

This is alien to me. All my life I've been something of an egotist. I've always been able to rub shoulders with pretty much anyone of any color or creed, as long as they were not acting belligerently, but rather communicating in good faith. If I have any bias in this discussion, it stems from that experience.

Still, my son's very life has shown me that differences *do exist*, and that those identities matter above all else. I had no opinion on what native American people did with their kid's hair. Why would I have an opinion on that? However, after I got custody of him, I wished to get him a haircut. For this, I got called a cultural genocidalist. (Natives usually let their kid's hair grow.) Yes, interracial procreation saw some problems for me, even if they weren't the worst of it. Suggesting that mixed couples should seriously take those differences into consideration before birthing children would be seen as a vile admonition.

And the people who chastise whites for declaring legitimate ethnic interests have no problem if other groups do so; Jared Taylor is right when he points that out, as he often does. The implications are reaching into the very language. How many Democratic Party members pander to the Hispanic vote when they speak their terrible Spanish? Tucker Carlson has a point when he asks that: even the language in which the founding documents were written in? "Think we're kidding? Yeah right." How soon before we have bilingual street signs? And does any community in this continent have the right to protest it? The proposal should not surprise anyone.

For today, I only wish for a moderately-sized yacht, so that I may take my son, books, beer, fishing poles, and then pray for a nuclear reset. You all can scream about which side was right as the shelters are shutting their doors. Fuck 'em.

Or—less hopeful—we can embrace individualism, communitarianism, sovereignty, and voluntarily separation, with virtually no ties save except for commerce and regulated tourism. Federal democracy is the real culprit. Groups see the political process as a way to "one-up" one another; in every sphere and domain, they need more representation and greater equality. It's been my contention that old-fashioned federalism should be restored, with the U.S. splitting up, along with the abolition of all federal gun and tax laws, a newfound appreciation for meritocracy, and basically letting people separate across the continent. We're running out of options.

(August 2019)

Thoughts on the Shots

LAST MONTH, THE World Health Organization held a summit on vaccine safety. Several of the experts there expressed concerns, all of which were unsurprising to those of us who have looked at the issue.

The concerns include that the safety of vaccines has not been thoroughly studied, specifically with the kind of adjuvants being used (safe and effective!); the growing number of doctors that are starting to question vaccines; and that the channels used to report injuries leaves a lot to be desired.

These problems were leading to a "miscommunication" between vaccine policy makers and the public.

In New Jersey, a bill was recently proposed that would remove religious exemptions. Luckily, because of the large number of vocal parents who showed up outside the congress, the bill collapsed. But the government and the vaccine manufacturers are obviously getting scared of this growing skepticism, as similar bills are being proposed and passed all around the nation. They're not going to give up their billion-dollar profit number without a fight.

As Del BigTree said, and I paraphrase: These chemicals have not met a high threshold for safety, there's little to no recourse if an injury does take place, and so the simple response, the only one consistent with liberty, is: "I don't want to risk giving my kids these shots."

It's no more complex than that.

There's no need for an unnecessary back-and-forth, no compromise of a delayed schedule, or letting you get away without giving the flu or Hepatitis shot. "I'm willing to risk diseases that were once commonplace rather than a lifelong injury."

And that's final.

Some will argue about where their tax dollars go, saying that they go to pay for public schools, and so I demand schools to force children to be inoculated. Anyone involved in this fight will know that the only side unwilling to compromise are the pro-vaxxers.

When asked if they would allow a voucher for school choice (i.e. get your money back, in full, so that you can use it to send your children to a private institution that doesn't require the shots), the pro-vaxxers give a reply of negative.

This is a despotic want for control.

But there're even more inconveniences, like fact that most adults are not up to date on their own vaccines. Or we might also wonder why no other private institution (malls, restaurants, amusement parks) requires paperwork before entering. In short, we've never realized the mythical—bogus—herd immunity, which is probably why we see so many cases of up-to-date people who end up getting a disease anyway.

But like everyone who panics when their faith-based system is challenged, or losing support, the pro-vaxxers feel their hands gripping tighter; hyperventilation sets in, head burning with rage and frustration. "I'm absolutely sure!" And so everyone else must be made to comply.

This is nothing short of neo-Stalinism—social ostracizing and encouraging your neighbors to rat you out. Never mind that a combination of even four vaccines (let alone a dozen) has never been tested against a true placebo; no 5- or 10-year studies with large groups of, say, 10,000 kids.

Pro-vaxxers claim that that study would be "unethical," because not giving the shots is innately harmful. This presupposes that the vaccines are safe, never having demonstrated that they truly are.

Thus, we are talking about faith.

Keep in mind that the laws set up by the UN state that a placebo test would only be unethical if there were no other means of treatment. Of course, this applies to none of the diseases that we currently vaccine for; measles and mumps and even pertussis can all be treated easily with bedrest, sanitation, and fever reducers. Therefore, there is no reason why they couldn't test these chemicals on a large group.

At the end of it, the Vaccine Paradigm is the oldest story in the book: the quest for the Fountain of Youth, eternal health. Now we learn of vaccines for cancer and Alzheimer's.

Scroll a pro-vaxxer forum some time, and, along with the despotism, you will see wishful delusions: "Yeah, a vaccine for my hemorrhoids! My cough! This rash!"

These are happy guinea pigs in the world's largest genetic engineering experiment.

As liberals like to say, "we're only one law away from perfection," and pro-vaxxers add, "were only one vaccine away from perfecting the human organism."

Paul Offit, who created the Rotavirus vaccine, is on record as saying that an infant could easily endure 10,000 vaccines. The sky's the limit! It is no parody to picture a newborn hooked up to a half-gallon of vaccine solution.

Let's call this project what it is: *Evil.*

In the new decade, I like to think that even the most faithful to the Vaccine Paradigm will begin noticing the cracks in the ceiling.

Hopefully, by the end of the decade, the whole edifice will have crashed down.

(January 2020)

Childless But Traditional

IT'S VERY FRUSTRATING to be lectured about the merits of starting and raising a family, especially if the lecture comes from young conservatives who don't have any kids but who always look to be enjoying every second of their free time.

Off the top of my head, I could probably name a dozen of these self-proclaimed champions of "traditional values." They travel wherever and whenever, doing their journalistic activism, while occasionally taking a break to rave about how "the Left is trying to destroy the family!" and that the "decline of birthrates is the end of Western Civilization!"

It is frequently implied that the best life is one served as a parent, manning the nuclear household. During these rants, no crying child is ever heard in the background.

Nevermind that that free time, that unquenchable thirst for study and artistry, the energy directed towards these individual passions, must necessarily take a backseat (even if a temporary 10 or 20 years) when one becomes a parent.

These irony-deficient loudmouths think that because they babysat their niece and nephew one afternoon that they are now qualified to encourage the hardship that is parenting: the endless fighting, screaming and crying, needing to stop whatever it is you're doing, the sleepless nights, the expenses, the inability to get up and go, the noise and the lack of solitude (never mind years of court battles with someone who tricked you into being a parent). This is on top of the fact that the 21st century newborn will be growing up in a technocratic hell.

And how to keep them safe from that?

But sure, it might be possible for a few privileged souls to juggle their passions with their progeny. However, you likely have some money in the bank, an education that takes you further, babysitters and schools that you can trust, and with a partner or family members willing to watch the kids. If not, then you're likely going through family court, with judges and lawyers negotiating child support and restraining orders.

More often, "traditionally," one parent works and the other rears, which takes up nearly all the ticks on the clock; there's precious little time in the week in which to read 3 books or write 3,000 good words.

Some people are more disposed to the parenting lifestyle, and there's absolutely nothing wrong with anyone deciding not to have kids. Not unlike the mythical Bigfoot, there are those of us who simply must have that time for ourselves, for all the reasons stated.

The need for quiet individuality is not a reaction to parenthood; it's what makes up our entire character, something developed long before we had borne any little clones.

Of course, you can argue for or against anything without being personally affected yourself. There's nothing inconsistent about that—just as I can argue against murder without knowing someone who's been murdered. But, again, it's the omission that's always annoying: "Good luck devoting 4-5 hours a day to your arts or studies or travels. No more quiet moments to do what you want. It'll be much more difficult to jump in a car or plane and go wherever. Now you must always be on call to take care of little people who need to be fed and have their butts wiped. So, if you can't devote your entire life to them, *don't procreate.*"

Why, young conservative, will you not make these admonitions a part of your program? Just say these words outright, dear young, happy, childless conservative. Be brave. Have some probity. Say it while you sip margaritas, out on your 10th vacation this year, whispering glibly about how "one day" you'll get around to creating your own little buggers.

Then think back to the heartache constantly seen on shows like Maury and Dr. Phil. Ask your partner if they plan on sticking around for 20 years. Or if instead you think the local family judge will soon know your faces. Ask the question again, this time in the mirror, maybe even with the honesty-inducing effects of intoxication coursing through your veins: *Are you sure?*

As I see it, if you're a young conservative in your early 20's or older, and you aren't currently trying to find a mate to settle down and raise kids with, then you should stop lecturing others about what they should be doing.

(January 2020)

Searching for the Silver-lining
in the Covid-19 Deathcloud

THE GRAVELLY FEMALE voice comes through the radio with all the steady, dull energy of an emergency broadcast. She needs to inform us of the latest bad news.

At the moment, there's a lot of it.

People are flushing massive amounts of non-flushable wipes down their toilets, which is clogging up the pipes and sewers. A couple of new celebrities have announced that they've tested positive for the virus by posting their smiling faces on social media. There's been a shooting in some supermarket in another state, the end result of two customers battling over the last roll of toilet paper.

Counties and states are enacting "stay home" orders, forcing the closure of all "nonessential" businesses, which will now leave a large part of the workforce trying to figure out how they're going to pay next month's rent.

And, most grimly, the total number of infected persons has doubled in less than 24 hours, while the fatalities have gone up by another thousand or so: respectively, almost 15,000 in the U.S. and 11,000 globally. These are numbers which will surely increase with every click of "refresh" button.

It's all so very apocalyptic, and I listen to the report as I hit 75 on the freeway. My son is in the backseat. I'm taking him to his bimonthly visit with his mother and her family. I turn the radio off and think of something that makes my heart skip a quick beat; because I really do hope that the other side of his family is practicing "social distancing," that term that will soon be etched into our vernacular. Collectively, we must all help to "flatten the curve" by exercising extreme individuality, or so we're told.

If the headlines are to be accepted at face value, the virus should be viewed as a serious threat to health, both to the community's and to oneself. A paper loaded with terminology was recently published by researcher Doris Loh, who provides much needed information on Covid-19 (even if the layman—myself—has to supplement the reading with some additional internet searches).

In fact, coronaviruses are ubiquitous; the common cold is a coronavirus. It's when the virus mutates into something else that it becomes deadlier. To demonstrate the severity of this current mutated coronavirus, compare it to the SARS-CoV epidemic of 2003, which infected over 8,000 people worldwide in 8 months.

In contrast, COVID-19 (or SARS-CoV-2) infected 120,000 worldwide in under three months (as of the publication of the March 14th paper). Loh says that COVID-19 is "up to 1,000 times more infectious than SARS-CoV or other coronaviruses." The reason for this is something called a "furin cleavage site," which was not found in SARS-CoV, but is found with the one we are currently dealing with. It seems that the virus has a tendency to really get inside the human tissues, and to then replicate with incredible speed.

Here's my big concern, quoting from the paper: "Patients suffering from cardiovascular diseases, hypertension and diabetes are often prescribed drugs that either inhibit ACE (angiotensin-converting enzyme) or block angiotensin 2 type-1 receptor (ARB). Both types of drugs increase the expression of ACE2." More:

> *The use of selenium during COVID-19 infections therefore, can be problematic. ACE inhibitors actually increase expression of ACE2, and SARS-CoV-2 infects host cells through binding with ACE2 receptors. ACE 2 receptors are found on lung epithelial cells, intestines, kidneys and blood vessels. Thus using ACE inhibitors either through medication or supplements risk elevating COVID-19 infection and developing severe or even fatal disease complications.*

Loh adds that:

> *The binding of SARS-CoV-2 to ACE2 exposes patients with CVD to higher risk for pneumonia and increased severity of symptoms. Reports showed that in China, among COVID-19 patients with severe symptoms, 58% had hypertension, 25% had heart disease and 44% had arrhythmia. Fatality data released by China's NHC showed 35% of patients who died from SARS-CoV-2 infection had a history of hypertension, while 17% had a history of coronary heart disease.*

"*Just great,*" I think to myself every morning as I pop my 30 mg of Lisinopril. (The only medication I take regularly!) It's for my high blood pressure, which might or might not have been properly diagnosed more than 10 years ago now. And it's an ACE inhibitor. A chronic dry cough, a permanent side-effect, is personal evidence that it indeed affects the lungs. It's also said that even if you survive COVID-19, you could suffer long-term or even permanent damage to the lungs, kidneys, or heart.

So, there's an obvious concern, and I've decided to treat COVID-19 seriously, starting by heeding the Surgeon General's recommendation to cancel all surgeries which are not life-threatening. Thus, my sinus operation will have to wait a while longer. Next, I've used the numbers to scare my son's family. They're older than my folks—in their 70's—and so they should also want to be cautious. My search for the silverlining has begun: for the time being, my son no longer has to attend church! There must be other silverlinings, I think to myself.

On this day, in this Target parking lot, I push him around in a shopping cart while waiting for them to come and pick him up. As usual, he's having fun, and I become thankful that the vast majority of children appear to be virtually unaffected by this virus; oftentimes asymptomatic, and with fatality rates that are near-zero for kids under the age of 10.

But your child can still be a carrier, which means that every time you pick them up from a visit, you're potentially standing 10 feet away from the adorable little vector who could soon give you a virus that'll end your life and thus put them in a foster home. Such is God's twisted design.

II

The virus has produced as many estimates as it has both persons fearful and carefree. There seems to be an equal amount of people who insist of the dangers as those who suggest it's nothing more than overblown hysteria. Both positions are forgivable, as we have seen the chaos captured in grainy videos out of China. And the second, too, as the average person watching the media will believe that we're always in the midst of some imminent crisis.

We can't easily forget the nonsense told to us about "swine flu." And wasn't it just last month that a girl named Greta was warning us all about climate change? Was there not some liberal on CNN last night who was railing against the NRA, which the city of San Francisco has declared to be a genuine "terrorist organization"? Nevertheless, I'm sure there was an evangelical predicting Jesus' return in the coming months.

How do we know to withhold our laughter with regards to this threat? It is possible that a society can become so weary from grappling with concocted threats that it fails to realize when a real threat presents itself. Then, can we trust the word of the Chinese government? No, and The Epoch Times has told us why: they've lied about the numbers. Our own government? Given history, there's reason to think not. Independent journalists and researchers? In a lot of cases, probably. What about our own senses? In the end, that's all we have, and the best and perhaps only way to start analyzing this situation is to look at the responses.

San Francisco often touts itself as a "sanctuary city," a place that undocumented immigrants can run to without fear of being persecuted by local officials, who are reluctant to work with federal officials during those hunting efforts. Yet Frisco was one of the first cities to enact a mandatory "stay home" order. Suddenly, everyone is a suspected cause of pain and death (albeit of course with entirely different motivations).

One minute, you're giving refuge to people that move illegally across national borders, and the next minute you're telling everyone not to move at all. Such is the power of the State.

Elsewhere, hospitals in Italy report being overwhelmed by

those infected, so much so that patients are getting transported to other hospitals in the country. This month, the city of New York says their morgues are almost full. When was the last time that a public health crisis resulted in that kind of scenario? Meanwhile, doomsday commentaries from Jason Warner and Joscha Bach have gone viral, arguing that we can't just "flatten" the curve, we must "squash it," this by using "social distancing" as our method.

More optimistically, biophysicist Michael Levitt, while agreeing with everything currently being done, still believes that COVID-19 is slowing down, and that society will soon resume normal operations. The Lancet finds that the death rate will be much lower than previously thought, somewhere around 0.66 percent.

The pattern is this: as soon as there's some bad news, there's some good news. As soon as there's some good news, there's some bad news. While everyone battles for the Correct Estimate, we should keep in mind that the person who dismisses the concerns of COVID-19 by reminding us that "X amount of people died of the flu" will probably think differently once bodies begin dropping dead right down the street. Furthermore, I bet if we could prove that COVID-19 is a true bioweapon that was cooked up in a laboratory ran by Bill Gates or the Chinese government, the narrative of "manufactured threat" would shift dramatically into one of caution.

Demonstrating the seeming hopelessness of this situation, there's a study out of the University of Otago that points to a strong correlation between unemployment and suicide. This news is quite bad when considering that the Department of Labor reports that 6.6 million Americans have filed for unemployment benefits since the COVID-19 deathcloud was first seen in the skies.

Another report tells us that calls to the suicide hotline have gone up 300% since this all started. If you do a simple Google search of "economic crash," and you'll have a lot of results to follow up on.

Based on the above, no matter how deadly the virus really is, there's little doubt that it's having a negative impact on our blue sphere-shaped spaceship. The whole machine, from small businesses to civil society to personal worship, can be shut down when confronted with the microscopic face of a very nasty virus. Still, it would be wrong to say that the world has shut down entirely. The major retail chains remain open, for example. Industries are still producing. The supply chain continues to chug along. There are no reports of widespread starvation—yet.

And there's something else I saw happening: every day I go for a walk at one of the three or four parks in my area. At first, I noticed an undeniable increase in the number of families who had come outside to get some exercise together. On the sidewalks, too, there were more joggers, walkers, and bicyclists out enjoying the fresh air than I can ever remember seeing before.

From my view, the interrupted daily schedule had entailed at least one positive thing. But, three months into this pandemic, the crowds are becoming smaller (though this could also be attributed to California's rainy season.)

Also, of course, crowds are a problem, and they have been thoroughly discouraged, oftentimes with legal threats. The families I see are almost always in small groups, broadly separated from others on the fields and trails. In Florida and California, the beachgoers had rebelled against not just the State, but also the virus itself.

We saw masses packed tightly together on the shore, wherein COVID-19 finds the perfect honeymoon suite in which to spread its horns and breed. Such behavior is risky, and it does not follow that we should champion the freedom to choose while also applauding every choice that's ever made.

That said, many people are in honest disagreement with these semi-suggestive lockdown orders. Fresh air and exercise is good for the immune system—correct? So who is to say that I cannot use the great outdoors to fortify myself?

Governments have responded to these feelings in kind. A bar I pass on the street has a notice posted on the door: "Sorry, the government made me close my doors." Lots of businesses share that same fate. National borders have also been shut down with a similar sadness. People in San Diego are getting fined for watching the sunset. This heavy-handed approach is captured best in a headline from The Atlantic: *The People in Charge See an Opportunity.*

The article gives some historical precedence:

> *There is nothing new about the sudden enthusiasm for aggressive government intervention during the health crisis. Throughout history, pandemics have led to expansion of the power of the state. As the Black Death spread across Europe in 1348, the authorities in Venice closed the city's port to vessels coming from plague-infested areas and forced all travelers into 30 days of isolation, which eventually became 40 days; hence the word quarantine. A couple of centuries later, William Cecil, the chief minister to Queen Elizabeth I, battled the plague in England with a law that allowed authorities to shut the sick in their houses for six weeks. A few years later, the Plague Act of 1604 made criticizing these and other measures illegal.*

That's all scary enough, but it's nothing compared to what can be accomplished in the age of so-called "surveillance capitalism." Everywhere we go, most modern denizens carry with us a helpful and less-itchy Mark of the Beast.

This item slides easily into a pocket, and it contains technology once hard to fit inside of a warehouse. A good state will dismiss the predictable cries of "Orwellianism!" and then seize the chance, as they now are. We know of a few governments for sure that have been analyzing data found on smartphones: Italy, Germany, Austria, China, South Korea and Taiwan—the last of which has set up "geo fences" that "alerts authorities when quarantined individuals leave their designated shelter locations or turn off their mobile devices," reports TheRegister.com.

Wild guess that many other states are doing the same. This is to can keep track of the smartphone's owners, who may have flown the coop, rebuffed their quarantine orders, and continued about their everyday lives. That's not allowed when there's a nasty virus in the air.

Shelter in place! The consent of the plebiscites has not been requested!

The New York Times opined that the measures used by the Chinese government were reminiscent of the era of Chairman Mao. In the Philippines, dictator Duarte has given orders to "shoot to kill" those disobeying the lockdown. The government of Hungary voted to give their president, Viktor Orban, what amounts of dictatorial power. In Russia, a country with 170,000 cameras on their streets, which has been used to arrest 200-some people for violations, the Moscow police chief was quoted by CNN as saying that he wanted "there to be even more cameras so that that there is no dark corner or side street left." Applause for brazenness.

The United States is following suit, or at least it's preparing to. The 2 trillion-dollar bill just passed by Congress and signed by President Trump provides for a "public health surveillance and data collection system."

This is on top of the door-to-door searches in Rhode Island, national parks getting shut down, and a few cases where judges have ordered people to wear ankle bracelets.

Somewhere, someone is having a wet dream: either those pushing a New World Order, or those who saw the whole thing coming. One of these people is Bill Gates, a name that frequents the mouths of the admonishers.

For years, Gates has been giving his take on global health. He's the loudest proponent there is for vaccines. It should be seen neither as conspiracy nor coincidence that two months prior to the first reported cases of COVID-19, in October, Gates and his foundation partnered with John Hopkins Center for Health Security and World Economic Forum to create a large-scale simulation of a global pandemic. Held in New York City, this was called Event 201.

Their purpose, per the official website, was to "educate senior leaders at the highest level of US and international governments and leaders in global industries," and also to "inform members of the policy and preparedness communities and the general public." Sounds entirely philanthropic. Sadly, humanity did not fare well: after an 18-month struggle against the faux pandemic called CAPS (for Coronavirus Associated Pulmonary Syndrome), 65 million people died. (Weird sidenote: participants in Event 201 were given adorable little plush viruses.)

Predictably, Gates is giving as much publicity as he can on the crisis. This is the same Bill Gates who has previously backed plans to cover earth's atmosphere with 500 surveillance satellites. Who was sued by the Indian government for testing vaccines on unwitting kids and teenagers. Today? A quote right from the serpent's tongue: "Eventually we will have some digital certificates to show who has recovered or been tested recently, or when we have a vaccine, who has received it."

Gates, who has no medical training whatsoever, tells us that "mass gatherings" will never come back until we've all been vaccinated. It's no wonder Gates seems so giddy when discussing COVID-19: he sees a partnership between lizard and virus.

Silverlining?

Now we know what some tyrants really have in mind.

III

It's frightening, but unsurprising, how quickly a public health crisis can turn so many people into enthusiastic fascists. Level-headed commentators should insist of a proper balance between taking the virus seriously and refusing to sprint headfirst onto a page of George Orwell's classic dystopia.

I, for one, am doing everything practical to keep myself safe: avoiding crowds, staying six feet away from the next person, and washing and sanitizing my hands religiously. And I'm even wearing a facemask and gloves when I go out shopping. But: I will not be respecting arbitrary rules that try to prevent me from going on my daily hikes and jogs. I go for my exercise every single day, without exception, and if we're concerned about "health," then my routine should be respected, as it's absolutely needed for my own health, both physical and mental.

Plenty of others would side with dictator Duarte and have me shot dead for stepping outside my house. They'll be quite upset when they learn about me running through the yellow caution tape that's been set up at my trailheads, snapping the tape as I throw my hands up as if I've just won a Gold Medal. Instead of exercise, they'll bunker down in their houses and treat their neighbors like they have leprosy. Indeed, this is likely the only time in which one can send money to random strangers in the mail and the recipient would send it back out of fear that the money might be contaminated.

I wish not to give arms and legs to this virus, and the question of contagiousness is one that, like every other detail, is still being debated. Measles is said to be the only true "aerosol virus," meaning that it's able to stay suspended in the air for long periods of time. If a measles carrier is in a room, leaves, and someone else comes in, it's a good chance that the second person will catch the virus.

StatNews.com reports:

> The weight of the evidence suggests that the new coronavirus can exist as an aerosol—physics term meaning a liquid or solid (a virus) suspended in a gas (like air)—only under very limited conditions, and that this transmission route is not driving the pandemic. But limited does not mean "no" conditions, underlining the need for health care works to have high levels of personal protection, especially when doing procedures such as intubation that have the greatest chance of creating coronavirus aerosols. "I think the answer will be, aerosolization occurs rarely but not never," said microbiologist and physician Stanley Perlman of the University of Iowa. "You have to distinguish between what's possible and what's really happening."

Updated studies in April find that the virus might be spread by talking and breathing, not just shedding droplets. Surface life remains a big concern, reaffirming the efficacy of handwashing and the wearing of masks and gloves. "We don't observe the transmission process...We actually don't know how respiratory diseases are transmitted," said Jeffrey Shaman, an epidemiologist and head of the Climate and Health Program at Columbia University in New York City.

While the conclusive evidence lies in wait, the virus itself is nonetheless *being treated* like a "deathcloud." All it would take, imply the doomsayers, is one bad windstorm, and then COVID-19 will flow through the communities and infect every person who's out by the mailbox retrieving their government check. And those checks are only one part of their solution. The other part entails an endless trust in Government, those that are expected to put all of society—economic life and personal life—into a deep freeze, only to be thawed out at an indeterminate time in the future.

By then, the UN estimates that up to 25 million people, globally, could be out of work. That number means nothing to the proud Marxists who are happy to see working people stay at home, because Marxists see all work—the small business owner and the recently promoted maker of six-figures alike—as an exploited member of the working class. To them, any workplace is far more oppressive than a democratic state. If anarchism is defined in this way, then what we see happening is a sort of "anarchy by decree"—except they only get halfway, as all other collective gatherings are put on hold as well. A state that can prevent you from going to work can also prevent you from attending your favorite Pride Parade.

So, if an anti-work ethic does gain traction during this ordeal, hopefully it coincides with other reconsiderations— such as spending money more frugally, holding off on another child when you can barely support the ones you already have, or thinking twice before agreeing to that tempting mortgage on the 3-bedroom house.

It's not enough to say, "It's good that you don't have to go to work tomorrow"; you then have to ask where one's food, housing, and resources will come from. If not, then how will those at home now pay their bills? Will we ask Big Daddy Government to reach deeper in your neighbor's pockets, or to ask their friends at the Federal Reserve to turn up the dial on the magic money machine?

There are problems with this. For one thing, the printing of more money will only further devalue the dollar, which subsequently depletes the value of one's savings.

Simultaneously, governments will have to tell property owners that they cannot demand their tenants pay any bills. If these commands are carried all the way through, it would render all incentives obsolete. What's the point of working harder when your boss can't afford it, as he's now getting taxed more and thus making other financial rearrangements? What's the point of saving money when that money might have to be used to pay for food when your job is gone next month? Is there any silverlining here? Why not appreciation of the irony that those cheerful fascists (most of them leaning to the Left) are no longer laughing at "doomsday preppers"?

Another thing: who can we actually trust to tell us when it's safe to come back outside?

Trump has been criticized for dragging his feet for a whole month before acting. So, it won't be the President. The World Health Organization had initially stated (via a series of tweets) that COVID-19 couldn't be transmitted from person to person, so maybe they're out too.

What group, at what level, will give us the One True Safe Date? The numbers, after all, are constantly changing; the models are changing by the day. It's possible that we'll never know, and the risk of contracting COVID-19 will remain with us for a good while longer.

What's certain is that the virus cannot penetrate through walls. Therefore, the person out on a hike or buying food should be of no threat to someone who has decided to bunker down inside their stucco-lined cells.

"But," they'll say, "if too many get sick, it'll overwhelm our hospitals, and that *will* affect more people needlessly." It's always difficult to calculate *who matters* and *who doesn't matter*, is it not? Yes, if the hospital beds are all full, then car crash victims will be inconvenienced along with women about to give birth. Is the lesson: drive safer and don't have babies? Or is it to tell the new father with a wife and daughter that he should obey his government and stay home, thereby quitting his job because it's wrong for him to risk interacting with customers whose purchases had for all this time been supporting his family?

What of the fact that 10,000 people committed suicide during 2008's Great Recession? Of course, that number isn't as high as those confirmed to have already died from COVID-19, so it should not matter if suicides are twice that amount once we witness the UN's unemployment estimates—correct?

Who is going to start making the wisest decisions? I vote for no individual, except the one who is impelled by his duties.

The real lesson comes from the caveat that's used too often when discussing the threat of COVID-19: that most of the people dying are old, or that they had "preexisting conditions." The implication is: "Well, they're old anyway. They had other health issues. So, their deaths aren't such a big deal."

So much for "not placing value on life."

But it's an agreeable recognition: the old and the unhealthy are expected to leave us sooner rather than later. One of these can be dealt with, and here I discuss my own country, for America is the most obese nation in the world. The standard American diet is notoriously unhealthy, filled with processed meats, high fructose corn syrup, and tons of additives and preservatives.

According to Dr. Amir Kahn, who cites a study of COVID-19 patients in China, obesity increases the chances of mortality and morbidity. Viewed cynically like this, it's obvious that obesity is something that's taken up voluntarily. Add to that tobacco smoking—said to be a major factor in the death rates of Italy and China—and things get even riskier.

In regard to "health," some of us have a lot to improve upon. For me, this could be the best reason to lose weight and try to get off my blood pressure medication. A virus like COVID-19, and the ensuing reactions, can make these shortcomings come into a better focus, showing us what we're doing wrong and what can be done differently. Therefore, I think the crisis could provide the opportunity for a reprioritization. This is the real silverlining. We can take Gates' plan for a New World Order and flip it upside down, creating a new, more Conscientious World Order. Gates speaks as if he knows what's best, and that the rest of us are idiots who need to be herded around like sheep. Admittedly, there's some truth to that, at least from the American perspective.

I wish for improvement and preparation to begin with personal impetus, not forced isolation. Rather than take the position that the household is the only true fortress, agreeing with the elites whenever they lock our doors, we should instead be viewing our very own bodies as a fortress, as well as our places of work.

Although it'll sound silly to those who have no intention of doing the following (and maybe wishful thinking on my part), should be said that we don't necessarily have to ideate suicide, drink excessively, or gain weight sitting in the house watching Netflix. Getting outside to exercise will require defiance in many quarters of the world, but it would be entirely justifiable, for one's health is at stake. This does not mean that we must hike and jog in crowds; indeed, it's probably a good idea to find spots that are as spacious as possible.

Most of the mandates don't prevent people from walking on the sidewalks; logically, if everyone walked on the sidewalks, there'd still be bodies coming into close contact with one another.

We might then start taking practical precautions against disease.

Gloves and masks will be worn regularly in the workplace and in the social sphere, with a small bottle of hand sanitizer hanging from the belt. Wired magazine, for instance, published a lengthy defense of face masks. Their piece points out the paradoxical stance of health officials, who tell us that masks don't work, but then insist that medical personnel should always be wearing one. It then cites several studies showing the efficacy of masks for reducing the spread of viral pathogens. "A 2011 review of high-quality studies found that among all physical interventions used against respiratory viruses—including handwashing, gloves, and social distancing—masks performed best, although a combination of strategies was still optimal," the article states, reminding us to not forget to wash our hands.

Handmade masks made from cloth are said to be less effective, but better than nothing if surgical masks and N95s are not unavailable. An entire industry for designer facemasks could be in the works!

We might always find ourselves standing farther away while in conversation, raising our voices a little louder so ask to make up for the adjusted distance. Businesses will hire extra hands to scrub and sterilize constantly. Cities will have someone who comes around several times a day to do the same on playgrounds and in bathrooms. Social gatherings will be smaller. Theaters will space out their seats. Yes, it's entirely probable that this virus will create such changes, whether permanent or in the short term. But in the end, these protocols and initiatives are far preferable to lockdowns, ankle bracelets, and "geofences."

If government has any role at all during a pandemic, it's to conduct studies on the disease at hand, to monitor the situation on all levels, and to keep the public informed of the latest discoveries. This way, we can make the decisions they feel to be most conducive to themselves and their families.

True: with this model, the rates of infection, and of death, might increase. But one must ask themselves: Is it more important to live with that risk, or live inside a world where Bill Gates can tell you when to step outside your house and what vaccines to put inside your body? Without a doubt, the COVID-19 virus is very dangerous. But with time, the virus will probably attenuate and become less deadly. Can the same be said about Bill Gates' proposals? Will they also pass with time? That's far more worthy of our doubt.

Then again, maybe I'm wrong: A click of the "refresh" button on WorldOMeters shows that we're up nearly 1,500,000 cases, globally, with 82,000 deaths. Perhaps we do need a dictatorial New World Order to save us from ourselves. I hope I'm not.

(April 2020)

Polling for Civil War

SOME TIME AGO, the scene in Portland, Oregon looked like a battlezone. It was one of many that sprung up in the wake of George Floyd's death. On 5 May 2020, the 46-year-old black man was killed by Minneapolis police officers, who were investigating Floyd for supposedly trying to pass a phony twenty-dollar bill. The video of his death went viral, sparking nationwide outrage, and not for the first time. As we all know, anger has been boiling for a while.

It's only a matter of time before the real war begins.

The *Claims Journal* is a publication which covers insurance news. According to them, the destruction and looting had spread to 20 states and 25 cities. "In the U.S., there has been no precedent for a riot catastrophe like this," said Tom Johansmeyer, Assistant Vice President of Verisk, a firm that analysis risk. Johansmeyer said that while major retailers were hit the hardest, "there are a lot of smaller losses out there as well."

He estimated that losses will exceed $25 million, deemed a "catastrophe" level. If this "movement" is a response to lost lives, then it would also be appropriate to mention the almost 30 lives that have been lost amid the chaos.

During his speech at Mount Rushmore, President Donald Trump said this would not be tolerated. Soon after, the President launched Operation Legend. Although Trump did say that he'd use federal troops to help local law enforcement squash the rioters, the operation itself was specifically for the protection of federal property, namely courthouses.

Not that local law enforcement had been sitting on their hands: According to the *Washington Post*, some 14,000 people across 49 cities have been arrested since the end of May, many for minor offenses, like curfew violations and failing to disperse.

Libertarian podcaster Eric July wishes the headlines would read: "Rival Gangs Battle in the Streets of Portland." Because there is violence to be found on both sides, this is an apt analogy. One gang wears helmets and camouflage, while the other is blackly dressed from head to toe. Let's start with the second gang.

II

"Peaceful." How many times have we heard that word used to describe the protesters, none excepted? These are black-hooded Gandhi's, we're always told, doing nothing more than peacefully exercising their First Amendment rights.

They're peaceful up until the second they drag someone out of their car, or beat another over the head, or throw things through privately-owned windows. Then we see the gears change: well, *yes*, those are acts of violence, but they're completely justified given that America's police are, according to most, empowered by a white supremacism which aims to either kill or incarcerate every last person of color.

The hesitancy to be forthright covers up an uncomfortable fact: That the rioters aren't much different from the ones blasting them with pepper spray. That isn't mere rhetoric, despite the chants that "All Cops Are Bastards" (ACAB). Drivers and business owners have been assaulted, and so those assailing activists have that in common with the police.

Adding to that comparison, who will argue that many of those now asking for libertarians and freedom fighters to come to their defense were, just a couple months ago, applauding the police as they arrested *peaceful* business owners who did nothing more than defy the lockdown? If my observation is true, then demilitarization of the police is hardly what they seek. Rather, and more explicitly, it's the end of so-called "white supremacy." The Black Lives Matter website uses the word "eradicate."

What *is* white supremacy? We can only guess at all the components.

The western-prescribed nuclear family structure finds its way to the gallows, where presumably some "nonbinary" person holds the lever. Private businesses are part of the oppressive capitalist system, so those can burn along with the courthouses and police stations. Monuments of figures as diverse as Albert Pike to Confederate leaders to the Founding Fathers—those come down quicker than any white person who tried to protest.

And as this eradication takes place, some "educator" named Robin DiAngelo tours the country, lecturing white people on their "privilege" and "fragility." Tucker Carlson's commentary on her book leads me to believe that DiAngelo wishes to indict all white people for a racism that's as unavoidably necessary as oxygen.

While the Democrats and the leftist media play their role as the promotor of and apologist for destruction, others are even more honest. The Nation, for instance, published an article titled *In Defense of Destroying Property*.

The article acknowledges that, "The destruction is too

widespread to attribute it to a few bad actors." And why the need for this destruction? Because the "police need to be defunded, and some police stations need to disappear."

Property is a "violent thing," the article goes on, and so "disavowing property destruction and even theft because of a spurious attachment to a reified notion of nonviolence is a mistake." Lastly, "the vandalizing of property and the theft of goods could just as easily be framed as the enforcement of a moral economy—the rightful reappropriation of stolen wealth." As I said, there's no reason to stop at the police stations and courthouses. Therefore, if I break into my neighbor's house or business and steal everything in the place, perhaps shooting them when they resist, I can simply justify it on the grounds that the property sits on stolen land.

Why is it so difficult to guess that the principles enshrined in Bill of Rights might also be on the cutting block? I start to get the feeling that, if those same police energies could be made to collect a "privilege tax" on the white middle class, it would be met with widespread approval. The sooner we all understand and acknowledge this hatred, the sooner we can start giving a more complete analysis.

III

Thinking they have an ace in their hands, some will try to argue against these generalizations. If ever a libertarian offers a collectivized assessment, they're swiftly castigated for it. Indeed, this is more of a tendency towards *unthinking*. Bifurcating with "them" and the "other" might often be wrong and lacking nuance—but not always.

Presumptions derive naturally from a recognition of patterns. For humanity, war is the rule and peace is the exception, so we've had to take notice of the symbols and appearances of our enemies. I'm thinking it's hardwired.

If you see a hundred people dressed in black running around a street that's lined with several burning buildings, but your eye had only seen a dozen of them with bottles and bricks in their hands, why would it be wrong to guess that the others might have been participating in the destruction just a second beforehand? You say, "they probably were" or "they might have been"; not, "only the dozen or so who I personally saw, and I won't entertain the possibility that some of the others were also complicit."

Try to view it another way: Somewhere on that burning street, there's someone wearing a helmet and camouflage. Suddenly, that person grabs somebody on the street and throws them into a car. Apparently, this has been happening in Portland. Now, if a libertarian were the first person to see those images, they'd shriek. Their first reaction would be one of outrage. Cries of "martial law" will be shouted for days.

And while the presumption is probably correct—that the official who physically removed the peaceful protester was and is a government actor—it's not obvious that said-strong-armed actions are necessarily unlibertarian, as an anarcho-capitalist society would respond to the chaos by encouraging shop owners to pool their resources and employ a private police force so as to protect their properties.

Likely, such a society would see a lot more rioters thrown into the back of buses. Of course, the only legitimate objective would be to grab or stop those who were seen destroying businesses, and any deviation from that goal would allow for legal action. (That an anarcho-capitalist society would also see every street and sidewalk privatized—not tolerating even those walking in the middle of the road—does complexify the problem a lot more. And so let's stick to the real world, and the fact that many businesses and institutions employ private security, or bravely defend their own property; see the McCloskeys).

Finally, if you were a business owner in the market for private armies, you would not pick a firm that had trained its soldiers to refrain from making collective judgments. You'd want those who were protecting your property to be vigilant of the many anonymous faces found as the Black Bloc. After all, that's the very tactic of these minor-terrorists: *All as one, and none as all.*

Again, that does not mean that the private army could indiscriminately grab whomever they wished. They'd have to have reasonable assurance that the one they're launching into the back of a bus had actually thrown the bottle.

Still, as I said, the presumption above is granted, as the officers in Portland are, in fact, agents of the federal state. Furthermore, the general criticism among the masses, which in my opinion is now only given as a pretense—that America's police forces often abuse an authority which was never properly given to them—is, in my view, and my experience, accurate. And so it's important that we discuss the other side of the spectrum.

IV

I don't know anybody who saw the video of George Floyd getting choked to death who did not believe it to be anything less than cold-blooded murder.

For those of us who recognize the existence of the so-called Blue Line culture, whereby police protect their own, we have to wonder: If that deadly encounter had happened on a dark street, and the video not captured by a civilian, would the police have faced criminal repercussions? Would they be charged and tried in a court of law? For we who say the term aloud—American Police State—we know accountability is not guaranteed.

After one has been abused so many times by the police,

your perspective of them changes. They begin to take on the appearance, not of noble and rational defenders of our rights (whether understood divinely, constitutionally, or culturally), but rather as a cold and blunt object.

Although this object is oftentimes wielded by corrupt lawmakers, it always has its own interests at heart. That isn't to say that all police are abusive; nor to suggest that no officer ever signed on simply because they wanted to make their community a better and safer place. I certainly won't be making the case that America's overwhelmed prisons are full of nonviolent pot smokers.

Not at all.

But power is what collectivizes America's police. It's what binds them. No matter how well-intentioned the individual officer is, they wield an authority which one-hundred years ago was regarded as unconstitutional. And the routine abuse of that power, with nary an instance in which "good" officers turn in their abusive partners, leading to disconcerting lack of accountability, is what makes it easy to throw out the whole batch as being rotten.

This power is awarded both by the federal government and the state governments: The Supreme Court, and their individual state unions, respectively.

We often hear the term "qualified immunity." Cornell Law School has a summary of all the Supreme Court rulings that granted such power. "Specifically, qualified immunity protects a government official from lawsuits alleging that the official violated a plaintiff's rights, only allowing suits where officials violated a 'clearly established' statutory or constitutional right," reads the website.

It's possible to sue an officer, but the Supreme Court has set the hurdle very high, and they have no desire to lower it.

Then there's unionism. While some police departments condemned the killing of George Floyd, the President of the

Minneapolis Police Union, Lt. Bob Kroll, wrote a letter to union members, denouncing the "despicable behavior" of political leaders who Kroll said were betraying the city's police.

Such language is familiar in a society whereby police unions shield their members from scrutiny. In New York, there was a long battle to "repeal 50-A," a state law that prohibited the public from attaining records of police misconduct. Efforts to overturn the law and release the records were repeatedly blocked by both the union and Governor Cuomo, who eventually gave in to the recent street pressure and signed the repeal legislation.

Nationwide corruption? JacobinMag.com reports on the work of scholars who have documented how police unions in California, Florida, and Texas have challenged efforts to "change sentencing laws, abolish solitary confinement, outlaw capital punishment, close prisons and jails, end commercial bail, and on and on."

My criticism of the rioters and looters is not meant to suggest that are no peaceful protesters. I'm sure there are many just expressing their grievances and demanding necessary reform.

That *is* their right.

And, of course, the police have abused those demonstrators too. Who can forget the video of New York officers shoving 75-year-old Martin Gugino to the ground, his head gushing blood as the gang calmly walked past his limp body? After two officers were charged for it, the entire fifty-seven-member unit resigned in protest. That's not unionism; that's brotherhood, and the abuses are not far and few between. *USAToday* found that "at least" 85,000 American police officers have been investigated over the past decade. To repeat myself: For many of us—no matter if we have black skin or white skin—these things are anything but shocking.

To someone like Patrick Lynch, head of New York's

largest police union, reform advocates are "pro-criminal." What Lynch will never admit is that when police beat up civilians, plant evidence on suspects, lie on reports, and use their badge to pressure women into performing sexual acts—they are *also* criminals. And the public is right to say as much.

V

Ammon Bundy might wish for "unity" and "coming together," but he should know that many of the activists he now aligns with will continue to see him as a privileged white man who was allowed to take over a federal institution without being killed for it.

Such ideological fault lines are ready to burst, and so it's time for Americans to start doing their own seismology—to try and measure the hatred and find out where the cracks are at. Social media provides an opportunity to conduct small, private polls. I can think of a few questions to get us all started.

For example: Is it not generally true that those now raging against police abuse were just recently praising the police as they arrested hairstylists who defied the lockdown? Did they not also praise the St. Louis prosecutors when they charged the McCloskeys with felonies, this for brandishing weapons at a horde of protesters that came through their property? Amend the poll: Do you *really* think the couple had no reason to fear for their lives and home? Could you honestly tell the McCloskeys that they had no reason to fear that the mob might destroy their property, especially since that mob falsely believed that the mayor lived at the address?

If you try to argue that police also murder white people— a la Duncan Lemp or, more recently, Ryan Whitaker—will their deaths be downplayed as rare exceptions? What if you aren't checking your white privilege as compulsively as an impatient man checks his watch? Moreover, will those who post any story about a white person being racist neglect to post when a young white woman is murdered by Black Lives Matter activists (her name was Jesse Whitaker)? What about a white 5-year-old boy? Not a peep, I imagine. Ditto for CNN and MSNBC.

It's our right to assemble peacefully, they assert correctly, so was that right granted for the white nationalists who went to Charlottesville? Were they screaming about how the rates of COVID-19 would skyrocket because of the anti-lockdown protests, only then to change their tune once these protests took off?

Will you or I still be an "ally" if we were to say something totally outlandish, like "woman don't have penises," or "the doctrine of Islam is not one of peace"? Such truthful claims will seem controversial whenever there exists a market for mistruth.

And then for the rightists on your friend list, another series of inquiries: When a civilian is killed by the police, are they quick to smear their character while ignoring the record of the officers responsible for the killing? Do they ever discuss any mysterious death at the hands of law enforcement, such as Elijah McClain and Breonna Taylor?

After all, conservatives insist that it's "only a few bad apples." Then why should they have a problem discussing those apples and bringing their abuses to light?

If they had done so, they probably could have prevented some of this chaos.

VI

We should not be forced to choose between America's overpowered police and those cosplaying as Che Guevara. If the latter ever got in control, they'd become just like the former, and so it's possible to take another position: The one that refuses to side with anybody's violence.

While I try to be realistic in my analysis, I'm *unrealistic* in my objectives, because I want nothing more than a world that cherishes reason, nonviolence, and peace—and, in my view, that won't be happening anytime soon. I am a misanthrope *before* a libertarian. I'm not fetched by any talk of "liberty in our lifetime." Such rhetoric is just plain silly to me. Human beings are many hundreds if not thousands of years away from that point. In short, a lot more evolving has to take place, and neither cops nor rioters are going to help us get there.

Unfortunately, the natural evolution of humans will likely be cut short by *un*naturally evolved humans, those who have upgraded with technology. What these metahumans will do to our kin will leave us begging to be choked to death on the street, if only to spare us the horror of it. Assuming we stand any chance against that grim scenario, I will continue to help evolution progress.

My "tactic" is to advocate for dialogue, voluntarism, and nonviolence: dialogue with those I strongly disagree with; voluntarism not only in the sense of *coming together*, but also *going apart*; and nonviolence where it matters the most— the next generation, who are the only ones capable of creating a world with little need for these violent gangs.

(August 2020)

Information as Immortality, Data as Damnation

WHAT WENT THROUGH the mind of the first primate that realized its body would soon decay and die? Likely, that fear found itself into our very DNA, something horrific but true which must immediately be screamed about at the top of the nearest mountain.

Even if lesser-evolved animals share with us the ability to understand their own mortality, could they build upon that epiphany, to then conjure up ideas of an afterlife, a standing legacy, a lineage that stretches far past the sunset? An animal that can envision the world in which their offspring's offspring will one day live is an animal indeed worthy of great respect!

Are we privileged or hindered in our distinct capacity to project ever-forward? Knowing of one's mortality can instill a sense of lazy fatalism, a "what's the point?" attitude, leading to thoughts of "god's grand design" or a "just making my way to the coffin" outlook; or, sometimes, it can give rise to think of a more permanent existence.

The monuments of the past would strongly suggest that mankind has attempted to make its own timestamp on eternity, all those efforts to be remembered forever. With some seeing themselves as literal gods, those ideas of "forever" resulted in forms of suffering and hardship that is hard to calculate. No pyramid or skyscraper gets erected any other way. The only ones more ambitious than Kings, Pharaohs, and Corporatists are those who wish to count the bodies underneath their gold-plated soles.

Mother Earth always proves to be a challenging obstacle. Ice ages, rainfalls, and seismic shifts were constantly throwing blows. Worse, the cosmos also liked to take swipes at earth's many species. It's believed that an asteroid hit earth 66 million years ago, destroying three-quarters of life on earth. Surely the would-be Gods of flesh considered such possibilities when they reached for the clouds.

The clouds?

Archaeologists, astronomers, scientists of all stripes, as well as UFO hunters imbued with the most credulity, would all love to find evidence of extraterrestrial intelligence. How exhilarating it is to think that just on the other side of the moon, the so-called eternal darkspot, hides some bubble, inside of which houses a community of gray-skinned, bug-eyed humanoids, who like to enjoy their space beverages while having a laugh at our collective ignorance.

I'll accept two premises as true. 1.) Although other lifeforms probably do exist in the universe, the proof for such intelligence has not been found—for if it had, it would by now have been uncovered and thus widely disseminated. And 2.) We have not only fired rockets and satellites out past our atmosphere, but we have also placed such technologies onto other astral bodies. If these are both correct, it means that our civilization is already more advanced than any that came before. No pharaoh or king ever accomplished such a feat.

For anyone curious about Information—what it is, how it's stored, and where it ultimately goes—this advancement in technology has terrifying implications. Because if we can place some beacon or satellite down on the moon, or have it situated far off in space, it would theoretically be spared from any earth-destroying catastrophes.

Now, think back to your life: How many things have you done that you wish you had not? As humans evolved, so has our sense of morality. Right and Wrong are matters explored in great depth, and we have often fallen short on our proclaimed principles. Consequently, most of us are plagued with the fantasy of going back in time and redoing certain choices from our past. Regret is an integral part of the human experience.

But even the most cynical could find some solace in knowing that, one day, far off into the future—or maybe sooner than that—our earth will witness another erasure, that which would destroy any memory of our misdeeds. Nobody would ever know about that kid you bullied in school, nor the name of the person you cheated on your spouse with. The murdered and murderer, the raped and the rapist, the burglarized and the burglar—all of these will be equalized in their nothingness, never a trace that any of them ever even existed.

While the evildoer could suddenly find relief, the few who called Christ's bluff and happily cast their stones find themselves despondent. The crimes of the higher-evolved are never to be forgotten, so says the Almighty and the Perfect. Not even oblivion should save the wicked and the godless! Our experiences, victimizations, and vices would have become nothing more than a faint flash in the infinite vastness of space.

Only in that primitive scenario would an alien explorer find it difficult to diagnosis the ills of the human psyche. If the latest asteroid had hit a hundred years ago, oblivion might have saved us, as the only evidence of our crimes would have been shards of earth rumble. "What made a Homo sapiens?" would then be much harder to deduce.

But that opportunity has passed.

"In the beginning," so the bible begins, "there was the Word"; but the words themselves were chiseled into rock, and with great labor carried through oral histories. As with morals and tradition, the ability to communicate evolved along with us. Communication is what gives us the advantage over the lesser-evolved; the need to speak and to write is therefore innate and reflexive.

No surprise, then, when we see the masses waiting in line to get the latest I-Phone, nor as they bury their faces in the screen, typing their Very Important Words on small buttons. Indeed, in the modern age, as the art of prose becomes ever more remote, words are all too abundant. We make sentences, not out of necessity, but out of compulsion.

And the words are no longer contained as an echo in the desert canyon; now they bounce through technologies far away from us. We search online for our desires, let cameras capture our expressions, and pay no attention as governments and corporations continue to store and harness such information. Even if towers turn to ash, many of the records and blueprints will still be digitalized. What a data overload!

With this, we discover the real Inferno of the technological age: the impossibility for one to obliviate, for its entirely plausible that such electronic data is also being transmitted to satellites in space and drones on the moon—if not at present, then soon.

With these thermospheric data collecting systems, we become the extraterrestrials. And if the earth below does explode, the data will still be safely held—ready to be studied by lifeforms not yet known to us. Our criminal allegations, perverted conversations, and strange searches—all that data will help those lifeforms to draw a more perfect image of humanity. We'll be remembered until that civilization too is destroyed, and by then what will they have done in terms of preservation? In this material realm, that's as close to *forever* as I can imagine.

At last, the would-be gods of flesh witness a kind of immortality. Might we ask: Is this state of being Heaven? Or is it Hell? Is our preservation as mass data something to fear, or to embrace? Will it compel us to behave less violently and more rationally?

Realistically, not every document in every institution will be digitalized. People who live on the outskirts and refuse to put their most personal information online will likewise be spared from analysis by our hypothetical aliens. Should the rest of us keep happily producing that data?

Or should we try to evade immorality, and thus avoid a damnation which would have us scrutinized long after our earthly demise?

(October 2020)

Resisting Medical Fascism

THE GOVERNOR OF California, Gavin Newsom, recently signed an executive order adding the COVID vaccine to the list of inoculations required to attend public school. Newsom's dictatorial pen stroke was preemptive, as the vaccine is not yet even approved for children under the age of 12.

The expected approval date, per Newsom's official website, is hoped to be sometime between January 2022 and July 2022. Then, it becomes the first state in the nation to make it mandatory for kids "K-12." Before then, I can only pity the luckless high schoolers.

All across the country, medical freedom is being trampled upon and California is happy to lead the way.

The Los Angeles City Council went further than San Francisco which passed vaccine mandate legislation back in August.

In either of those two major cities, if you want to walk through practically any door—be it restaurants, gyms, theaters, or shopping centers—you will be asked to show proof that you've been vaccinated. (It's something that still needs to be answered: How many businesses are doing this by their own volition, and how many are doing so under pressure from the state?)

I consider myself a refugee from California, having recently resettled—happily—in Arizona. I refer to my former native state as the Pyrite State, because California is no land of gold.

Rather, it is full of high-class tyrants and low-level criminals, neither of which care about the rights of parents, business owners, or taxpayers. Too many otherwise decent people, who could move if they wished to, choose instead to tolerate those abusive policies. It's full of fools, thus comprised of pyrite.

My family chose differently, and we truly feel like we've dodged a bullet. It is so very nice to breath freely, never having to worry about some maniac screaming at you for not wearing a mask.

But being a paranoid of a different sort, I can't help but worry: what about the rest of the world, or at least here in America? What about my new state? As it is, an Arizona judge just struck down Governor Ducey's ban on mask mandates, so now we're waiting to see if the schools are going to make us suffocate our children.

Elsewhere, we find President Joe Biden, who's barely able to string together a coherent sentence (it's meant as no offense to the elderly, but senility is common for that age group), but still somehow manages to lie as only a career politician can.

In December of 2020, Biden said there would be no such mandates. Now he's instructed his labor department to give a citation to any business (with more than 100 employees) that refuses to force the injection upon their staff, or else subject them to weekly testing.

Of course, the diktat compels all businesses in the nation, accounting for some 80 million people.

While getting his COVID booster shot, Biden was asked how many Americans need to get vaccinated. His answer: "Look...I think...we need to get the vast majority...like some industries, some schools...97, 98 percent."

There are a couple scandals running concurrently here.

For one thing, because the CDC stopped tracking "breakthrough cases" earlier this year, we have no idea how effective the vaccine really is.

And while we keep hearing that the vaccinated are far less likely to contract the virus, anecdotal stories and reports strongly suggest otherwise. A bunch of fully-vaxxed democrats who took a drip to DC got it. Israel's population is highly vaccinated, and their infection rates seem to be through the roof. Then there's the prison in Texas, where a whopping 70% of fully-vaxxed inmates also contracted the virus. Doesn't seem like a very effective vaccine at all.

And this is on top of the other scandal: the absolute refusal to acknowledge *natural immunity*. Because the COVID tests have never been reliably accurate, we still can't be sure how many people—both in this country, and around the world—have recovered from the virus. Despite these people having stronger and longer-lasting immunity, the bile-inducing huckster named Anthony Fauci continues to insist that they too receive the vaccine.

Fauci is no more a scientist than Newsom is a leader. Both play important roles in what Klaus Schwab calls The Great Reset, which is basically a restructuring of the entire world. And you? You're nothing more than a cog in the machine.

Be quiet and do as you're told.

For this we must resist.

We who believe in medical freedom and the right to control our own bodies (Yes, I alone will include the right to evict a fetus from your womb), must find the courage to say *enough!* Businesses that have mandates should be boycotted. Legislators who pass vaccine mandates should be replaced by ones who won't. Meanwhile, we must make use of all such exemptions, be it religious or personal. (Thankfully, some exemption clauses remain in California's mandates).

If there's any way out of this, it only comes after we've rediscovered our backbones.

(October 2021)

Protesting Medical Fascism, in Phoenix and Beyond

On Wednesday, Nov. 3, there was a rally in downtown Phoenix, which I've only recently learned is the capital of my new state, Arizona. The rally was hashtagged with "Stop the Mandate," and was yet another gathering of freedom-loving Americans who are pushing back against this emerging medical fascism. In brief, this is a dictatorship in which the federal state (and, if Klaus Schwab gets his way, the global state) can forcibly inject you, and me, and our kids, with an experimental vaccine.

There are many people, ordinary and unexceptionable like me, who will not stand for it. The scaremongering, as per all good propaganda, is only a pretense for more sinister intentions.

It's unnecessary anyway, what with new treatments being developed and made available. There are also the masses who have recovered from the virus, thus conferring on them lasting immunity, with no need for anything more than that. Scandalously, they've been ignored. Then tell us, pray, why does everyone, from St. Fauci, to a recent massive study done by a Harvard professor, to even the lizardman himself, Bill Gates, all say—or might that be concede?—that the vaccine is a total failure at stopping transmission?

This is an intrusion into our privacy as well as an insult to our intelligence.

At the end of it, we don't wish to bequeath to our children a world in which they'll be forced to get a booster shot every six months, proof of which to be shown every time they enter school, or a restaurant, or an entertainment venue; or, most frighteningly, the emergency room, where we might have to rush them if they happen to develop myocarditis. Could we imagine a long line of bodies, both young and old, all waiting to get admitted into the hospital, but who all must first prove their vaccination status, only minutes before insisting that very thing as the cause of their health crisis?

Not counting all the bots on Twitter, everyone else who argues in favor of these scenarios would do well to reread their favorite dystopian novel. Only an optimist—which I am not—would have the slightest bit of hope that a ton of irony would drop down upon their conscience and awaken them as to what they're helping to usher in.

I wanted—do want—to help awaken the masses. And the protest scene is where I'm in my element. No need to think too hard as to my angle. I am, after all, a refugee from the state of California. My former state seems to have the most draconian restrictions in the whole nation, which is something I can certainly testify to.

So, the night before the rally, I went over to Walmart to get supplies so as to make my own personalized protest sign. I bought a white poster-board and some red nylon rope: a message to be hung around my neck, leaving my hands free to give out business cards, or perhaps use my bullhorn (it wouldn't be useful at a rally this small). The first side was easy. It read: "Resist Medical Fascism!" I added a little syringe with a skull, filled with green liquid.

Cute and quant, but in the end, too simple and mundane. The other side was sloppier but was more aligned with my unique position: "I Didn't Escape California Just to Deal with the Same Shit Over here." Perfect!

The protest was scheduled to begin at 1:00 PM. I arrived fifteen minutes after the hour, never having been to this side of town. Took a left on Jefferson. Up 17th. Then I saw the crowd on my right-hand side, across from what I assumed to be the capitol building. There, the signs and the canopies; and just beyond those was the large, mostly empty parking lot. I circled the block and pulled in, parking my car at the far back edge of the lot.

I took the backpack with my bullhorn, but I likely would not use it, as that noisy thing is usually reserved for crowds of nearly a thousand. I packed water and business cards. Locked up the machine. Finally, I hung the sign around my neck, with the side indicating my refugee status facing out. While I didn't figure this crowd as being partial towards victimhood, I still might be able to invoke some sympathy. "Native Californian…it's really bad over there…we barely made it…could be traumatized for life…don't let it happen over here."

The tears would gush, I was sure!

Walking over, I asked the first person I came up to if it was readable. He laughed and said it was. It was the first of many laughs I'd be greeted with. By my guess, there were a couple hundred people here. I spent the next three hours doing laps around the park, meeting the attendees, and handing out cards.

There were representatives from Robert Kennedy's Children's Health Defense, the Pima County Libertarian Party, The Patriot Party, The Arizona Coalition of School Board Members, and EZAZ, a grassroots organization of which I have recently become a member.

If one of the speakers had caught my attention, I'd go over and listen. I once again neglected to make any notes or recordings myself, but thankfully an activist named Tzadik recorded the entire program. Tzadik, for his part, recently started an organization named EarthWalk which, as the name implies, plans on organizing several long, awareness-raising walks in all the states.

The woman from Children's Health Defense, whose name I didn't catch, was organizing the list of speakers. She spoke first. "If COVID vaccine shot were a perfect vaccine, one that was perfectly effective, and perfectly safe, it should still never be mandated."

Indeed!

Dru Heaton with the Pima County Libertarian Party admonished libertarians who felt that private businesses could make their own rules regarding vaccination. "That is BS," she said to loud applause. "It is actually statism that is allowing you to open your business, or it will shut you down." I was a bit confused by this statement and am still without a firm position as to whether the individual states should be allowed to tell businesses what to do.

Merissa Hamilton, cofounder of EZAZ, gave one of her fiery and impassioned speeches. When she mentioned that we were fighting for "parental rights," I initiated that round of applause. Of course, who else ought to be in control of our public schools? But when she asserted that those who don't vote—and presumably, vote for Republicans—are "contributing to totalitarianism," I offered a quiet "boo," unbelieving of the idea that the ballot contains all meaningful power and influence.

Surely, the people can do more than just drive over to the voting booth, as Mr. Tzadik intends to prove. Tzadik plans on walking from Sedona to the US-Mexico border, and then back to Phoenix, by which time he'll have some two million people in tow.

Electorate need not apply!

During and in between the speeches, I was making laps around the small gathering, stopping several times so as to talk with someone new. My sign proved popular, with a dozen or more people requesting to snap a picture of it. "I'm a refugee from the pyrite state," I'd say, striking up conversation. They'd ask what part, and I'd tell "outside LA, in the county." I was not the only one who had fled the state, but most of the others had done so years earlier, when they first saw the storm clouds gathering. Then I'd tell them I'm a correspondent for Stairway Press, handing out a card.

A guy named Doug told me that Phoenix and the larger valley are home to the largest concentration of 5G towers in the whole country. Even with no real knowledge of 5G, knowing only of the fears held by many others, a natural paranoid as myself would quiver upon learning of that fact—not that I needed anything more to add to my anxiety. Well, my ideal home wasn't Arizona anyway; I wanted a cabin up in Montana or Idaho.

But Arizona is home. And it's a relief living in a place where there's so many people who readily acknowledge the horror that humanity is now staring down. No need to hassle my neighbors about the need for medical freedom; perhaps just to educate them a bit about The Great Reset.

In California, life is already hell: the prices, the traffic, the fires, the oppressive policies. But none of these, save for the Antifa/BLM riots of last year, have riled up Californians *en masse*. It wasn't until the vaccine mandates that Californians found themselves backed into a corner, only then able to feel their spine against the wall. Now we watch and read as literally thousands have taken a stand against the mandates—workers, students, parents, police, and firefighters. Look at the schools, as waves of students and parents walk out and away from them. I would be lying if I said that I wasn't a bit shocked. Yet I was proud. How encouraging! Maybe I won't have to wait until California turns to ruins before I decide to move back.

And it's not just my two familiar states: uprisings are

happening all over the world. Elsewhere, we have surreptitious striking by those employed with Southwest Airlines. In Australia, where medical fascism has already hit an apogee, there's been clashes between the people and the police. Similar scenes are seen in Italy and New York.

So loud have these dissident voices become that's its nigh impossible not to hear them.

If you can't hear it, nor see it, certainly you can *feel it*. Aside from street clashes and rallies, all family gatherings, workplace settings, and checkout lanes have borne witness as to what is happening. This is most unlike day-to-day "politics"; you don't usually start talking about who or what you'll soon be voting for, even if those choices affect others.

Tax policies are something complained about in private; but vaccine mandates are experienced in a manner that is much more tangible and immediate. This in turn induces feelings of despair, right before rage and anger.

Tapping into this generalized resentment is like taking a sharp knife to a large water balloon: you can't miss, and the result will be dramatic. One will see how much relief their neighbor gets when they realize they're not alone in this fight.

Hopelessness fades, if only a little bit.

Besides, it could be an opportunity to find common ground with people whose face you would've before spat at. Who knows, together we might just stand a chance of putting a stop to it.

(November 2021)

Littering in California

IN MANY PARTS of California, the streets and sidewalks are piled high with garbage. As it is my hometown state, I should know. On a heavy day, a relaxing walk can quickly turn into one in which you're dodging debris almost at random. You might find yourself jumping over cartons and dried dogshit, while trying not to let that food wrapper coil itself around your calf.

If one stood on a high spot above downtown Los Angeles, they might mistake the city for the world's largest landfill.

Suppose you're inside of this landfill, and with trash in hand. The natural thing to do would be to throw the trash on the ground right below your feet. The action would be as carefree as if you had walked up to a waste container.

This perception stems not only from the experience of living and sloshing and mucking through these streets; indeed, studies show that some of the dirtiest cities in the US can be found in California.

So, if you were so convinced that you were inside of a

genuine landfill, the urge to throw your trash on the ground would likely be forgiven by everyone unpersuaded by delusionary labels, like that of the Golden State.

Of course, California is neither a "golden state" nor a giant landfill. Instead, it's a semi-Communistic hellhole, as well as being an enervated limb on the body of America. Luckily, I've recently fled that horrible place, making for the greener and freer (and hotter) pastures of Arizona. But, alas, every month I must make a weekend-long return to my former state, per court orders.

For years, living in California, I've been an avid litterer. It's a bit of a reflex. I didn't really think of it at all, aside from the quickest of glances to see if the police were around. It's done with such ease: trash in hand; trash on the ground; walk or drive away. And my conscience doesn't ring with the faintest twinge of guilt.

However, recently my littering habit has been much more deliberate—something I do as an act of rebellion, disgust, and hatred. Since I can't burn the whole state down, the most I can do is saturate the streets with my wrappers, bags, and bottles.

In the back of my mind, I believe that every little scrap gets me that much closer to seeing the state's total downfall. So instead of merely tossing the trash casually onto the ground, these days I throw it down fiercely, as though I were bludgeoning the whole society with my refuse.

Immature?

Sure, it is, but such are the times we're living in, when decorum, likewise, has also been discarded down the gutter.

As an addict, I can rationalize my habit several different ways. For instance, soon after making the move, I would always ceremoniously toss a few items out my window immediately upon crossing the border.

But now I figure that: nobody would see it in the desert. There's so little out here; small towns and trucker outposts.

And why blemish land that has yet to be desecrated by the building of metropolises? Therefore, I now wait until I arrive in the counties of, first San Bernardino, and then Los Angeles. Then the trash flows out of my windows as if the garbage collector had forgotten to close his container.

This compromise was still met with disapproval. My family didn't like it. Friends on Facebook and in real life both offered strong criticisms. Impenitently, I would then resort to charging them with bigotry, telling them that, as a native Californian, this was just part of my culture. "How dare you insult my culture!" I would retort.

It's said that all cultures should be respected, so why not California culture?

But my critics do have one valid point: my trash does not stay in the gutters and streets; it flows out into the ocean—the Pacific Ocean, for those who have never seen a map. And what do the fish have to do with my private beef?

Unlike sewage—what goes down your sinks and toilets— stormwater is not treated or cleaned. One can think of "stormwater" every time you look underneath a curb and see a storm drain: what goes down there eventually ends up in the ocean. The onus to keep it free of debris, therefore, is on...well, me. And you. And the homeless guy you just saw, whose condition you'll blame on capitalism. After all, when the homeless litter, it's only a chain reaction stemming from external circumstances far out of our control.

Depressing facts also start adding up.

In 2016, the United States generated the most waste in the whole world. According to a report by the Associated Press about a study published in Science Advances, between 2.7% and 5.3% of that waste was mismanaged—"not burned, placed in landfills or otherwise disposed of properly."

Plastic products seem to be the focus here, because, while plastic is ostensibly recyclable, many plastic products never get recycled. Yet we live in a plastic world. Plastic—which is oil—is ubiquitous and is perhaps why the average person consumes thousands of plastic particles every year.

The same study in *Science Advances* estimated that some 560,000 to 1.6 million tons of U.S. plastic waste "likely" finds its way into our oceans, making the U.S. the third worst "plastic polluter."

The U.S. used to export a great deal of its plastic waste over to China, but a few years back, the Chinese prohibited dirty plastics to scale back its own pollution. Now we're trying to dump our trash onto Malaysia, Thailand, and Vietnam, according to the SierraClub.

All this garbage has to led to the freakish creation known as the Great Pacific Garbage Patch, a massive island of trash, twice the size of Texas, which floats adrift in our oceanic beyond. This is a monstrous testament to mankind's endless producing and consuming and disposing.

As for my homestate, communities in California try to do their part by spending roughly half a million dollars a year—collectively—to clean up the streets and gutters, per a 2013 report by the Natural Resources Defense Council.

Guilt at last: I participated in the destruction of the ecosystem! Yet no matter how much Californians are bilked, their tax dollars will never buy a shovel or mop large enough to clean up all the trash they throw on the ground.

So, again, the responsibility is largely on us, the public. Suddenly, the adage echoes in my mind like an empty beer can tossed down an alley: "Be the change you wish to see in the world." This means bettering oneself, which is right in line with my brand of anarchism.

Well, believe me when I tell you that I have not littered one single time in my new state. This is because I have respect for Arizona, the streets of which are comparatively cleaner. It's a different class of citizens, I reason. Then why can't I help myself in California? Why does the "imaginary line" turn me into a Mr. Hyde? The gutters almost cry out for my garbage.

The state is just so moribund. Leaving trash on these streets is a lot like taking the wristwatch off the corpse of your worst enemy. I could try to control myself, but even if I had properly disposed of my trash, it would make no dent in the damage that's already done.

So, who should start cleaning California up? As mentioned, the homeless situation in California is dreadful, as the state has the third highest rate of homelessness in the country. Homeless encampments are notorious for their abundance of garbage, and if the authorities and green thumbs really cared about the littering issue, they would want to clean out those many encampments.

Heartlessness! Heresy! Those are human beings!

Where would we put them?

I'm unsure, but wherever it is, it would likely be cheaper than what we're currently spending on cleaning up the oceans.

In fact, the effort seems to be the inverse: that they're trying to produce more waste in the streets. Consider the mask mandates. When the pandemic started, California was one of the first to implement lockdowns—and mask mandates. Two years later, masks are still required for most indoor settings.

The results? No need for Sherlockian powers of deduction. Disposable facemasks are now found all over the coastal regions.

A December 2021 report from EcoWatch tells us that "disposable face masks littered in the environment increased by nearly 9,000 percent from March to October 2020." The masks, too, are made from plastic. Some 29,000 tons of this stuff is estimated to be floating in the world's oceans. Don't be surprised if Anthony Fauci tells us that those masks are helping to keep the sealife safe from the virus.

"Then just throw your masks in the trashcan," I'll then hear. If masks have any utility whatsoever—which I now doubt—then they should probably be worn once and then thrown away.

Imagine how many masks one would go through in a day or a week. Has the state unleashed an army of mask-collectors onto the streets?

I don't think it has.

If it's inconvenient for them to pick it up, it's more convenient for me to throw it down. Likewise, for everyone else.

Maybe I'll just start identifying as a homeless man.

That way all my littering will be excused.

(January 2022)

Inflation, a 40-Year High

JUST A FEW short years ago, when one went to a gas station, one could see the happy or at least content faces of people at the pump filling up their tanks. The Trump presidency, for all its drama and guffaws, oversaw steady gas prices that usually stayed between $2.25 and $3.00.

During the worst days of the pandemic, gas prices occasionally dropped down to a buck-fifty; when people are not allowed to go anywhere, they won't be needing much gasoline. Then the faces became a half-smile: the total was cheap, though whatever you saved would have to be carefully rationed, as meals and mortgages were no longer a sure thing.

Today, in the middle of 2022, the faces are not sad; they're angry. Not only must people go to work, they must also pay nearly double for the gasoline needed to get them there. And it's not just gasoline, either. *Inflation Hits Four Decades High*, the headlines read as we angrily crumple up the grocery receipt. The Washington Post "fact checks" the latest bad news out of the Labor Department. By their estimate, the Consumer Price Index (measuring prices) had risen to 8.5 percent, "the fastest 12-month pace since 1981." High food prices are felt nearer to the stomach, but it's the eyes that catch those digitalized numbers right above the pump.

"It's criminal!" you can sometimes hear from the other side of the station. Make the first grunt that it's "Biden's fault!" and see what happens. And below those digitalized numbers, one can sometimes find a sticker—placed there by some guerilla activist—which features President Biden pointing dumbly: "I did that." Indeed, I might've posted one or two of these stickers myself.

But is that true? Is the Biden administration to blame for this inflation? For these gas prices? Plenty of people—including those in the administration—have had their turn at spreading the blame. If they can confuse and obfuscate, it's all the better. Likely, we're just seeing corrupt, dishonest, war-thirsty politicians doing what they do.

On June 10th, Biden addressed these issues. As if at the hip, the President blamed Russia. Biden has even tried to hashtag the "Putin Price Hike" into the language. He then congratulated himself for reducing the deficit. Then more blaming, now with the supply chain; but he can fix it, just need to make it easier to move things along. Next on his list of scapegoats was some nine shipping companies ("foreign-owned," Biden said, summoning his predecessor) that have recently raised prices one-thousand-percent, in the process making 190 billion in profit.

Putin-controlled Russia is the easiest to blame. Putin is state enemy number one, a much-hated warmonger, and so a little extra hatred won't be noticed. Or will it? Rick Newman at Yahoo News argues that the "Putin Price hike is real—and huge." But whatever argument Newman tries to make backfires the second he puts the blame, not on policies enacted by Russia, but on policies enacted by the U.S. To "punish Russia for its barbarity," Biden made sanctions, which "have cut into Russian sales, leaving a supply shortfall." Russia is also a major food exporter, but "while nobody is sanctioning food directly, financial sanctions are making it harder for Russia to export nearly everything." The headline alone would suggest that Putin is the one putting these sanctions on Russia.

Previously, Biden had placed partial blame on "the pandemic," which must necessarily follow using the word "virus." While viruses can infect the human body and replicate therein, viruses cannot operate the levers of government. Were the effects of COVID so lethal that it slowed down the supply chain by killing off those who ensure it runs smoothly? Or was it U.S. government policies that acted as the Red, White and Blue monkey wrench? The first seems unlikely.

Even Janet Yellen thinks the problem can be traced back to the second. In early June, the former Fed chair and current Treasury Secretary feigned ignorance (which is standard practice for Federal Reserve Chairmen) while taking her turn at blaming the Bear. Then, a couple weeks later, Business Insider reported that Yellen privately believed that the price hikes could be the result of "unexpected 'self-sanctioning.'" That is, companies that voluntarily stopped doing business with Russia, this out of fear that they might eventually run afoul of the sanctions. According to the same article, some in the Biden administration share this view, worrying that the sanctions are resulting not so much as a help to the Ukrainian resistance as they do a harm to the U.S. consumer.

And Russia does seem to be doing well. Gerald Dippao at the Center for Strategic & International Studies informs that Russia is still raking in some billion dollars a day from oil and gas exports, half of the proceeds going directly to Moscow. It's also said that what Russia isn't exporting to us is instead going to their other big trading partner: China.

One thing that Biden did not mention is the amount of new

paper that's been pumped into the economy. The president continues to deny the disastrous role played by the printing presses. Such an admission would not be good for the reelection campaign.

Biden's "America Rescue Plan," the "pandemic relief bill," totaled $1.9 trillion. Bill Clinton's Treasury Secretary, Lawrence Summers, a man who for his entire career has argued in favor of hyperactive printers, had nevertheless forecasted the incoming inflation as early as February 2021, with the primary "source in the massive fiscal stimulus of the COVID recession," so writes John Cochrane.

But that can't all be put on Biden. Number 45 did some stimulating too, as did a lot of other Republican politicians. That first "pandemic relief," signed in December of 2020, cost $2.3 trillion. Here, the blame can justifiably be attributed to both parties—both-aisleism if you will—which also came together to give many more billions in U.S. tax dollars to the Ukrainian resistance. It seems the U.S. treasury is nothing more than a piggybank; the U.S. taxpayer, as the hammer used to break it open.

One thing that Biden did get right is pointing out that other countries are also getting a "big bite" (his words) out of this inflation crisis. In other words, we're not the only ones who are suffering. "An analysis of inflation across 111 countries from Deutsche Bank puts the U.S. near the middle of the pack," writes Dave Lawler at Axios. That made me curious.

On June 14th, I participated in a webinar featuring representatives Thomas Massie and Chip Roy. Massie, a vocal opponent of out-of-control spending, tried to force the Congress to give a recorded vote for the first stimulus.

For that, he was properly chastised. I was allowed to ask several questions, only one of which reached the ears of the representatives. It was about the above, global inflation. While Massie retorted by saying that he gets asked this a lot by "Leftists on Twitter," he tacitly acknowledged the fact, admonishing us "not to point to other countries who did it worse," and warning that "printing money is going to cause pain and suffering."

Certainly! And as we've seen, my query was not meant to suggest that Biden is blameless. All countries have a central bank capable of conjuring up an endless supply of cash. Those mechanisms have been used for their own "pandemic relief." However, as far as the other contributor to inflation, it's the politicians in the U.S who have spearheaded the sanctions against Russia. Or, perhaps Putin's invasion did disrupt Ukraine's supply chain, as that country is also a major grain exporter. Why Putin felt the need to invade their neighbor and historical ally? That's a matter for another time.

Humbly admitting our own ignorance, we're just like the heads of the Fed, or even Paul Krugman: "We had *no idea* inflation was going to get this bad…it came out of nowhere…we're so sorry, but we'll get it right next time."

Others will see the outline of a larger project. After all, during his presidential campaign, Biden promised to "end fossil fuel." That might be a good thing, or it might be a bad thing, but it can't be *anything* without some sort of viable alternative in place before it happens.

Most damning was Biden's response when asked for how long we drivers, here and abroad, should expect to pay these exorbitant gas prices. The president: "As long as it takes…Russia cannot defeat Ukraine and move past Ukraine." It's good to know that the President of the United States has the backs of the Ukrainians—even if it breaks everyone else's back. If there's anyone to blame, voters will know who that is come election cycle.

(July 2022)

Happy News about Antidepressants

THAT MANY MILLIONS of people around the world have been prescribed dangerous drugs, with no beneficial effect whatsoever, has now found conclusive evidence of the fact. A recent peer-review metanalysis, published in *Molecular Psychiatry*, debunks the decades-old theory that depression is caused by a chemical imbalance in the brain—the key chemical being serotonin.

The lead author of the study, Joanna Moncrieff, says:

> ...*we can safely say that after a vast amount of research conducted over several decades, there is no convincing evidence that depression is caused by serotonin abnormalities, particularly by lower levels or reduced activity of the brain.*

This latest review included tens of thousands of people. Those with lower levels of serotonin did not fare any worse, psychologically, than those with higher levels of serotonin. Genes, likewise, played little to no role.

Tom Cruise, feeling vindicated, is probably somewhere jumping on a couch. During a 2005 interview with Matt Lauer, the megastar and scientologist expressed criticism of both medical theory and the companies that profit from pushing it.

While those clips now see new life on social media, we should keep in mind that Cruise wasn't the first or only person who said as much. For a couple years, I've been slowly making my way through a couple of Dr. Peter Breggin's volumes. Breggin, who is described as the "conscience of psychiatry," has been critical of these drugs for a long time. I'll be referring to him here.

The big news comes far too late for millions of others who already have a pill halfway down their throat. This class of drugs are called Selective Serotonin Reuptake Inhibitors, or SSRIs, which are intended to raise your levels of the chemical, thereby easing your depression.

According to the stack of articles I'm reading from, some research has even found that these pills *reduce* one's serotonin levels. *Not* so salubrious. It's so depressing that it might even lead to an increase in refilled prescriptions. All addicts are familiar with such a cycle.

It's said that some 80 percent of those surveyed believe in the "chemical imbalance" theory, resulting in worldwide bamboozlement. How did they all fall victim to the theory? It was probably less bamboozlement and more of mankind succumbing to its innate need to believe in something.

Daniel Carlat, a psychiatrist and the editor of the *Carlat Psychiatry Report,* gives support to that idea. In an interview, Carlat described the average conversation he'd have with one of his patients: "The reason you're depressed or anxious is that you have some sort of deficiency. And I say that (laughter recorded) not because I really believe it, because I know the evidence really isn't there for us to understand the mechanism—I think I say that because patients want to know something."

The person in the white coat wouldn't possibly lead you astray—just look at the credentials proudly displayed on that wall! (Interestingly, Wikipedia tells us Carlat is a critic of the current paradigm.)

As it is, doctors have a lot of practice with the "all in your head" line. Just ask someone who's suffered from chronic pain and they'll tell you about the number of doctors who've dismissed them in the same fashion. For psychiatrists, it's even more convenient. Suppose you do have a good doctor, and you're suspected of having a broken bone, then you'll get an X-ray; if it's a bad sinus infection, a CT scan; for liver disease, blood work.

No such diagnostic equivalent exists in the field of psychiatry. Therefore, "try this pill."

II

Side thoughts. The problem with meme culture, useful and humorous as it may be, is that it often opens one up to ridicule. Nowadays, whenever someone points out the dystopic thing, others immediately laugh at you for stating the obvious, or for being a nerd, or whatever. After all, Aldous Huxley's *Brave New World* came out in 1931. The premise of the novel involves a population that daily consumes a drug called "soma," which lets them forget about the general meaninglessness of their existence.

Almost thirty years later, Huxley wrote a lengthy afterward to his classic. In that, he explored the possibility that he would be proven right with his prediction, and that his nightmare of a painless but pointless society was being constructed faster than he had anticipated. He concluded that it was already almost here.

Since that initial publication of his book, there had been a "tidal wave of biochemical and psychopharmacological research." Huxley mentions the isolation of both adrenochrome and serotonin. As real-life somas, beer, tobacco, and amphetamines are crude and unreliable. "A more promising candidate for the role of soma," Huxley opined "…is Iproniazid." Iproniazid is considered the world's first antidepressant.

And how, Huxley wondered, would we get the population to take these pills? Simple: "In all probability it will be enough merely to make the pills available." Prediction made manifest! So *of course* this stuff is handed out like candy. It's not a secret, and so it's not a scandal. Cue the cheesy commercial featuring someone happily sliding down a large mound of, not dirty pebbles, but colorful pills. One can hardly watch a news program without being bombarded with a dozen such advertisements.

"That a dictator could, if he so desired, make use of these drugs for political purposes," felt Huxley, "is obvious." A properly numbed population won't protest when the government spends another half trillion of their money. It won't pay any mind when someone puts bizarre lesson plans into their child's school curricula. It will ignore the slow brewing of a new war. These things don't enter the thoughts of a man or woman who's been "emotionally blunted," to then borrow a phrase from Dr. Breggin.

III

Returning to Moncrieff's study, it would, as expected, find some critics. Psychiatrists Pies and Dawson (Dr.'s P&D from here on out) had seven "serious problems" with the study. I'm a journalist, not a scientist, and so I'll try my hand at a few of their points.

Dr.'s P&D reject the view that there's been "a full-blown theory of depression proposed by a monolithic entity called 'psychiatry,' asserting that depression is directly *caused* by abnormal levels of 1 or more neurotransmitters." They then quote psychiatrists Joseph Schildkraut—who is reported in the news as the man who first proposed the "chemical imbalance" theory—and his presumed partner, Seymour Kety, who make basically the same point.

Here it is in full:

> It should be emphasized...that the demonstration of...[a catecholamine] abnormality would not necessarily imply a genetic or constitutional, rather than an environmental or psychological, etiology of depression...it is equally conceivable that early experiences of the infant or child may cause enduring biochemical changes and that these may predispose some individuals to depressions in adulthood...[and] any comprehensive formulation of the physiology of affective state will have to include many other concomitant biochemical, physiological, and psychological factors.

Dr. P&D then tell us that their own review of medical textbooks and journals yielded exactly zero references to the "chemical imbalance" theory, at least none within the last thirty years. "Very few—if any—US psychopharmacologists and academic psychiatrists have ever endorsed a sweeping chemical imbalance theory of mood theory," they write.

Which is interesting.

I wonder if these statements are at odds with the current position of the American Psychiatric Association. One of the "risk factors," according to them, is: "Biochemistry: Differences in certain chemicals in the brain may contribute to symptoms of depression." As of this writing, that remains the first item listed on their website.

Reconfigure the words yourself. Is it an imbalance of only serotonin? Or a hugely complex neurological system, involving countless chemicals and transmitters, not working as harmoniously as they should? I don't know. And neither do the people who get paid handsomely for putting their names on studies and prescriptions.

Then Dr.'s P&D tell us what they really think. In brief, a lot of medications work wonders for people, and for many of them we have no idea exactly why that is.

In more technical words, "the mechanism of action" is unknown. To grant themselves more insurance, Dr.'s P&D add that such brain pills should be used cautiously and conservatively.

But that's a little *after the fact*, isn't it? As they know, the whole pharma program is a semitruck driving on a dark night with no headlights on.

Thankfully, "there is convincing evidence that most antidepressants are safe and at least modestly effective in the acute treatment of moderate-to-severe major depressive episodes." Dr. Breggin, and plenty more these days, would beg to differ.

For instance, Dr. Breggin long ago pointed out that antidepressants eventually replaced sedatives as the drugs most frequently involved in successful suicide attempts. "Obviously," Breggin wrote, "there is a built-in danger to giving such lethal drugs to depressed patients who have a high and unpredictable suicidal potential."

Powerful stuff, both the pills and the observation.

IV

As for the big study, Dr. Breggin would agree that it's nothing new. Way back in 1991, when he wrote his book *Toxic Psychiatry*, he reported on several studies that had the same nonexistent findings. "No causal relationship," he wrote, "has ever been established between a specific biochemical state of the brain and any specific behavior, and it is simplistic to assume it is possible."

Again, to this day that remains so.

One might notice I haven't even attempted an exact number of people taking these drugs. *Millions.* Worldwide, its probably nearer to a hundred million. Most disturbingly, this includes a lot of young children (I specify *young* children because I don't only mean 16- or 17-year-olds—I'm talking children in elementary school) who are also victims of the pharma-vortex. Dare I once again use the word dystopia? But then neither have I tried to estimate the billions in profit accrued from the abuse of these drugs.

My last point is a slight regret. The studies reviewed herein indicated that "stressful life events" had greatly contributed to someone developing depression. Just so.

But I've only focused here on antidepressants, and not depression itself, as that would require an entirely separate piece. Importantly, and as Dr. Breggin himself has stressed, someone currently taking these drugs should not simply stop taking them, as that very well could lead to painful and devastating withdrawal symptoms.

Instead, that person should seek help in carefully waning themselves off, hopefully with the help of a professional who can closely monitor their progress.

That this news might provide the incentive for someone to do that is, all in all, good news.

(August 2022)

On Jeffrey Tucker's Techno-Optimism

IT'S PERFECTLY fine to come to a different conclusion after looking at new evidence and considering other perspectives. Jeffrey Tucker has that same right, and he has exercised it. Starting in 2015, Tucker began warning of the threat of fascism that he felt was growing on the Right. Actually, some of us told him, and political parties aside, the real authoritarians were to be found *on the Left*. Let us not, we stressed, be fooled of that fact just because Donald Trump happens to like the police and national borders. When it came time, the animal-like spontaneity of the Left would be what was needed to enact and maintain authoritarian superstructures.

Our words of warning would be borne out during the lockdowns and mandates, which found their biggest cheerleaders on the Left. Careless acts of door-closing, cage-linking, arm-poking, and struggled breathing would be things championed by those who speak wildly about "civil rights." (No, that's not exactly fair, as I estimate some 500 temperature scans for myself over the last few years…hoping of course that everything turns out well for us all!)

"You were right," Tucker replied to one of my replies on Twitter. More people than me pointed this out, to be sure, but finally some vindication afforded by one of the world's best libertarian activists!

That was pleasing.

For Tucker (and as he says again in an essay I'm about to look at), the lockdowns came as a great shock. He didn't think a modern population would be fertile ground in which to institute such draconian measures, let alone to tolerate those cages for as long as we did. There was too much civilization, too many enlightened minds, too much to remind us of what happened nearly a hundred years ago.

One can imagine what went through Jeffrey's head as he learned about the measures taken by even worst regimes than ours. Maybe Tucker had long ago accepted Fukuyama's kneejerk impression about humanity finding itself at the end of history. Perhaps he thought that from here on out, the people of the earth would work in total cooperation as we completed the stairway which went up past the clouds. Pray, Jeffrey, you didn't think it was going to be *that good*.

In fact, it might be worse than he's aware. Yet, to his credit, Jeffrey Tucker shows himself as not only a great activist and thinker for liberty, but also someone willing to admit when he's wrong. I think that will soon be a cherished quality. Although I've only had fleeting conversations with him on social media and quoted him once in each of my two booklets, this really isn't surprising. I've appreciated Jeffrey's marketplace activism, whereby he defends the things gifted to us by innovation, hard work, and trade—in short, the fruits of industrialization.

But there is everywhere to be found excess, corruption, and decisions so awful and so catastrophic that they often appear as having sinister intent.

At this moment, I can't find the speech Tucker gave at the inauguration of the Brownstone Institute, which he founded as a response to the lockdowns. Instead, on YouTube, I find a speech he gave a few months ago, in April of 2022, where Jeffrey is seen having a difficult time with a microphone.

While it's always nice to see someone else beating up on technology, the video I'm really looking for features Mr. Tucker referring to himself as a sort of "optimistic techno-utopian." (please don't sue me for libel, Jeffrey). No surprise to be found there either, as one of Tucker's essay collections is entitled *It's a Jetson's World*.

Tucker also recently penned a truly remarkable column asking: *How Could We Have Been So Naïve About Big Tech?* He first refers to the 1998 thriller *Enemy of the State*, which sees the NSA hunting down a lawyer using all the interesting real-life gadgets available at the time. In the decade that followed the release of that film, Tucker excoriated those simple-minded Luddites who refused to run down to the nearest Best Buy, so as to meet the newest "smart"-whatever which could help them forget about their teetering stack of bills and dwindling bank accounts.

Then we find ourselves at the end of the first quarter of the 21st century, when Big Tech joined hands with the State, helping it to craft official narratives regarding lockdowns and vaccines, leading to the soft corralling of we livestock with bigger brains. Turn the corner in cyberspace, and we find a dejected Jeffrey smacking himself in the head as he answers his own question: "It's rather obvious this would happen because it's happened with every other technology in history, from weaponry to industrial manufacturing."

Sadly, some of us took the Black Pill a long time ago. We were, unfortunately, given early membership to the misanthrope community. A few of us even remember reading—gasp, it's true—the manifesto of one Theodore Kaczynski (How right he was about Leftists!) No surprise from us, then, as we admit to our own distrust of both humanity *and* Big Tech—which is, for at least a few more years, still controlled by humanity.

For us misanthropes, the lockdowns were no kind of shock; they only reinforced our bleak and hopeless worldview. *Of course* people would gladly turn around when told not to open the door of their business, or do nothing more than clean up the caution tape as it unraveled and fell off the playground equipment.

Why is that? How did it happen? I hope to join Jeffrey in forever asking, and one day answering, that question. No list of reasons would suffice here. History is all around us. Wars, torture, deception—it was all there just yesterday. Most remember the Attacks of September 11th, and then the wars and programs that came in the aftermath of that day. It shouldn't be that shocking that some of us did not blink when we saw more people acting terribly.

But somehow this time it feels a little different, doesn't it? Cue the hopeful retorts: "It's been bad before…Count the number of apocalypses that did not come to pass…We'll pull out of it."

No matter how many times these have been stated, it truly seems that humanity stands at a crossroads, unlike anything that came before. We've never had technology like we do now. There's a lot more than just the printing press, the musket, and the gallows; more than just the television, the telephone, and the tanks. How ancient those gadgets! Having been outlined in novels and movies, we then move swiftly into a higher-tech dystopia.

"As for escaping," Tucker writes, "any truly private email cannot be domiciled in the US, and our one-time friend the smartphone operates now as the most reliable citizen surveillance tool in history." And we're just getting started!

The elites of the world are soiled with giddiness. For them, the prospects look great. Klaus Schwab and "Great Reset" trends several times a day on Twitter, showing that others are aware that *he's* aware. Clips of Schwab's top advisor, Yuval Harari, have also become popular.

Harari gets very excited when explaining how we big-brained livestock will soon have devices implanted beneath our skin, which will be able to monitor things like heartrate and temperature. Hollywood never foresaw that one! That's more reserved for the comic books, with the villains having leapt off the cheap page and landing onto the expensive stage. During those forums and events, they scheme and plot and design their future—which doesn't include all of us.

For now, that's the best I can do in defining *technocracy*.

The People, disparate as that concept can be, will have many different reactions to these developments. For those who lean more towards optimism, they will seek reaffirmation of older ideals.

For instance. Plastic makes up a good deal of the modern world. So much so, that scientists have recently found microplastics in our blood. Dr. Shanna Swan seems to think that the chemicals in plastic have contributed to the drastic plummet of sperm counts and testosterone. Just ask a friend if they know someone who's had to seek help at one of the numerous infertility clinics. Our predicament is so bad that, according to Swan, the human race should consider placing itself on an endangered species list.

And so I don't think it's a coincidence that during a time in which the human race struggles not only to justify its own history, but also to maintain its very existence, that the act of abortion is greeted with the most virulent kind of opposition. Those who couldn't give a damn about the thousands of children shuffled around the foster care system, nor the shameful number of suicides, will justify the punishment of a teenage rape victim should she regain control of her body and then terminate the life of a month-old fetus. Twisted as that is, it serves as an easy and costless way in which to reaffirm the importance of human life.

These days, we also find hyper religiosity, and with no specific religion in mind. There's talk of "making us fear God again," with no mention of any theological doctrine: merely something bigger than ourselves. This is because the Schwabs' of the world position themselves as the overseers of a new epoch.

In one way, and as much as loathe to admit it, the U S of A is a religious society. It is home to a lot of devout people, even if they haven't read the writings of any of the very skeptical Framers. Jeffrey himself is Catholic. And does he not feel the need to apprehend those mere mortals who claim to represent a sort of Data-godhood? Other believers will feel repelled by this too.

Notice that most nationalism—which Jeffrey might have given a thought or two about—comes with a religious tint. Here, I recall a second sentence in Tucker's reply to me: "I still worry about that backlash." The Right is speaking more loudly about "civil war," which, along with "national divorce," are also trendy on Twitter.

Which takes us by the midterm season. Elections. Voting. *Democracy*. The collective effort to grab hold of the reins is the most civilized and sensible of reactions. "There's nothing we can't do together," as it goes. There won't be a civil war or secession or a technocratic hellscape if we all just vote to "conserve" our wonderful way of life.

But, as the Joker says, there's no going back to the way things were. The changes might be irrevocable.

Then what? The problems, therefore, are insoluble. Good options are rare, but then again, for us misanthropes, none of the options ever look that great.

Moreover, my referencing a mass murderer is not meant to imply that we're about to go to war against technology. It's only to highlight some of these extreme reactions: when even political candidates like Blake Masters, who came from Big Tech, cites Kaczynski as one of his heroes. Conservatism to the point of primitivism: so much for the White Man's building of the modern world! Strange times indeed.

But we're obviously not going to do away with all technology. Who really wants to give up their traveling-machines? I know Jeffrey likes his airports. As for me, the only place I truly feel alive and free is traveling 80-plus on a mostly empty highway. Neither cars, planes, or air-conditioning are going anywhere. And we don't want to give the impression that a regulatory state would do anything beneficial anyway. (We only wish that the seats on the plane would be spread farther apart! And that the car doors stay open like the DeLorean, never having to worry about your leg being crushed as you attempt to fetch something from the other seat. Only one of these has been provided by the market.)

Well, how about we just do away with evil men (and women!)? If we didn't want a war against technology, then maybe just a war against the technocrats. This is an even more impossible task. As stated, humanity has a great capacity for evil. So while some want to change who sits in the seats of Power, others like myself want to evolve beyond Power.

How to do this? Certainly, it's a long-term project. Interestingly, Jeffrey also has another recent column in which he discusses Mary Shelley's Frankenstein. He reminds us that Shelley's parents were two of the great thinkers of the Enlightenment—Mary Wollstonecraft and William Godwin. Godwin's *An Enquiry Concerning Political Justice*, published in

1793, has been a huge influence on my thinking. The perfection of mankind! Such an old fantasy, but when living in a time in which elites talk of such lofty ambitions, like that of merging with machines, the fantasy might be more relevant than ever. The goal, then, would be to outpace these transhumanists.

There are signs that people are evolving, which would be the real "Great Awakening." If we stand any chance against the technocratic elite, we should keep doing that.

If not, then our future might be even bleaker, a future in which the next most popular gizmo turns out to be suicide-pods.

(September 2022)

Peter Thiel's Man in Arizona

THE 2022 MIDTERM elections are *here*. For the last couple weeks, in the state of Arizona, the Democratic incumbent, Mark Kelly, has been neck-and-neck with his challenger, Blake Masters.

Everyone is very excited about Masters becoming "the new senator from Arizona!" Kelly, we know, is the astronaut whose wife, Gabrielle, was shot in the head by a psychotic madman more than a decade ago. But who is Masters? Wikipedia tells everyone that he was born in the state and raised in Tucson. He then went to study law and politics at Stanford. While there, he met the billionaire tech magnate Peter Thiel.

Masters was mesmerized by Thiel's lectures, writing a series of notes which became fantastically popular after they appeared online. The two became such good friends that Blake later went on to become COO of Thiel's investment firm and president of his foundation.

The average voter might ask: Where's the big briefcase full

of court cases? Or military service? Or the mayoral campaigns? As it appears, Masters' resume looks to show only that he's been an employee of Peter Thiel. This is the rich guy who is known as one of the primary builders of Silicon Valley, as well as the man who gave Donald Trump a huge injection of cash in the lead up to 2016. For that gesture, he was the main speaker at that year's RNC.

So, it comes as something of a shock that very few people mention Mr. Thiel's name when discussing Arizona's senatorial race. Even libertarians shy away from it, which would disappoint the late libertarian sage Murray Rothbard. In 1984, Rothbard wrote a long essay detailing the nexus between powerful interests and their trigger-happy recipients vying for a comfortable seat within the state apparatus (the title is emphasized: "*and* American Foreign Policy.") After all, someone has to pay for all those signs and T-shirts, and maybe we should know a thing or two about them. Those questions never used to be controversial.

Aside from the small details—those regarding Trump's campaign—I hadn't really thought about Peter Thiel, even when I picked up a copy of Max Chafkin's biography from a Barnes and Noble earlier this year. *The Contrarian*—hey, just like me! But what was Thiel being a contrarian about? I wouldn't find out immediately, because I put the book on my shelf, where it sat for several months uncracked.

But politics! Arizonans do love their electoral season. Some street corners have so many political signs, you can't even see what businesses are behind them. When it gets too windy, they fly across the intersection, and your car tires will soon give a black mustache to Mr. Masters, or a full head of hair to Mr. Kelly. As for knocking on doors, election volunteers give even the Jehovah Witnesses a run for their money. One never has to worry about hearing someone say, "What election?"

I'd made several attempts to wade into my new state's

political atmosphere. For instance, on June 23rd a senatorial debate was being hosted by FreedomWorks. I intended to attend. But first, do more Googling, find out about our candidates. There was Jim Lamon, a businessman who made billions in coal, gas, and solar power; Mark Brnovich, the attorney general of Arizona who claims to have launched more lawsuits against the Obama administration than any other AG in the country; Mick McGuire, a retired Air Force general; and then Blake. Although I don't remember anyone telling me specifically, the race was winnowed down between Lamon and Masters.

Masters and I have at least one thing in common: we both have exactly one article posted up on Lew Rockwell. (Rockwell was Rothbard's best friend and co-publisher, and so another household name in libertarian circles). Masters' 2006 article was a synthesis of G. Edward Griffin's classic work on the Federal Reserve and another book about British Naval intelligence. In it, he argues that the United States government lied the people into World War One.

My article was a report about the rampage of one Christopher Dorner and the subsequent manhunt that took place over the course of several days. (My article can still be found there if one looks hard enough.)

Rockwell himself is an avowed secessionist and talk of secession is in the air. It trends on Twitter all the time. The issue is also pertinent considering that the Texas Republican Party had, just a few days earlier, approved a platform that included the right to secede. It was a fair question to pose to Mr. Masters, or anyone else who would entertain me.

So, I went to the debate. Watched and listened. Lamon said Thiel by name—"one of Facebook's board members!" Masters rejoined with a corrective: "Former Facebook board member. I'm proud of Peter," he said, calling him the "only America First billionaire."

When it finished, I looked around, seeing who was hanging out. Blake was standing to the side of the stage, talking and taking pictures with his fans. I approached, and it was apparent that Blake enjoyed the adulation. He wanted nothing else, and cheerfully argued with some CNN reporters when they asked for an interview.

Then I approached, with a "quick question": "You used to write for Lew Rockwell. Rockwell is an avowed secessionist. Do you…?"

Blake looked at me, waved me off. He said I was "trying to make him look bad," adding that he'd "rather talk to CNN."

Trying to make him look bad?

I was trying to do no such thing. Besides, only he can make himself look bad. Plus, I thought this was a grassroots movement. And I am the grassroots! And I felt secession was a perfectly relevant subject. But Masters did not want to talk to me that day. It seems not everyone appreciates ambush journalism.

I kept up with the campaigns as best I could. Masters got the nomination. I then started "following" him and Kari Lake on Twitter. The two started a statewide campaign tour—which, to the outside observer, appears to be confined largely to the massive Maricopa County, and with Phoenix, the capital, being the very center of the state. They always hit all the high notes: fentanyl poisonings, caused by a Southern border left wide open by Biden; inflation, also Biden's fault; gender ideology, pushed by the insane radical Left.

And as the campaigns heated up, so did the war between Russia and Ukraine. In September, Putin annexed several parts of Ukraine. Zelensky then asked for "accelerated ascension" into NATO, with Putin quickly repeating his decades old warning that if this were to happen, it would trigger World War Three.

For whatever reason, the conflict was left off the table. It didn't seem to be discussed very much at all in ads or speeches.

On October 6th, the three senatorial candidates—Masters, Kelly, as well as the libertarian lawyer/candidate Marc Victor—had a debate, if only for a single hour. Again, there was not a single mention whatsoever of the war.

This omission of was made all the more striking when it was reported, less than two weeks later, that Mr. Masters' benefactor had invested seventeen and a half million dollars in a drone manufacturer that had already given 42 drones to the Ukrainian resistance. Thiel said the company, Quantum Systems, was "leaps ahead" of the competition.

More Googling revealed that Alex Karp, Thiel's hand-appointed CEO of Palantir (which I'll come to), had flown to Ukraine back in June and met with Zelensky, who said he was "delighted that Palantir is ready to invest in Ukraine and help us in the fight against Russia on the digital frontline." The reports note that Karp was the first CEO of a major company to offer such support.

There was also Blake's "tweet" from March 1st, in which he wrote that, while we should "obviously not go to war," that we should "supply the Ukrainians as they fight for their country," as well as "sanction Russia so that Putin and his cronies feel the consequences." Our own military, the Twitter thread concluded, should keep out of the conflict.

Another townhall-like event was coming up. Scheduled for October 18th, it was being held in downtown Chandler, between two of the many bars in the town. That night, I would once more attempt to ask a question to our candidates.

The place was mostly packed. About a half hour into it, on the path that led to the parking lot behind the event, I saw our candidate for Attorney General, Abe Hamadeh, who was about to share a stage with Blake. Abe was very approachable, and only had one large security guard following him around. I told Abe what my concerns were: Masters is Thiel's employee, and Thiel is "kind of all over the place," as I said to several people here.

Now there's news of this drone manufacturer he's investing in. "I'm glad I don't make those decisions," Abe said with a smile. I shook his hand and walked off.

Abe went on stage and was soon joined by Blake. An iron gate separated the stage from the attendees. They repeated the same old crowd-pleasing pans against the Democrats. When it was over, I got on the side of the gate where they were supposed to walk alongside to get back to the parking lot. I managed to shoulder my way to the front and got an arm way out there. Blake came around in front. He grabbed my hand. "Are we going to give any more money to the Ukrainian resistance?" I yelled it as loudly and clearly as I could. Blake shrugged, and I think he said, "I don't know." Then kept walking.

Not totally satisfied with that response, I followed him around the side, but soon came up to a huge crowd that leaned against the iron gate, leaving me no way to continue. I went the opposite direction, out of the crowd, and ran around the entire building—tripping on my face one time, due to a dark corner— and then headed to the back.

I turned my camera on. Masters was hugging and taking pictures with a few of his admirers. "There he goes," I said to myself, "running off." "Blake," I said louder, "some kind of comment *please*...one question, about arms going to the Ukrainian resistance." He walked off, between the cars, to the hotel beyond. "That man," I fumed to the security guard who began following me, "is a coward."

As expected, Tulsi Gabbard was tonight's surprise guest. Tulsi had recently defected from the Democratic Party, something any idiot could see coming. I think she came out first. Then Kari. Tulsi gave her endorsement of our candidates. When they were finished, Tulsi sort of disappeared into a crowd that seemed to have grown larger.

Then Kari Lake came into the crowd. She shook some hands and said some hellos. I got on the side and asked my question. She glanced at me, then kept walking. I then yelled it: "Is Blake Masters going to give any more money to the Ukrainians?" Afterwards, I argued with some of the attendees, who needlessly reminded me that the governor doesn't make such decisions. That I know; but she's campaigning with the guy who does.

So, did I get my point across? Well, maybe.

Soon after the event, Masters went on two prominent libertarian podcasts. The first was Ron Paul's "Liberty Report," hosted by the great man himself and his wonderful cohost Daniel McAdams. These two men, both principled anti-warriors, asked about Ukraine, with McAdams bringing up Blake's earlier tweets.

Blake said these aid bills, a result of the "bipartisan foreign policy consensus," were "increasing the chances for nuclear war." He then talked about how Ron's son, Rand, had asked for an audit of the bill, since there was too much momentum in stopping it. "I look forward to joining forces with him," Blake said.

McAdams, not wanting the interview to be just a "lovefest," then asked Blake about his tweets. "I don't think I said we should send weapons," he replied, saying that perhaps food, fuel and medical supplies might be justified. "I've drawn the line at weapons," Blake said, "I don't think we should be engaging in a proxy war in Ukraine."

So that's good. And then Blake appeared on libertarian Dave Smith's podcast, where he was again asked his stance on the war. This time, Blake said we should do everything in our power to get Russia and Ukraine to the negotiating table. "We want to stop the war," he said, adding that all this aid is just pouring more fuel onto the fire. Of course!

Now, I'm not saying that I gave Blake the impetus to appear on these shows. I only point out that I was the one who made the concerns clear to those touring on the election roadshow—and especially with my elaboration told to Mr. Hamadeh. In any case, they're fans of Trump, and so perhaps a little hubris and self-aggrandizement will be appreciated.

But notice that neither Paul, McAdams, or Smith had mentioned the name Peter Thiel. They neglected—forgot?—to discuss Thiel's investments. I figured this was a good time to crack open Chafkin's book. It was important to learn more about the man who *was* Blake Masters' campaign. And while I won't go over every chapter of this 337-page hardcover, I'll highlight a few details I feel to be concerning.

Mr. Thiel has been described in various ways. He's a libertarian. He's one of the main builders of Silicon Valley. He's a thought leader of the New Right. The first is a description Thiel has even used himself several times. As for the second, if one considers his cofounding of PayPal, as well as his early investment in Facebook, then it's just a matter of fact. As for the third, that's one used more and more these days.

I've been reminded that Thiel had been a main bankroller for Ron Paul's last two presidential campaigns. And so doesn't that make him a libertarian?

Two counterpoints here. First, Thiel is the founder of Palantir, which Chafkin calls his "thoroughbred unicorn." The author reports that Thiel was in New York City on September 10th, and was unable to find a flight out of the city. He was told to wait until a United flight the next morning, but instead opted to wait until there was room. Thiel made it out that night, but it's likely that some other passengers who did wait until morning became victims of the Attacks. Perhaps for this reason, Thiel had become "increasingly consumed by the threat posed by Islamic terrorism..."

Palantir was created in 2003 when Thiel had ordered a group of employees to see if Igor, a software developed by PayPal cofounder Max Levchin to thwart Russian cybercrooks that threatened the company, could be upgraded to catch terrorists. Thiel named Palantir after the mythical "seeing stone" in Lord of the Rings and hoped to "mine the governments near endless trove of data, including financial and cell phone records, and use the network analysis to find terrorists," according to Chafkin.

Thiel then picked his old classmate, the left-leaning Alex Karp, to run the company.

In February 2017, *The Intercept* ran a piece explaining what Palantir did for the U.S. government. The company first gained attention with Edward Snowden's original revelations. The relationship between Palantir and government spy agencies goes back to at least 2008, with the British government being especially impressed by Palantir's demos. Within a few years, three of the "Five Eyes" countries—that is, the spy agencies of the U.S., the U.K., Australia, New Zealand, and Canada (which all share information together)—were using Palantir.

Specifically, Palantir was made for data analysis. The governments were taking in so much information from people's online activity that they became overwhelmed by it. They needed help organizing this data, which is the function that Palantir was designed to do. According to Chafkin, Thiel was even courting officials he had known in the Bush Administration, including John Poindexter, who is considered the architect of Bush's "Total Information Awareness" doctrine; in short, knowing everything about everyone.

In the years that followed, Palantir would be given a lot more U.S. government contracts. This is despite the fact that the government didn't always want to use the company. Indeed, in 2016, Thiel sued the U.S. Army, because it claimed the army had left Palantir out of the contract bidding. Thiel won that case. During the Trump presidency, Palantir would do a lot more business with the U.S. government, working with ICE, and later, with COVID, helping to keep track of vaccines (it also had contracts with hospitals, monitoring cases and supplies).

The second counterpoint to the "he's a libertarian" talking point is Thiel's relationship with the Paul campaign. In the 2012 election, Thiel gave $50,000 to Revolution PAC, a group supporting Paul. Then another $85,000. Finally, he gave $2.6 million to Endorse Liberty.

But these donations left the Paul campaign bewildered. Officially, Super PACs and the candidates work independently, though normally they remain somewhat close, making sure to play by the same rulebook. Jesse Benton, Paul's campaign manager, said: "We had none of that with Peter." Chafkin tells us that neither Benton nor Paul had so much as shaken Thiel's hand prior to 2012.

Thiel never again made mention of Paul. Why? Thiel later said that supporting Paul "was for 2016." One can see the strategy. Thiel was laying groundwork on which he could later build upon. Now, one can start a company that helps the NSA spy on people around the world—and still be seen as a libertarian! How very clever.

Chafkin sees these self-contradictions all over the place. "Contrarian" isn't about Thiel taking a controversial stance; it's about Thiel contradicting himself at every turn. Which is not to say I agree with all Chafkin's observations.

For instance, Chafkin wonders how a man who is so interested in extending life (Thiel is a big believer and investor into life extension) could be so critical of the COVID lockdowns (a reason given as to why Thiel didn't really support Trump's reelection bid), as those were supposed to save lives.

For plenty of others—us real libertarians—we recognized how preposterous it was to think you could lock everyone in their houses until the virus just disappeared. Instead, we worried about those who would gain weight, or would miss doctor's appointments. That, too, would lead to death.

The contradiction I've tried to highlight here is the War Question. Supposedly this meant a lot to Kari, who is said to have switched parties in 2008 so as to vote for Obama, because Obama said he wanted to end the Iraq War.

As for Thiel, since his initial endorsement of that war, he has become a critic of America's endless and pointless wars. He even said as much during his RNC speech. Yet he and Karp still run Palantir, which, as said, fought the government to make them buy their product. Now they're doing business in Ukraine. Then there's this drone manufacturer, which was just reported the other month.

I certainly don't wish to be a gossipy publication like Gawker, which Thiel helped put out of business. Moreover, I can also say "thank you" to Kari for being so vocally opposed to vaccine mandates, as well as gender ideology inside our schools.

Thank you!

These things are important.

But Ron Paul brought me into the political fold—*also*—and his consistent criticism of the imperial state has stayed with me. So, excuse me if I'm a bit concerned about special interests.

One possible way to project the future is by looking at three other candidates supported by Thiel. Ted Cruz was the first politician Thiel helped to elect. Josh Hawley was the second. Now there's JD Vance, and of course Blake. Cruz voted in favor of military aid. Hawley did not. Vance has been critical of the aid, saying he "doesn't really care what happens to Ukraine." And then we have Blake's position. Let's hope he sticks with it.

During an interview with Marc Victor (who then endorsed Blake), Blake said to *hold him accountable!* Almost sounds like I've been invited into his house. Yet when Blake rebuffed me, I really did feel like the grassroots, if only because I was being stepped on.

Hopefully, the grassroots don't get salted.

(November 2022)

An Army of the Awakened?

ON THE 16TH and 17th of September in 2022—a Friday and Saturday—Charlie Kirk and his organization, Turning Point USA, hosted an event in Phoenix, which was called "Defeating the Great Reset."

Hey, I thought, that's what I want to do. I told my publisher about it. He decided to pay my way—*and his*, which I didn't know about until the day of. "Carpool?" Sure, why not. The first day started in the afternoon. For this event, I decided to dress up a bit. I had picked up a bowtie some years earlier, but it had lay dormant in a drawer. Might be a good time to take it out. Yes, I felt overdressed, but at least the pictures got a good reaction.

The publisher picked me up and we headed out. We arrived at the Arizona Grand Resort and then went searching for the party. As soon as I saw the people, I realized *I was* overdressed, and so took off the tie. Still, a black jacket and a white button up is more than I've worn all summer. My publisher estimated there to be about 400 people inside the main room. That sounds about right. We stood in a line for check-in; one must get registered, then get a lanyard with their name on it.

Alongside the line was a guy campaigning with several posters. Vote for Kari Lake! Well, okay, maybe, if I did vote. And also vote Blake Masters! Upon hearing that second name, I felt the urge to argue. "I don't trust him," I said. "His boss, Peter Thiel, started a surveillance company that was used by the CIA." Actually—common mistake—it was the NSA, which is much more secretive and globalized than the CIA.

The guy tried to get a word in, but I talked through him. "He's also been all over the place with abortion." These two facts get the Masters-baters every time. "He's better than Mark Kelly," said another woman in the line. "It's always lesser evilism," I said, "Isn't it?" You don't vote *for* someone; you vote *against* someone.

"This is why I'm a principled nonvoter," I said finally. The guy then castigated me, saying how it's my responsibility as an American, then asking something like: "So what do you do to change things?"

"I'm a pamphleteer," I answered, pulling out a copy of my booklet on the Great Reset and handing it to him. "I change minds—or hope to."

"You wrote this?" he asked.

"I did."

Right before we got in the door, I turned around and saw who I had come to see—James Lindsay, author of *Cynical Theories*, among others, and who has made a name battling "the woke." Lindsay had no bodyguards orbiting him. How human! He shook my hand and I mumbled some kind of hello. Then he heads in; he's one of the speakers.

Me and the publisher got inside, checked in, got our lanyards. The first room was the "merch room": shirts and buttons and more shirts. Into the next door, the main room. It's dark in here, with two huge screens on each side of the podium. Doors were in the back, which were open for now, but were soon to be locked, and then used only as an exit. You'd have to get in through the front doors.

For now, most of the people were outside, where three bars were set up. Why yes, I would like a margarita. But just one! And, seriously, no more than two. Those orangey margaritas were so delectable and refreshing in the 95-degree blaze. I walked around, trying to find the restroom, should I need it. I then saw the host himself, Mr. Kirk, coming out from the back door, accompanied by a security man. I followed them through the glass doors.

As we were walking, I asked Charlie: "Taking questions today, Charlie?" He turned his head: "Tomorrow."

Oh good.

I limped behind—bad knee—until I saw them go into the restroom in the corner. Another security guard came out, and together they stood outside the door. "Do I have to wait outside until Mr. Kirk is done?" They said yes. A bit elitist, that. I couldn't help but wonder if Klaus Schwab had similar protocols in place. *I kid.* No comparison to be seriously made.

Back outside. Met up with the publisher. By now, food was being brought around on trays: chicken and fish, mostly. My publisher enjoyed these appetizers, as did I, even if I didn't "sample" as many as he had. The event was starting. Most of us went inside. It was sometime around 4.

Kirk was first on the mic. (It's all there online, if one is curious.) Kirk is a smart guy, if a bit milquetoast for my taste. Some even refer to him as the face of Conservative, Inc (although I only cite myself).

As I said, I was here for Mr. Lindsay. And when Lindsay got up there, he gave us all an education. He went from Marx to Marcuse, China to the Club of Rome, from Schwab's founding of the World Economic Forum to what we're now dealing with today. Excellently informative and informatively excellent. I took more notes and details to follow up on.

The last speaker was the man who helped Number 45 get into the White House: Steve Bannon came to Kirk's event. Unlike the other speakers, who gave us all lessons, Bannon's speech was meant to rally the troops. He called us an "Army of the Awakened," which is involved in "spiritual warfare" against the "demonic" party of Davos, with their appendages on Wall Street and in the City of London.

What's their endgame?

Well—and we must thank Kirk and Bannon for taking this issue into the mainstream—those elites want to eventually merge with machines, thus becoming immortal, while the rest of us wither and die on the vine. Our "battlefield," said Bannon, "is the ballot box and the precinct." I wasn't so sure.

Bannon laid it out: Advanced chip design, Artificial Intelligence, Quantum computing, CRISPR gene editing, and nanotechnology—these will converge into Homosapien "Plus" or "2.0." (*I think* Bannon listed five but stated a few more. I'm unsure if any of these are the same thing.)

I wondered if any of the pro-lifers in here—which certainly there were a few of in this crowd—would be in favor of the transhumanist agenda. At least then a few of us will have the "luxury" of never dying. The retort would likely sound something like "protecting innocent life"—which the elites are not. But not everyone at the top of the totem pole is guilty of genocide.

Right?

Why wouldn't the ultra-wealthy (and hell, maybe even Blake Masters' mentor) recognize the ultimate investment: that of immortality? After all, the dream of achieving godhood can't be all that uncommon. As for me, being trapped in this material realm with no exit has always sounded like Hell. Talk about "life without the possibility…"

President Biden hopes to help someone get their wish. His recent executive order, signed in mid-September, was titled: "Executive Order on Advancing Biotechnology and Biomanufacturing Innovation for a Sustainable, Safe, and Secure American Bioeconomy." The order calls for the development of: "Genetic engineering technologies and techniques to be able to write circuitry for cells and predictable program biology in the same way in which we write software and program computers; unlock the power of biological data, including through computing tools and artificial intelligence…" Whew, boy.

"We're living in the biggest inflection point in human history," Bannon said. He then asked that most important of questions: "Why did divine providence put me here and now in this place? Every generation coming down the road is going to look back at this time and say: 'Who stood up and fought?'" That one hits any parent in the gut.

That was it for this evening. The publisher and I went outside. We wanted to see if we couldn't find Mr. Bannon, so as to get a picture with him. We walked around the back of the building. Nobody.

Then a door opened.

Tall guy comes out.

"Is Mr. Bannon around here?" I asked. "We wanted a picture." He said: "I can neither confirm nor deny, but you can't be back here." We kept walking. He walked with us. Then he got a call on the radio. "Bring the car back?" And then a black SUV backed up and into the area we just were.

No luck tonight in getting a picture with a leader of the revolution.

The publisher and I agreed to drive separately tomorrow, as he wanted to get here early for breakfast.

II

I arrived around 11 on that Saturday. The second day was scheduled to be longer than the first, and so it featured more speakers. No margaritas today, as there were no bars set up outside. My option for alcohol was to make a small walk to the hotel lobby, where a bar was off to the side. Three beers and no more! The pierced and tatted bartender girl did not seem like she was having a good day. I was, but still I did not tip her merely for taking my credit card, ringing up 9 dollars for a single bottle of Heineken, then popping my cap.

So I would make my rounds: walking into the event room, standing in the back, listening to the speaker; if he—I don't think there was a single female speaker—caught my attention, I'd listen for a while. Then I'd go outside, make that walk to the lobby, or maybe use the restroom or sit outside and make notes or try to finish reading an article I'd started earlier.

One of the first panels of the day was a joint interview with Charlie Kirk and James Lindsay. I struggle to remember the details of their conversation and can't seem to find it online. As promised to me, Charlie was going to take a few questions. I jumped up, ran over to the mike. Two other people were front of me. Boring questions. Then me. "Hey guys, I appreciate it," I started.

> *The event has been great. Charlie, last night you said that every in the room agreed basically on two things: that we all believe in God, and that we are not God. You're standing next to a man who a little while ago you said is not a Christian. I know James has written some books that are quite critical of Christianity. Question for either one of you: What would you say to we secularists, those who don't necessarily believe that America was founded on*

Christian values—we read Thomas Jefferson, primary author of the Declaration of Independence and the Bill of Rights, of course he edited the bible down to a quick pamphlet—where is our place in this fight? We would like to have a place as well.

Kirk replied by telling me that I am "always welcome aboard the 'truth train.'" But he quickly caveated, America is "undoubtedly a Christian nation." After thanking me for being here, he provided some evidence. "Fifty-five of the fifty-six signers of the Declaration of Independence were bible-believing, church-attending Christians," he says. "John Adams was very clear—he spoke fluent Hebrew—and said the United States Constitution was founded by and for holy and religious people and was wholly inadequate for the people of any other."

Kirk then told us that George Washington was a "very devout and a very focused Christian." America didn't come about only through the work of Thomas Jefferson, he says. It was also who "mentored them and who actually laid the foundation for it": Johnathon Edwards, and May Hugh, and George Whitfield. These guys gave "anywhere between forty and fifty thousand sermons that talked about how God, not King George, should actually be the person in charge, the head of your government." In the Declaration of Independence, Kirk reminds us, "god" is mentioned four times.

Then he says something that's inaudible to my ears. "But all that aside, despite the fact that America was a Christian nation, that every single state, state-by-state, had Christian laws, not just the federal government." What's the place of those like myself and Mr. Lindsay? "We need to build coalitions for liberty and for truth. Liberty is God's idea, not man's idea." Then more inaudibility. "And if James, who I consider to be the world's most expert on these issues, we might have theological differences, is going to come here and just drop the bomb on the evil people...are you kidding me?"

He then gives an airplane analogy—people do like their airplane analogies: "Okay...you get on an airplane and say, 'Hey, I only have Christians as pilots.'" Now a doctor analogy. "Or, when you have heart surgery, you say, 'I only have Christians as heart surgeons.'" Not at all. "You want the most qualified, and you want the best, for your mission, for your goal. And I can say this: I wish American Christians had as much clarity, wisdom, and courage as James."

Whew.

James then chimed in. "I'll be brief," which he was: "But you actually said it: if you don't believe in God, you don't believe you're God. Their religion is that Man, as a collective, has forgotten that he's God. If you don't think you're God, you're on the right side. That's all it takes."

Charlie made one last comment: "All are welcome, unless you're a Marxist." I had stepped aside after asking my question but was right there listening intently to their replies. "I'm not a Marxist," I said loudly enough. The room laughed. With me or at me, I don't know, but the vibe was positive.

Though I did regret walking away, as I wanted to argue a bit more with Charlie over America's founding. For one thing, George Washington's diaries indicate that he had attended church no more than twelve times a year. And in the last three years of his life, he went as few as three times. More, although it was custom at the time, Washington made no request to have a man of God present at his deathbed, and so he heard no prayers as he took his final breaths.

As for John Adams, Kirk might have missed his other opinions. Like this one: "Nothing is more dreaded than the national government meddling with religion." Or another: "Books that cannot bear examination certainly ought not to be established as divine inspiration by penal laws." The last was in reference to an "embarrassing" law that punished blasphemers.

(These selections come from Brooke Allen's *Moral Minority: Our Skeptical Founding Fathers*).

To sum up, Kirk has the story exactly backwards. Prior to the Constitution Convention in 1787, the individual states had an assortment of laws that discriminated against one religion or another. The Framers purposely chose Thomas Jefferson's revolutionary new law in Virginia, which guaranteed freedom to both believers and nonbelievers, as the model for the new American government.

Madison, very much concerned about the possibility that the individual states would become tyrannical, even tried to include in the Bill a Rights an amendment that would prohibit the states from making laws interfering with the freedom of conscience. That amendment did not pass, but less than a century later we got the 14th Amendment. (This information comes from Susan Jacoby's *Freethinkers: A History of American Secularism*).

Anyhow, a little later, I went to get another beer. Coming back, I saw Lindsay standing outside the door talking to a woman. He looked at me as I walked up. I approached, interrupting with little guilt. "I think you're great, James," I said. "I read your book *Cynical Theories*." Then I asked for a selfie, which he was happy to grant me. I handed him a copy of my Great Reset booklet, which he also took. "How about an interview sometime?" I asked. James seemed open to the idea. "Sure," he said. "We'll try to make it work."

The woman he was talking to then turned to me. She was also something of a researcher, and if I remember correctly— because I was still trying to talk to Lindsay—we began a joint criticism of Masters and his mentor, Peter Thiel. Another man joined us, getting into Lindsay's ear. Eventually I walked into the merch room, asking someone who was now speaking. "Alex Jones." No way! So that was the special guest! I walked into the main room and was greeted with the sound of Jones' trademark gravel. He was visiting us via video. Charlie was at the podium.

And I'm sure Charlie knows who Alex Jones is, and what he has said in the past. As soon as someone says "9/11 was an inside job," you know you're talking to someone who has a very different set of politics. Those politics go far beyond mere partisan bickering: we're talking the real "deep state" here, the kind of evil that transcends political parties. (For the record, I *also* believe 9/11 was an inside job, with Bush and the Neocons at least knowing the Attacks were soon to happen). Jones had a few more interesting things to say today. "Energy is the Queen," Jones told us. "If you know anything about chess, you know that the queen is the most powerful piece on the board. It can move in any direction."

Now I went into the hotel's main lobby and found a cushioned bench to lay down on for a few minutes. When I went in this time, there was a gentleman explaining how Christian institutions have "gone woke"—which means they've taken up the social justice, anti-white agenda. He then showed a clip of Schwab talking about one of his main influences, a priest named Dom Helder Camara. "Values cannot be justified by the intellectual process alone," Schwab is quoted as saying, "faith must be included."

Suddenly I recalled something else about Jefferson, a quote he made: "In every country and in every age the priest has been hostile to liberty. He is always in alliance with the despot, abetting his abuses in return for protection of his own." For the attendees here, learning of such corruption within their church will only embolden them to reclaim it. For me, it only further demonstrates as to why people should question, if not their faith, certainly their congregations. The true freedom fighter would never be persuaded either by exciting oratory or the colorful fabrics worn by their church leader.

Next came one of the most interesting speakers of the event, a gentleman named Terry Schilling. He's the president of the American Principles Project, which he described as "the NRA for the family." Living up to the project's name, Schilling told the audience that he and his wife just welcomed baby number six.

Schilling wants us to know that the elites wish to abolish the family, and that the plan is nothing new. He tells us how, in 1963, a Congressman from Florida had entered a list of 45 goals, Communist in nature, into the U.S. congressional record. Oddly, Schilling doesn't name that politician. It was Albert S Herlong Jr.

What are those goals? Schilling tells us some of them: promotion of pornography and obscenity; presenting homosexuality, degeneracy, and promiscuity as healthy and normal; infiltration of the churches; eliminating prayer from schools; discrediting the constitution as outdated; same with the founding fathers; and the family, with the state eventually taking complete control of their upbringing. Schilling also mentioned the dismantlement of the FBI, something that a few Trump supporters might be in favor of in the aftermath of the raid on Mar-a-Lago.

Schilling's tactic of fighting the Great Reset was predictable: get married young and have a lot of babies. Then "raise your children to value family and child-rearing the same way you teach them to love America and our founding fathers, the same way you teach them to love God, teach them to have large families and to be open to letting God determine how many children they have."

Noted: I will educate my child about the Founder's thoughts on religious tyranny! For it seems the Founders and the Communists had at least one thing in common.

The last speaker at the event was the reporter Jack Posobiec. He was here to debut the first episode of TPUSA's minidocumentary on…well, the Great Reset. The barely 30-minute film wasn't horrible. My publisher and I laughed in terror when we saw Yuval Harari, Schwab's top advisor, acting as his usual sinister self. "Look how excited he gets!" my publisher said. "He loves what he does," I said.

Afterwards, Posobiec told a story about a visit his family took to the "holy land" of Israel—sponsored, of course, by TPUSA.

During their walk up Via Dolorosa, his father broke down and cried. "Do you honestly think," Posobiec said, "that Klaus Schwab, and these programs and these agendas, can ever compete with that? With true belief in the risen Christ; true belief...in something greater than ourselves?" Recently, Mr. Trump "retruthed" (shared) an article on his "truth social," which gave a subtle comparison between himself and the Lord.

Certainly, Mr. Schwab, aware of the power of faith—as we've seen—intends to give Christ a run for his money, just like the man adored by so many in this crowd.

III

In the weeks after the event, I've done some more reading and reflecting. I think we should take Bannon at his word, and thus acknowledge that the human species—*indeed*—stands at a precipice. We *are* living in a time unlike any other, this due mainly because of the kind of technology that has never before existed. Not hearing that last part, one will then argue that mankind has always suffered war and slavery and "manmade horrors beyond our comprehension," as the meme goes. But then we'd have to acknowledge that the agenda of Klaus Schwab isn't really all that unexpected. Since Schwab is still a man and not yet a robot, it would not be surprising that someone should aspire to be the world's first ever fully realized techno-tyrant.

Where does that put us, other than inside of rooms filled with more faith-based individuals who wait patiently for their own god to come back and thus cast Schwab into eternal hellfire? As for myself, Schwab only serves as my weekly reminder of an observation made by the late Eric Hoffer: "The savior who wants to turn men into angels is as much a hater of human nature as the totalitarian despot who wants to turn them into puppets."

Guilty.

For I am a misanthrope, a hater of mankind, and don't dare think I shield myself from that hate. Trusting my neighbor is already difficult enough, but I trust them even less if they refuse to at least admit to the evil they're capable of unleashing. Luckily, even Charlie Kirk can say as much. Everyone at the event received a short booklet, "The American Response to the Great Reset." On page 10, quote: "Indeed, one look at human history suggests that man's nature is at best volatile and at worst vicious." *To put it mildly*, say we who realized that some time ago.

One might think of this as an obscure worldview, but that's hardly correct; all activists, changemakers, and curmudgeons have their favorite evil to focus-in on.

This would then assume the most disturbing of all dilemmas: What if Homo Deus actually managed to put an end to these evildoings? I can't be the only madman who's ever wondered that. For instance, wouldn't it be nice if the annual baby genocide that is abortion (900,000 abortions every year— in just America alone) was a thing of the past? A good development. But what if that was because mankind was made completely sterile, this due to plastics or radiowaves or whatever? Wouldn't it be worth relinquishing our most natural of all rights if it meant that no more fetuses were ripped apart inside the womb? If otherwise, can we then come to accept that we will continue to give in to the third most natural impulse (aside from eating and excreting), thereby resulting in a lot more unwanted humans? I would argue for what I've deemed "responsible natalism," but then that sounds eerily close to eugenics.

Or, what if the old arguments for World Government was shown to have merit, and then warring between nations soon made a relic of a time when Homo sapiens ran the show? Then let me remind everyone that we are again teetering on the edge of nuclear exchange.

I could be tempted by such proposals. But then I would sober up and realize that such lofty outcomes would not happen without a high moral cost and no absolute guarantee.

Contra my friends on the Right, life is a lot more than a heartbeat. Children have a right to life, they'll argue; and I'd argue that children have a right to an upbringing that wasn't deliberately made painful. Which is pretty rare.

In my view, the primary role of parents should not be that of imparter of values. Rather, the main roles of parents should be that of custodian and guardian, ensuring that children are brought up mostly unharmed and able to come to understand certain truths by his or her own faculties. (This is not to say that we should not impart values to our children. Only that it raises more questions, like what those values are: big government or small government? Christianity or Islam? Which school, tradition or denomination? Subjectivity!)

Scroll through the WEF website and you'll soon realize that Schwab and his cohorts are also disqualified from fulfilling any of these roles. For starters, the WEF has articles on its website that promote vaccine passports. We're just starting to find out how dangerous the COVID vaccines are. There's an abundance of stories and studies coming out about myocarditis and the harm done to the female reproductive system. If Schwab really did care about people, as he always insists, he would advise caution while pushing for recompense as well as better reporting systems.

There's also a slew of articles dealing with "gender affirming" healthcare. Puberty blockage is a chemical maiming of children, and Schwab's organization is all in favor of it.

Finally, there's an emerging atrocity, one that was hinted at during the event but not elaborated upon. In both Kirk's booklet and in their film, carnivores were demonized. "It'll become a treat," the WEF says in regard to meat. And how do they plan on forcing us to go meatless? How do they intend to curb our consumption of cows, our feasting of fish, and our devouring of fowl? No writer of horror could invent the forthcoming answer.

I have a friend that I've known on Facebook for many years. Some months back, she told me that her middle child, a boy, had developed "alpha gal" after being bitten by a tick. Alpha gal, or alpha gal syndrome, refers to the name of a sugar molecule found in mammals, which one can become allergic to. Her son's symptoms are typical for an allergic reaction, except that he's allergic to meat, which is something that would seem odd to most of us. (He's receiving a combination of allopathic and homeopathic medicine and seems to be recovering slowly. He's even gradually reintroducing meat back into his diet.)

My friend then passed along some articles discussing the WEF's work with bioengineering, a favorite item on the agenda. One of these articles, written by Alicia Bittle at *Evie Magazine*, tells us about Bill Gates' investment into "mosquito research." Accordingly, this research has the end goal of ending malaria worldwide—the lethal virus carried, of course, by mosquitos. Turns out, mosquitos also have the potential to induce alpha gal syndrome.

So, we find it odd that the WEF has hosted a bioethicist who believes this might be necessary in order to get the population to go meatless. Dr. Matthew Liao, director of the College Public Health Center for Bioethics at New York University, says "people eat too much meat," and if we could curb our consumption, it would help save the planet. Humans must become a "cat-eyed, meat-allergic, semi-genius, hobbit" creature. (Really, that's what's reported). In short, if they can't convince us to stop eating meat, then they'll just have to make us allergic to it.

This is all so very depressing—is it not?—and I'll soon be told not to be so negative. I would reply that the depressive state is a consequence of "being awake"—because "army of the awakened" cannot be just a longer way of saying "woke." Nowadays I happily call myself "black-pilled," just as I readily admit to being a misanthrope.

However, I take issue with any comparison between the extreme forms of cynicism and that of nihilism. I reject entirely the notion that being aware to evil automatically means that we have submitted to it.

Think back to that most allegorical of all Hollywood films: *The Matrix*. Neo escaped his simulacra prison, then joined up with others who had also escaped. They who had plugs in their bodies now lived in the shoddy conditions of Morpheus' ship, eating gruel while constantly on the run from the machines who wanted to hook them back up to the system. Did these awakened warriors appear "happy"? They looked downright miserable. The sense of loneliness was also hard to miss.

One member of the team even found life "awake" too unbearable to endure. He then turned on his friends by making a deal with the machines, giving them access to the ship in exchange for a blissful life back inside the Matrix. This would be 90% of us, I assume. Slumbering along in our daily existence, we generally like to be lied to. As I like to say, for the intelligent creature that is not quite perfected, deception must be the most precious commodity. Such as we are, such as it is.

So I think: Here we are, living on the brink of nuclear annihilation; WEF is pushing ahead with its transhumanist project, with all its mandates and allergies and goofy flesh-and-blood puppets; inflation is skyrocketing, with people unable to afford food or gas; politicians and teachers are telling children that they might have been born in the "wrong body," thus selling them extensive surgeries in the hope they'll get it right; there's still hundreds of millions of babies conceived by irresponsible parents, thereby finding themselves in the predicament in which they'll either die in the womb or else live with an increased chance of being abused or drugged or trafficked, thus possibly making them fantasize about that missed abortion; and, worst of all, Kamala Harris might very well be the next president of the United States, because Joe Biden, loyal servant to what used to be called the New World Order, is seriously unwell.

So maybe I should be offended when someone tells me not to be so negative. As far as I'm concerned, to be "black pilled" is simply to realize how bad things are. After all, it was Kirk who welcomed me aboard the Truth Train. But as written by "depressive realism" scholar Colin Feltham in his book *Keeping Ourselves in the Dark*: "[W]e all know that we have to be judicious in the truth, that we must exercise utmost discretion in determining to whom we may speak openly." To put that more poetically, we zip our lips so as not to risk an offense.

Therefore, we're living in something of a delusion, which for some is a pleasant dream and for others a monstrous nightmare. For the latter, we must scream—and, by all means, feel free to make a buck or two by perfecting your pitch (I'm still trying!) But how to get out, and how to make sure the same thing isn't repeated a second time? We can hardly claim to be slapping ourselves awake when we continue to push snooze on all the alarm clocks set by other truth-seekers. Some of those alarms might be too far away. If I haven't already, perhaps I could nudge a few of them closer to those who are still asleep.

Alarm one: Posobiec had regaled us with his trip to the Holy Land of Israel. Kirk has also been to the country, multiple times. And one of the speakers did say that Americans should not be more concerned about Pakistan's borders than we are our own borders. Myself, I would have added two more borders: those belonging to Iraq—and to Israel. Number 45 had agreed with me on the first, calling that disastrous and illegal war a "beauty" of a blunder, and telling his fans that the Bush administration deceived the people about WMDs. For a Republican, that was quite contrarian! Yes, veterans, you fought bravely in defense of our country; but no, the whole war was based on a lie. These are the ways in which conservatives like to approach the question of the imperial state—delicacy to the point of elusion.

I can forgive anyone trying to find their way on the right side of that murderous mistruth.

And who helped goad us into the Iraq War? It was all about oil, wasn't it? I too had always assumed this to be "the truth," before I learned that there was more to the story, a story that includes our "close ally" in the region, Israel. According to Mearsheimer and Walt, in their excellent book *The Israel Lobby*, the Iraq War was "intended as the first step in a larger plan to reorder the Middle East in ways that benefit long-term American and Israeli interests."

This wonderful work of scholarship provides a great deal of evidence showing how Christian Zionists in America, as well as the many groups that lobby on behalf of the state of Israel, made sure that Saddam Hussein was deposed—even if that meant lying to the whole world about his potential to acquire weapons of mass destruction. "For the sake of Israel," you say. I say that if American Christians believe they have a sacred duty to protect "God's Chosen people," the policy will always be "America Second." ("I'm a big supporter of Israel," the god-fearing Jones reminds his host on this afternoon.)

Alarm two: I think it was Bannon, at this event, who had called our political leadership the "Uniparty." It's a term often invoked, so much so that it seems redundant at this point. How many activists and commentators throughout the decades, and from all "sides," have explained how both parties are corrupt to the core?

Yet here we are, almost a quarter into the New Century, when we're certain to face a future that will witness irrevocable changes, and *still* we plead with our neighbors to vote for one of these two parties. This would be the doctrine of "lesser evilism."

And how exactly do we measure what amounts to "lesser" evil, especially when Republicans and Democrats have always come together whenever there's a new war waiting for the green light? War is the great unifier. Along with their fellow major players in Wall Street and the pharmaceutical industry, the menace spelled out by President Eisenhower provides the very definition of *bipartisanship*. They don't disagree when it comes to asserting dominance around the globe, and only when negotiating the best deals on all that oil and territory, all those guns and drugs.

Type the words into your search bar and guess how close we are to nuclear exchange with Putin-controlled Russia. Perhaps the most frightening report is about the Biden Administration purchasing $290 million worth of radiation sickness drugs. Nothing to worry about, I'm sure.

Then we remember how Republicans in congress joined with the Democrats (who are leading the war) in giving some—how many billions was it now?—of U.S. tax dollars to the Ukrainians in their fight against Russia. Together, they escalated the conflict. They wage war against Putin by pushing buttons and pulling levers on their surrogate, the Ukrainian resistance as controlled by a bunch of Neo Nazis, and themselves led by some salesman/showman named Zelensky. And that's America...*First?*

The American people did not have a proper debate as to what we're committed to with these countries. My own assumption is that *their* national defense is not *our* concern.

"But this time it will be different," says they who could be paying their mortgage by stating it. After the Republicans sweep this election, we're told, they will at last shrink the State! It will cut the hose that feeds all these corporate parasites! Why anyone would be shocked if this doesn't happen—especially since Republicans often assert the opposite objective—I do not know. Surely, there's someone out there who can feel their IQ lower whenever they utter the sentence: "I will help elect a Republican and they will fix the country's problems."

Alarm three: Throughout this essay, and appropriately coming right after some notes on war, I've hinted at the possibility that mankind could stand to use some improvement. Specifically, I mean moral improvement, this as opposed to technological improvement, which is something desired by people with massive bank accounts and a lot of connections. The first is something we've all expressed at one time or another. We've all been dismayed when seeing our neighbors behave in ways untoward to their fellow man. When that polite husband slaps his wife around, we say "how could he?" When that father is found to be shooting dope in front of their kids, we think "that slime!" When the 20-something female high school teacher is raping her teenaged male student, we…well, too many of us shrug.

When they want to give us the full blueprint of their plans, the inability of mankind to act wonderfully will be the reason asserted most forcefully by the technocrats. As I've tried to show here, in some respects, that's obviously true. Their reasons will include our diet, which includes a strong element of carnivorism. And they won't let us forget our "carbon footprint," seemingly the main "wire" that hooks us all up to the rest of the industrial machine.

For me, I'd say it was the penchant for inflicting pain upon our children. After living with corporal punishment for eons now, we've had time to study the results. They're not good. Despite the absurd premise that inflicting pain and fear upon young minds will result in peaceful and rational adults, the evidence points very much to the contrary. Hitting your kids gives them one lesson alone: that, under the right circumstances, violence is perfectly acceptable.

This has broader implications, the importance of which affects all of us. We always hear about crime, and how best to prevent it. "More cops!" It almost seems that civilized society is willing to accept a number of criminal actions so long as it has institutions capable of prosecuting and locking away those who commit them.

How many actually said "I wish they had not murdered, raped, or abused in the first place"? Silly utopian thinking impels me to find a way to have a world with little violence, addiction, or malfeasance—because that world was full of individuals who simply behaved better. A whole world full of human beings that are not defined by their trauma: think of the possibilities!

This thinking is, to be sure, utopian; but I did say I wanted to be part of this Great Awakening. I also agreed with those at the event, who explained how the elites are already laying the groundwork for their own utopia. If it's a race between us and them, why not try to beat them to it?

I consider the real cynics to be those who merely want to change who's in charge of the government, or who heads the newest tech company or weapons manufacturer. As for me? I'd like to change our understanding to the point where we hardly even need a government. Nor any makers or weapons of war, or tools of mass surveillance, or bioengineered insects. These schemes would be inconceivable if humanity truly understood peace, negotiation, and nonviolence.

This could be a new, and perhaps last, avenue for anyone who calls themselves an activist.

(November 2022)

The 2022 Midterms, and Soon Thereafter

WE WERE TOLD to expect a "red wave" for the 2022 midterm elections, a nationwide clean sweep by the Republican Party. Instead, according to most analysts, we got a "blood clot" or a "red trickle." You can pick your own analogy, but I always thought a blood clot was life-threatening. Actually, while the Democrats did hold onto the Senate, Republicans took back the House. Dems also won most of the gubernatorial races, Florida excepted.

All in all, Republicans failed to perform as many had hoped.

Fingers are now being pointed. Maybe it was Mitch McConnell's fault, because he withheld important funds from candidates like Blake Masters. Or perhaps it was Donald Trump's doing, as he only seemed to endorse candidates who would declare that ego-inflating certainty—"the 2020 election was stolen!" With that, Trump would fly out to your state, record an endorsement, and then try and grab the attention of your wife or attractive staffer. Everything else about the candidate was irrelevant.

And that whole endorsement—anointment—was expected to be no less than celestial, like the movement of the sun or the moon, that unfailing precursor to the waves. Republicans on surfboards. Here they come! Clearly, some of that Trumpian magic was gone, and some people, as well as a few bots, got stuck in the sand.

Or maybe it was the crummy candidates; as I maintain with regards to Blake Masters, who indeed did appear as a programmed robot, always saying the things that Republicans wanted to hear, and in exactly the right order.

But I suspect part of the reason Republicans underperformed is due to their fingers being pointed at the typical targets—the Democrats. At once: same old, same old. Any problem in the world can be attributed to those on the other side of the aisle.

Inflation alone can illustrate why this can't be the whole truth. Conservatives have neologized the word *Bidenflation* to show that rising prices are the result of policies made by Biden and the D-dominated congress. The causes of this historic inflation are myriad, but at least two main sources can be pinpointed: massive government spending, and wide-ranging sanctions against Russia. (Although I've written about inflation before, it's possible I didn't say as much as I could have in regard to this latter cause.) What sane, sober, or savvy observer of politics would argue that Republicans have no blame here?

That's absurd and should not stand.

To start, Republicans were all too willing to sign off on Trump's "pandemic relief." Those bills totaled a few trillion. Apparently, Republicans felt differently about such relief once

Trump's successor took office. Did that time, less than half a year, make all the difference? Or was it both bills, and all the bills printed in that time, that contributed to the inflation? One can guess my answer, and then come up with their own.

Of course, the bipartisan orgy resumed when the Democrips demanded billions to give to the Ukrainian fighters. No one is quite sure where that money even goes, as there isn't even an inspector general assigned to the case.

As for sanctions, all presidents feel they have unilateral authority to implement them, followed by the rest of the Western countries signing even more economy-crushing decrees. This is something Biden believed also. Aside from a handful of notable exceptions, the president felt no pushback from Republicans, whom in April even voted to suspend "normal trading relations" with their target. (Many more Republicans, to their credit, are becoming critical of the aid bills, even as they stay quiet about the other contributor.)

And there is another possible factor in the inflation equation. In a 2021 article for *Unherd*, Philip Pilkington argues that the lockdowns did just that. According to Ballotpedia, in the first part of 2020, 19 of the 26 Republican governors had implemented lockdowns.

Are Republicans going to start blaming Republicans, along with the Democrats? To be sure, lately there has been some internal divisions within the Grand Old Party. We hear more and more talk about "rebuilding" and "reforming," this by kicking out all the establishment elephants. McConnell will stay, even as Arizona's own radical, Kari Lake, tells all the McCainites to "get the hell out." Instead of abiding Reagan's "11th Commandment," never to speak badly of those who wear the same gang symbol, such radicals wish to get their axes and shovels into the chasm that number 45 had created with his first meteoric descent onto the world stage.

That said: in my view, it's politics as usual. Just as it was with most of Trump's presidency. Even though Trump wasn't the disaster everyone thought he was—with inflation very low, and without directing his (never *our*) military generals to begin any new bloodbaths—Trump nevertheless allowed swamp creatures to continue sucking at the fumes. For instance: The Clintons were never prosecuted; the Federal Reserve kept pumping; Assange and Snowden were not pardoned; Trump formally recognized Jerusalem as the capital of Israel; he wrote a foreword to Mitch McConnell's book (Trump now denies writing it, even calling McConnell a "piece of shit." He probably did write it, or most of it); and finally, when COVID struck, Trump became best friends with Big Pharma and the biosecurity state.

All normal here. Suppose, then, that our crazy clown world hasn't yet flipped completely upside down; we must only be halfway through the black hole we started drifting into back in 2012.

Deep and open politicking is one thing, parties are the vestigial twins, and principles are the risky surgeries perennially unperformed.

Let's look at one such principle. If the polls were to be believed, abortion was going to take a backseat in these midterms. There were so many other important issues to focus on. I believed this too. But after seeing what happened to two ballot measures in Kentucky and Montana, I've come to think I was mistaken.

The second of these laws very much did disturb me: In Kentucky, the voters struck down a law which would have affirmed that their constitution does not allow for abortions. In Montana, they even tried to penalize doctors who refused to offer life-saving care to babies who were victims of "botched" abortions, or who were born prematurely. These measures, in two fairly Red states, were soundly defeated.

What does that tell us, aside from now calling them pink

states? Gazing upon the Twittersphere, one would have thought there to be nary a person in America who believed that abortion should be legal, let alone acceptable. The online consensus was not dismayed by the handful who would allow exceptions for rape or incest. Obviously, whoever controlled those Twitter accounts—bot or not—were wrong. There were at least a few C-and-R-identified (that is, conservative and Republican) voters who just had a word to the contrary, showing perhaps that the issue did weigh heavily in the minds of the Post-Roe electorate.

The polls were likely right on this one: the majority of Americans, parties to the side, would surely permit the procedure in "some or most" cases, as the gray-and-black reports might read.

Even Republican candidates seem to realize this. After all, Tucker Carlson never makes an explicitly pro-life argument. Tucker believes—*believed*—that the individual states would make their own decisions at the ballot box. Imagine, or recall, the tempering of the message, with confident statements about the need for *limitations,* along with a few stipulations, rather than a full-blown federal prohibition.

Thus, when recalling the adage that "the personal is political," we wonder how close today's politics were felt against the skin of the individual. Seeing how 900,000 abortions happen every year, with an estimated 1-4 women eventually getting one, one could guess the distance of the policy from the womb.

As for other controls on the body, in the last two years, vaccine mandates and lockdowns had followed with plenty of protesters taking to the streets. Little of either was said during the midterm "season." But then nor was much said about police brutality and misconduct, which does happen often, and when captured by a Screen, always seems to unleash the larcenists.

Despite what some conservatives aver, the Biden administration is no foe of those most lethal and best equipped of Americans: the police, which also enjoy a bile-inducing amount of impunity. In August, Biden announced his "Safer America Plan," which would fund police departments to the tune of $37 billion. Someone is going to feel something, *somewhere*. And what line *did* Biden succeed in pushing into the Narrative? Something like "you can't be both pro-insurrection and pro-cop"—referring to the Day That Most People Forgot. We hope there's no more lockdowns or mandates, as I've grown tired of guessing how many of our "blue" will enforce them. Again.

As for Israel, they have no complains about this election. Their biggest lobbies, AIPAC and J Street, both celebrated big wins. According to Haaretz, J Street candidates—a lot of them Democrats—picked up 105 wins, while AIPAC says that 95 percent of their endorsed candidates came out on top. "We congratulate the elected and reelected senators and representatives from both parties who will be joining an overwhelmingly pro-Israel Congress," AIPAC said in a statement.

What, I ask, is unusual here?

Yet, as I've said, of which I do not make light of, there's nothing *usual* about the times we're living in. I often joke about mankind crawling like big-brained bugs over a green and blue spherical spaceship as it hurtles through some dimension unknown by all astronomers. As we slowly realize the harsher truths about mankind, we also witness the daily onslaught of unreality, the explosion of inverted events. This makes for an abundance of memes that poke fun at "ClownWorld."

Does it not seem like we're living in a time unlike any other? Resoundingly, yes.

Perhaps soon even gravity itself will lose its grip, and then we'll all drift up into the clouds, where we'll contact monsters worse than Man. Could that be our reality? The good news is that that's only a dark fantasy programmed into your personalized Metaverse.

Going back to my stack of articles, we learn that Klaus "Mr. Reset" Schwab had attended the G20, which was held a few days after the midterms. (Actually, it was the "B-20," an event *sponsored* by the G-20 and hosted in the same city, Bali).

In his speech, Schwab spoke about the way that the "internet has changed our personalities over the last 20 years." The Metaverse, Schwab assures us, can be used "in order to create much deeper and more extensive and comprehensive global dialogues."

So, there's the bad news: the Metaverse—what will be Soma made perfect—is coming to a store near you. Soon, you'll be able to plug in and let the monsters of the real world be tuned out as imaginary monsters start flashing before your eyes. Battling these monsters will be fun and harmless, which will free you from having to fight monsters that can cause harm. No more elections. No more Uniparties. Forget about the mountains and the lakes. And even your loved one's smiles.

Most sinisterly, you can't see the technocrats laughing. Now we see that this unparalleled epoch is the result of the lightning-quick pace of technology, with advancements that Schwab gloats about having predicted.

During a phone interview with Hrjovi Moric, I told my host that Schwab is already very close to getting his wish, and all one must do is look around to realize it. Arms up, device in hand; face down, with eyes not only opened, but locked. The human race is falling ever faster into its Screens. Most ironically, a great deal of these election campaigns are run and conducted through those very Screens. The average voter, likewise, views and interprets these events in the same way.

Meanwhile, acceptance of Uniparites and compliance with lockdowns and mandates is a "glass half full or half empty" scenario: there was pushback, but perhaps not nearly enough considering how much they eventually got away with. We

wonder what will happen next, as the G-20 also declares the need for global digital passports. In the states, and on cue, Biden asks for more billions to give to Ukraine. Elsewhere, the Federal Reserve announces plans to test-run a CBDC, or central bank digital currency. End times? I won't be mad if any of my Christian friends say as much.

I hope those willing to resist soon realize that they have about as much a chance of grabbing hold of the reins of the centralized state as they do in stopping the real wave coming at us, that of transhumanism. Both of those reins are out of our reach.

The best chance mankind has for a future which includes us in it is by learning how to outpace the technocrats in the race that is evolution. This would oblige us to broaden our understanding, and to make a few personal changes.

We should start sprinting, as the finish line is well within sight.

(November 2022)